GORDON BENNETT
AND THE
FIRST YACHT RACE
ACROSS THE
ATLANTIC

GORDON BENNETT
AND THE
FIRST YACHT RACE ACROSS THE ATLANTIC

SAM JEFFERSON

ADLARD COLES NAUTICAL

BLOOMSBURY

LONDON · NEW DELHI · NEW YORK · SYDNEY

Adlard Coles Nautical
An imprint of Bloomsbury Publishing Plc

50 Bedford Square
London
WC1B 3DP
UK

1385 Broadway
New York
NY 10018
USA

www.bloomsbury.com

ADLARD COLES, ADLARD COLES NAUTICAL and the Buoy logo are trademarks of
Bloomsbury Publishing Plc

First published 2016
This edition published 2017

© Sam Jefferson, 2016

Sam Jefferson has asserted his right under the Copyright, Designs and Patents Act, 1988,
to be identified as Author of this work.

British Library Cataloguing-in-Publication Data
A catalogue record for this book is available from the British Library.

Library of Congress Cataloguing-in-Publication data has been applied for.

ISBN: PB: 978-1-4729-4102-2
ePDF: 978-1-4729-1675-4
ePub: 978-1-4729-1674-7

2 4 6 8 10 9 7 5 3 1

Text design by carrdesignstudio.com
Typeset in Goudy Old Style Std by Deanta Global Publishing Services, Chennai, India
Printed and bound in Great Britain by CPI Group (UK) Ltd, Croydon CR0 4YY

To find out more about our authors and books visit www.bloomsbury.com.
Here you will find extracts, author interviews, details of forthcoming events
and the option to sign up for our newsletters.

CONTENTS

I

THE BIRTH OF TRANSATLANTIC YACHT RACING

꩜

> It is a time when one's spirit is subdued and sad, one knows
> not why; when the past seems a storm-swept desolation, life
> a vanity and a burden, and the future but a way to death. It is a
> time when one is filled with vague longings; when one dreams
> of flight to peaceful islands in the remote solitudes of the sea,
> or folds his hands and says, What is the use of struggling, and
> toiling and worrying anymore? Let us give it all up.
>
> MARK TWAIN, *THE GILDED AGE*

The sleek black hull and white sails of the schooner *Henrietta* looked like the ghost of summer gone as she foamed across the start line that cold December afternoon in 1866. She and the two elegant yachts that sliced through the water alongside her had no right to be racing out of New York Harbor on such a day as this. That flat, hard sheet of water with the Atlantic beyond was no place to play in winter. Out past Sandy Hook lay a serious, uncompromising ocean, which these three yachts, playthings of their wealthy owners, were going to cross. They were bound for England on the whim of gentlemen's honour. Death or glory.

The three crossed the invisible start line to a puff of smoke, the crack of the starter gun and a cheer from the thousands of spectators who had gathered to see them off. Sails were hardened up to the keen breeze and all three vessels leaned purposefully toward the horizon. It was 1pm and the westering sun, pale and watery, shone low, glinting off the mighty icy rollers in pea green and snow white that were visible beyond the shelter of New York Harbor. The seas were running at 8 or 9 feet that day. The open sea offered little but desolation – what a contrast to the comforting band of well-wishers, betting, drinking, squabbling and screaming aboard the pleasure steamers that accompanied them.

The three beautiful schooners leant their sails to the icy breeze and headed away into the emptiness. Six men would be dead before the race was out; the final price of a careless roll of the dice.

To understand why these three yachts were out there dicing with death, we have to head back to a late October evening of the same year, 1866. New York was already commencing its long descent into winter and the last glow of an autumn that had suffused the city with a golden light was almost gone. High up in the trees that lined Fifth Avenue a handful of gilded foliage clung to the trees like tattered bunting from a long-forgotten party. They rattled uneasily to that first breath of winter, while down below great mounds of brittle, fallen leaves scuttled and swirled, scratching the ground, hurled around as the wind howled down the avenue's wide walkway. As the evening gave way to darkness and chill, a passer-by would have seen three figures dashing across the street and plunging into the Union Club, one of the oldest and most opulent gentlemen's clubs in America. These three young men, James Gordon Bennett, Pierre Lorillard and George Osgood, were on the verge of making yachting history.

The trio shook off the cool night air and made themselves at home within the dark panelled walls, glittering chandeliers and banked fires of New York's most exclusive gentlemen's club. The newcomers felt fully at ease here among the cream of New York society; this was a place where rich gentlemen could go and be rich together. Everywhere you turned there were people of consequence. There in the corner would be General Ulysses Grant – hero of the Civil War and soon to be President – brooding as he puffed on a cigar and tried to forget the stench of death from the battlefields of Shiloh, Vicksburg and the Appomattox campaign. The big hitters, however, were the financiers and industrial magnates emerging from the conflict, men like JP Morgan and Cornelius Vanderbilt who were grasping America by the scruff of its neck and hurling it into the industrial age with a ruthlessness that took the breath away. These were the kind of men to be found at the Union Club: they had turned the place into one of the great engine rooms of New York. Fortunes and even reputations were made and lost within these walls. In those days after the Civil War, the place was alive with possibility. Its parlours, thick with cigar smoke, reeked of wealth.

Our three young gentlemen were little more than wallflowers in a place where the fates of many were decided by the few. Yet yachting history was there to be made and who better to do it than three of the brightest young lads who ever sipped a cognac or popped the cork from a bottle of champagne: Pierre Lorillard, a tobacco merchant, George Osgood, a successful financier, and James Gordon Bennett Junior, whose father owned the *New York Herald*, the most successful newspaper in America at that time. All were regulars at the Union, and they immediately spotted a pair of old friends, Franklin Osgood, brother of George, and Leonard

Jerome, who sat, brandy in hand, luxuriating in front of a roaring fire at the heart of the club. They made a beeline for the pair.

Seating themselves comfortably in the wing-backed leather chairs, they took to drinking, smoking cigars and bragging. As the party warmed to their task there is no doubt they earned their share of censorious glances. The Union Club was a deeply conservative place. Women were only allowed inside in 1914, and then only to serve as waitresses. Yet, despite the hidebound atmosphere, there was still room for merry-making, and the group pickling themselves by the fire were probably the merriest of all. Their ringleader was unquestionably Gordon Bennett Jr.

Bennett was 25 at the time and just getting into his stride as a playboy and hell-raiser. As contemporary novelist Edith Wharton might have written of him, he was one of the first of a new generation who knew virtually nothing and expected everything. His father had risen from poverty and obscurity to set up the *New York Herald* and such had been his success that he had accumulated an indecently large stack of money into the bargain. The upshot was that his only son bore all the familiar marks of having been born with a silver spoon jammed firmly in his mouth. He had an annual allowance well over $1m a year in modern terms and this stupendous income had given Bennett a very poor understanding of the value of money, but a very clear understanding of what high-class debauchery entailed. His high jinks were to become legendary, ultimately leading to his banishment from New York society – the phrase *Gordon Bennett!* originates directly from his catastrophic behaviour. In 1866, however, he was but a beginner. Nevertheless, he was already finding his way as a world-class playboy. His present obsession was driving a coach and four horses at absurd speeds around

New York and the surrounding countryside. Coaching was considered a genteel activity, fashionable among English aristocrats at the time, but in Bennett's hands it became an altogether wilder pursuit. Oiled up to the eyelids, he would roar around streets and country roads with no apparent regard for his own or anyone else's safety. Rumours that he was clinically insane were fuelled by bizarre late-night encounters where Bennett, full to the back teeth with the good stuff, had become so braced by an exhilarating night ride that he had ripped off his clothes and rattled through the streets atop his coach, coolly puffing his cigar, naked as the day he was born barring a white silk top hat. Many felt it was only a matter of time before his father had him carted off to the 'nerve specialists' for a serious assessment.

This was the leader of the group that clustered around Leonard Jerome in the Union Club, and it wasn't long before the whole party was suitably awash. Talk turned to yacht racing and the merits of the various vessels they owned. Lorillard had just purchased a brand new centreboard schooner, the *Vesta*. He argued that this 106-foot-long, shallow draft, light displacement boat was far superior to Osgood's *Fleetwing* or Bennett's *Henrietta*. These heavier, narrower vessels would be no match for *Vesta* over a long course, he declared.

As the argument waxed and waned, it would have been obvious to the sober observer that the participants were being prodded and cajoled by Leonard Jerome. This made sense; if Bennett was the apparent leader of this little group, Jerome was the ringmaster. He was the only man without a racing yacht, yet it was he who seemed intent on stoking the argument, frequently refreshing the parched participants and steering the conversation back to yachts when it meandered off down some drunken cul de sac. Jerome was 49 in 1866 and while nowadays he is famous for

5

being the grandfather of Sir Winston Churchill, back then he was the 'King of Wall Street' on account of his stockbroking prowess. A shrewd yet careless man, he'd made and lost several fortunes by 1866.

It was not his business acumen, however, but his capacity for fun that had enraptured the likes of young Jimmy Bennett. Jerome was the elder statesman of this party and all present looked up to him. A pioneer debauchee, he could light up any room through his flamboyant personality and legendary largesse. To be around Jerome was to be part of an event; 'People like Jerome do not enter Society, they create it as they go along', a contemporary had noted. It was true. At that moment he basked in the glory of his latest venture: the previous month he and his brother Lawrence had hosted the inaugural race of the American Jockey Club at Jerome Park, his own 8,000-seat purpose-built race track. The great and good had reclined in the opulence of his clubhouse and the Jerome brothers had soaked up the champagne and the adulation when Leonard's horse, Kentucky, came in first. The Belmont Stakes, which they and fellow financier and friend August Belmont set up, remain a cornerstone of the horse-racing calendar in America.

But that was last month's game. Now there was yachting to be discussed and young gentlemen to goad. His ammunition was a recent article in James Gordon Bennett Sr's own *New York Herald*, urging yachtsmen to be a little more adventurous, exhorting America's 'smooth water gentry' to:

> trip anchors and start out on a cruise on blue water. Get off your
> soundings, trust your sea legs for a while, reciprocate the visits of
> your English cousins, visit your own coast, go to South America,
> try Europe, call on the Sultan; or, if you have got the pluck,

*circumnavigate the world, then come home and write a book. It will
perpetuate your memory, reflect lustre on your deeds, and resound to
the honour of your country.*

As the evening wore on, the group grew increasingly incoherent, and
Jerome continued to needle the substantial egos of the three yachtsmen
on the theme of racing further afield. As it happened, he had an agenda
of his own; he had invested heavily in the newly laid transatlantic
telegraph cable, the brainchild of Cyrus Field – another Union Club
member, incidentally – which promised to revolutionize the way America
communicated with the UK and Europe beyond. The transatlantic cable
had opened for business on 27 July 1866 amid intense fanfare yet, so far,
interest had been modest, with many put off by the extortionate charges.
Jerome was sure that it would only take one major publicity stunt to get
the whole show on the road and the dollars pouring in. It was at this
point that he introduced the idea of a race across the Atlantic to his
intoxicated companions.

All three took the bait eagerly. The rivalry between the three owners
and their yachts was keen and Bennett was smarting from defeats
inflicted on his *Henrietta* by both Lorillard's *Vesta* and Osgood's *Fleetwing*
that summer. All were veteran members of the New York Yacht Club and
leading participants in the summer programme of races. A noteworthy
offshore race was from Sandy Hook to Cape May, some 127 miles; this
was considered far enough to establish the innate superiority in speed of
a yacht. For Messrs Bennett, Osgood and Lorillard, however, it wasn't
nearly far enough.

There was more to the argument than that, too, and more at stake
than a yacht race. Pierre Lorillard IV was heir to the Lorillard tobacco

empire, which dated back to 1760. If ever a family deserved the term 'old money' in the US it was Lorillard's. He had watched with dismay as a grasping, avaricious new breed of wealth had scrabbled around, fighting for its slice of the pie, and he loathed it. If you needed evidence of that, you only needed to look at the pivotal role he had played in ensuring that that old rogue Cornelius Vanderbilt was denied a seat at the grand opera of the New York Royal Academy of Music. To Lorillard, Vanderbilt was a jumped-up crook who was crass enough to dabble in the stock market. Never mind that he was feared and revered by all Wall Street, to Lorillard he was trash – trash to whom he would eventually sell his beloved family home of The Breakers, but trash nevertheless. It didn't help that both the Osgoods and Leonard Jerome had close ties with the Vanderbilt family. As for Jimmy Bennett … well, he was a law unto himself and highly amusing at that, but he wasn't so much new money as freshly minted. Not only that, but his *Herald* was a muckraking rag of the lowest order. This parvenu had no place challenging a man of his pedigree. It was an affront and a sign of the times. Something must be done.

Spurred on by Jerome, aggravated by drink and awash with testosterone and braggadocio, three men who weren't accustomed to losing anything bellowed and roared at each other until the only logical thing to do seemed to be to follow Jerome's suggestion and race the entire width of the Atlantic. Surely this was the only sensible way to decide the matter of whose vessel was quickest, once and for all.

The stakes were almost as high as the level of intoxication that fateful night, for the entrance fee was to be $30,000 per yacht, with a 'winner takes all' incentive. The final pot of $90,000 is about $1.35 million in today's terms. A more powerful example of value might be this: a farm labourer in Georgia earned about $10 a month at that time. It would have taken such a man 750 years of continuous work with no expenditure on anything to earn the stake. If that in itself bordered on madness, the three then took things one step further and agreed on a start date of 11 December. Why wait until the spring when the weather would be more clement? Hell, if something is worth doing, it's worth doing right.

You may think that all the men involved, perhaps with the exception of shrewd old Leonard Jerome, had lost their heads, but in truth they were simply part of a madness that had engulfed America in the wake of the Civil War. It was a little over a year since the last of the 750,000 casualties were laid in their graves at Appomattox, and the country seemed to be in the grip of a kind of fever. Fever for money, fever for expansion, all of it driven by the relentless clatter of the steam engine, the roar of the foundry bellows and the sharp clack of the Wall Street gavel signalling the opening of another trading day and the promise of another mad scramble for wealth. The madness had come with war, as the Union mortgaged its own future in order to put down the Confederates. For the first time borrowing – mass borrowing – became a real option.

The decision was taken to debase the dollar by printing off reels of paper money 'greenbacks' as legal tender. The banking house of Jay Cooke whipped up patriotic fervour throughout the north and drummed up millions for the government by selling high-yield government bonds on the back of these greenbacks. Troops had to be paid, weapons purchased and the rebels defeated, whatever the price. The national debt rose from $65m to $2.8bn during the war years. All the while financiers fattened themselves in the day of slaughter. Banks clawed in 6 per cent interest from the government annually on these war bonds and then were allowed to issue their own greenback banknotes on the strength of them.

Using their newly manufactured wealth they could charge borrowers an extortionate rate of interest. It was a double income with no risk or effort required. Between 1863 and 1878 the government had paid out £252,837,566 to banks in interest on these war bonds and financiers had made a killing. 'There's good fishing in troubled waters,' noted financier Daniel Drew, known as the 'Great Bear' of the New York stock exchange. No one knew that better than up-and-coming young banker JP Morgan, who supplied the funds to buy damaged carbines from the government for $17,486, ship them to the front line at St Louis, and then sell them back to the government for $109,912. That is a profit almost as obscene as the stakes of our gentlemen's yacht race. The guns, incidentally, were so defective they were liable to shoot off the thumbs of the men who used them.

Then there were the railroads being built at an absurd rate to open up the West. Even as the war went on, the iron rails were spreading out across the great deserted heart of the continent, their metal grasp reaching out for California, the promised land. Great swathes of the country were carelessly thrust into the hands of speculators by the government to achieve this goal and even greater piles of dollars were strewn all across the land. With the railroads came more borrowing, more stock, more shares. In New York the tempo of the city, already quickening, rose to hysteria; Wall Street reverberated to a great golden boom; the city's great temples of commerce echoed with the clamour of money.

At Wall Street's heart was the Gold Room, and at the centre of this great hall of money stood a serene fountain designed to soothe the fevered brows of the traders. While this trickled and babbled to its own gentle cadence, men roared and bellowed in one united language of wealth. It seemed like nothing they proposed to do could be withheld from them, for this was an heroic age. If a railroad could have been laid to the moon, this was the time. Never mind that the ironwork was so inadequate it would have to be replaced only a few years later. To hell with that. People reached for the sky and dared to believe, thrust their hands into that vast untapped continent and started to extract the potential of those great virgin prairies. Between 1869 and 1900, Gross National Product tripled, industrial output and urban population quadrupled, farm output and rural population doubled, exports quintupled, bank assets grew seven-fold.

From the ragged, muscular Irish and Chinese immigrants out there breaking their backs on the mountain passes of Colorado, sweating and shivering as they drove in the new rails, to the farmer out on the plains upping productivity year on year to satisfy the ever-growing demands of the cities, it seemed like a slice of the new American Dream was within the grasp of one and all. Pure Horatio Alger.

New York was right on the pulsing jugular of this new age. This was where the vast majority of the 2.3 million immigrants who arrived in America between 1860 and 1870 stepped ashore. The city throbbed and heaved as wave upon wave of migrants arrived. The Irish spearheaded the charge following the potato famine in their country. Thousands sailed across the western ocean to this land of hopes and dreams, almost forcibly ejected from the British Isles by the eye-watering avarice of their English landlords. In their wake they often left a trail of dead, with 30 per cent death rates for the voyage in the notorious 'coffin ships'. Tailed into port by hungry sharks, once ashore a different set of sharks sank their teeth into this fresh meat. They were worked until they dropped and vilified for failing to integrate and refusing to give up their traditions and religious practices. The melting pot often threatened to boil over with sectarian violence. In this seething atmosphere the city thrived and expanded out of control.

With wealth came breath-taking corruption. 'Boss' Tweed of Tammany Hall – an extension of the Democrat Party – ran the city in outrageous fashion. Tweed was the ultimate bloated fat cat, always skimming the cream off the top. He operated unashamedly on a regime of bribes, kickbacks, patronage and money laundering. Fraud was committed on a grand scale, with civic works being used as fronts to siphon off money into the pockets of Tweed and his cronies. The construction cost of the New York County Courthouse, begun in 1861, grew to nearly $13 million – about $178 million in today's value, and nearly twice the cost of the Alaska Purchase of 1867. In a single incident, a 'carpenter' was paid $360,751 (roughly $4.9m today) for one month's labour on a building with very little woodwork. This was paid for by the men running the city. Nowhere did corruption better than New York. Opportunity was out there for everyone, you just needed to grab your chance with both hands.

Yet it was down to a handful of mighty men to display the grit and ruthlessness required to fully realize the true potential of these unregulated times. Men like Cornelius Vanderbilt were consolidating their vast fortunes while young upstarts like that porcine little peacock of Wall Street Jim Fisk, Daniel Drew, and the sly, sickly, avaricious Jay Gould were starting to make an indelible mark on Wall Street, treating the financial markets as their own private plaything and gambling with lives and livelihoods with no consideration for the consequences. These were the heroes of a new reckless, unregulated age, an age with no federal income tax, no inheritance tax, no Federal Reserve Bank, no Securities and Exchange Commission, no Commodities Trading Commission, no Federal Trade Commission, no unions and no minimum wage.

By 1890, the top 1 per cent of Americans owned 51 per cent of all wealth, while the lowest 44 per cent owned just 1.2 per cent. This was the age of the robber barons. The true outlaws who won the west did not canter across the Great Plains, they sat in the clubs and money houses of the east and took what they desired until they could pretty much make the stock markets dance to their own tune. As Cornelius Vanderbilt, that towering titan of commerce, put it at the time: 'What do I care for the law? Hain't I got the power?'

This was the brave new world that our heroes staggered out into in the chill of the New York dawn, our merry band of one-per-centers. If James Gordon Bennett had looked up at the distant silver moon and decided to reach up and grab it, he should have been most surprised if it had not come away in the palm of his hand. In almost any other time and place a race in the face of death for stakes that can barely be conceived would have been scratched, written off as madness. In 1866 in America it seemed like the only sensible course of action. There was no going back, either. Before departing the club, all concerned had formalized the wager in the club's betting book. It read as follows:

George and Franklin Osgood, bet Pierre Lorillard and others thirty thousand dollars ($30,000) that the Fleetwing can beat the Vesta to the Needles, on the coast of England. The yachts to start from Sandy Hook on the second (2nd) Tuesday in December, and to sail according to the rules of the New York Yacht Club, waiving the allowance of time. The sails to be carried are mainsail, foresail, jib, jib topsail, fore and main gaff topsails, main topmast staysails, storm staysail and trysails.

The yacht Henrietta enters the above race by paying $30,000 dollars ($30,000). Any minor points not embraced in the above, that cannot be *settled by messrs Osgood, Lorillard and Bennett shall be decided as follows: Each shall choose an umpire, and the umpires chosen, in case of disagreement shall choose two (2) others; twenty per cent of the money to be deposited with Mr Leonard W Jerome on Saturday the third of November, balance to be deposited on the first (1st) Tuesday of December – pay or play.*

We the undersigned agree severally to the above matter.

JG Bennett Jr

Franklin Osgood

George A Osgood

P Lorillard Jr

There were also a couple of later addendums, perhaps the most significant and cavalier being that the race would 'start at one o'clock pm, blow high or low'.

This was to be the framework for the first ever offshore race of any great note, and thus a new form of yacht racing was founded on the drunken whim of three boors in a gentlemen's club. A new age of leisure was being ushered in and, in the warmth of the Union Club, with fiery brandy coursing through their veins, three men were willing to gamble their lives, and the lives of others, in the name of sport and for the sake of their own vanity.

2

THE FIRST OF THE INTERNATIONAL PLAYBOYS

There is no place like it, no place with an atom of its glory,
pride, and exultancy. It lays its hand upon a man's bowels; he
grows drunk with ecstasy; he grows young and full of glory, he
feels that he can never die.

WALT WHITMAN, WRITING ABOUT NEW YORK IN *THE BROOKLYN EAGLE*

I n the cold light of day, all must have wondered what they had done.
James Gordon Bennett, however, had the advantage that he was
accustomed to waking up after a heavy night with a nagging feeling of
impending doom. You see, Bennett was a voluptuary who could remain
as brandied and incandescent as a Christmas pudding for weeks on end.
The results of these sustained periods of hedonism were often alarming.
An example of his ability to make a first-class fool of himself can be
witnessed following a night of boozing and fine dining at his favourite
New York eatery, Delmonico's, where he was considered a particularly
objectionable customer. His arrival and departure were often announced
by the tinkle of crockery and the roars of outraged patrons as he made
his way through, grabbing tablecloths and depositing food and wine in

laps and on the floor. You will not be surprised to discover that on several occasions Bennett was punched while under the influence.

Anyway, on this particular night he had managed to get to his table without any great mishap and was working his way towards being thoroughly soused when he gathered, from a great din occurring in the street, that a fire had broken out in a nearby building. Bennett was not a man to miss out on even a minute's action, and he was certain he could be of great use to the fire service. He dashed out into the street, cognac in hand and cigar blazing, and set about directing the harassed firemen as to how to put out the blaze in the most effective manner. His ideas differed strongly from those of the captain of the fire service team. In desperation, the exasperated captain ordered his men to turn their high-pressure hose upon Bennett and, to the satisfaction of all, the would-be firefighter was hurled across the street and deposited, cigar fully extinguished, in a puddle. He was now soused in more ways than one.

On that occasion, Bennett had awoken the following day with a very thick head and a feeling that something wasn't quite right. He racked his brains to work out what had happened but drew a blank. In desperation, he sought out one of his drinking companions from the previous evening. 'What the hell did I do last night?' he asked. 'Made a big fool of yourself,' was the blunt reply. 'How so?' 'You interfered with the firemen by trying to tell them how to do their work, about which they know a good deal more than you do.' 'Order a rubber overcoat for every man in the department,' said Bennett wearily. 'Send me the bill. I was never so wet in all my life.'

This gesture was, by all accounts, well received. Yet high-spirited antics like these were nothing when compared to signing yourself up for a race across the Atlantic in December. The North Atlantic in midsummer can be a foul enough place; in December it was capable of unspeakable cruelty. The thought of it must have put even the gung-ho young daredevil Bennett into a cold sweat and there is little doubt that he headed down to Hoboken shortly afterward to look over his yacht, *Henrietta*, and gain some reassurance from her presence.

A visit to *Henrietta* would mean a break from Jimmy's strict regime, which generally consisted of rising late and breakfasting on plover's eggs, before heading to the *Herald*'s headquarters to smoke a cigar and be browbeaten by his father, James Gordon Bennett Sr, who remained in 1866 the editor-in-chief. This was followed by lunch at Delmonico's, a further brief spell of mooning about at the *Herald*, followed by dinner at the Union Club and drinks – plenty of drinks – until the early hours. A visit to his yacht would be a welcome break from this arduous routine. For Jimmy more than any of his monied associates, his yacht had a real resonance and meaning. She was one of the few things in his life that gave him a feeling of any worth. There were many reasons for this, the main one being his relationship with his father.

Jimmy endured a somewhat tricky relationship with Bennett Sr, who could perhaps best be described as a hard-boiled character. A Scottish immigrant of Catholic stock, Bennett Sr had grown up in Banff, where his parents had wanted him to become a priest. Instead he had renounced Catholicism and turned his back on God but retained that faith's sense of being the eternal outsider. There is no question that he had known hard times, particularly in his early years in the new world. He was not a man favoured in the looks department; his mouth was hard and mean and he had developed a disconcerting squint from too many years peering at print in murky, smoke-filled rooms. Bennett Sr was the kind of hard-hearted old bustard who could curdle the blood in your veins with a single piercing glance from his squinty eye.

He was a self-made man who had set up the *New York Herald* in 1835. Back then he was a disillusioned 40-year-old, mired in debt. He had emigrated 16 years previously and in the intervening years had struggled to get by as a journalist and sometime teacher. Thoroughly fed up, he had decided to take one last shot at setting up a newspaper and had scraped together $500 in capital. His editor's desk was a rough plank slung across a pair of barrels. His staff consisted of himself. Yet from this dingy cell, Bennett Sr had succeeded in putting together one of the most innovative newspapers the world had seen. In an era when newspapers were often little more than fiercely partisan rags supporting the political, financial or social views of their backer, Bennett set about delivering impartial reports, presenting news as news, unbiased by political allegiances. The public liked it. Likewise, his financial pages were well researched and impartial. Then, at a time when newspapers were only available by taking out a costly annual subscription, Bennett came up with the wild idea of making his paper available to the masses by pricing it at one cent. It was a recipe for success, and into this mix he added salaciousness and spice. He was at the forefront of a new wave of sensationalist journalism which used death, crime, scandal and celebrity to drive the news agenda. The public loved it. He was the original Dirty Digger. If a phone could have been hacked in 1835, Bennett would have been the man to do it.

In 1859 the *Herald* published the first ever interview in an American paper. Illustrations were introduced as Bennett's restless, active mind constantly sought to innovate. Rival papers were totally bamboozled. In fact, he was a key figure in setting newspapers along the furrow they generally still plough to this day. The *Herald* was the centrepiece of an explosion of mass media which saw the number of newspapers in

America shoot up from 150 in 1800 to 30,000 in 1900. On Bennett's death in 1872, Horace Greeley, who as editor of the *Tribune* was his great journalistic rival, noted: 'He developed the capacities of journalism in a wonderful manner but he did so by degrading its character. He made the newspaper powerful, but he made it odious.'

The eternal outsider, Bennett Sr was not precious about who he stomped on in order to get his story. His pen made him many enemies. On a number of occasions he was singled out in the street and 'horse-whipped' by disgruntled victims of his ruthless reporting. Even this he turned to his advantage, gleefully relating how he had been assaulted in the street by some notable member of society, including having his 'jaws forced open and throat spit into'.

He had won success through cunning, nous and, most importantly, hard work. As he once wrote with great pride in his own newspaper:

We do not, as the lazy Wall Street Editors do, come down to our office about ten or twelve o'clock, pull out a Spanish cigar, take up a pair of scissors, puff and cut, cut and puff for a couple of hours and then adjourn to Delmonico's to eat, drink gormandise and blow up our contemporaries. We rise at five o'clock in the morning, write out leading editorials, squibs, sketches etc, before breakfast. From nine til one we read all our papers and original communications, the latter being more numerous than those of any other office in New York. From these we pick out facts, hints and incidents, sufficient to make up a column of original, spicy articles...

It is perhaps understandable that Bennett Sr viewed the behaviour of his son with a mixture of incomprehension and despair. Bennett Jr's typical day boiled down to almost an exact copy of what his father had searingly condemned in his editorial a few years previously. In fact, his son was a constant reminder of one of Bennett Sr's only forays into frivolity. In 1840, at the age of 45, he had fallen madly in love with Henrietta Agnes Crean, a bewitching young Irishwoman some 25 years his junior. While he was rich and coarse, she was poor but accomplished, and had previously eked out a living as a music teacher. Bennett was impressed and for some time it seemed as if he had lost his head. Readers of the *Herald* must have been bemused to read the following rather touching announcement, nestled among the gruesome accounts of murder and mayhem:

TO READERS OF THE HERALD

Declaration of love – Caught at last – Going to be
married – New movement in civilisation

I am going to be married in a few days. The weather
is so beautiful – times are so good – the prospects of
political and moral reform so auspicious that I cannot resist
the divine instinct of honest nature any longer – so I am
going to be married to one of the most splendid women
in intellect, in heart, in soul, in property, in person, in
manners, that I have yet seen in my interesting pilgrimage
through life.

… I shall be married according to the holy rites of the
most holy Christian church to one of the most, remarkable,
accomplished and beautiful young women of the age. She
possesses a fortune – a large fortune. She has no Stonington
shares or Manhattan stock, but in purity and uprightness she

is worth half a million in pure coin. Can any swindling bank
show as much? In good sense and elegance another half a
million; in soul mind and beauty, millions on millions…

So he drivels on in the most sentimental yet strangely fiscal manner,
giving the clear impression that he is not so much hard-boiled as
poached. And, while all this is rather touching, the marriage was not 100
per cent successful. Although there was clearly affection there – affection
enough to see Bennett Sr sire young Jimmy Bennett in 1841 and also a
daughter, Jeanette – his beautiful young wife soon tired of her husband's
siege mentality. He was the ultimate social pariah; as the great editor
himself sagely noted: 'New York Society consists of people who don't
invite me to their parties.' It didn't help that she married him near the
high-water mark of this siege, when Bennett was locked in battle with
Horace Greeley, editor of the *Tribune*. Greeley set up the *Tribune* as a kind
of moral counterpoint to the *Herald* and Bennett took him on with great
aplomb. One of his most amusing battles was against the prudery of other
publications. At the time it was considered indelicate to use the term
'arms'; the more obtuse 'branches of the body' was preferred. Likewise,
trousers were termed 'inexpressibles' and petticoats 'unmentionables'.
Coarse old Bennett saw the absurdity of this and railed against it in an
editorial that concluded with the infamous lines: 'Petticoats! Petticoats!
Petticoats! There, you fastidious fools, vent your mawkishness on that!'
Such actions meant that he was considered beyond the pale in polite
society. As Greeley snidely observed: 'You cannot make him a gentleman,
it has been tried a hundred times but you may make yourself a blackguard.'

The upshot was that Bennett was shunned by society and his
unfortunate wife was infected with his social leprosy. She also had to

withstand stinging attacks from rival newspapers which called into question every aspect of her character, including frequent suggestions that she had extramarital affairs. None of these allegations had so much as a sniff of truth to them. In fact, one of Bennett's most satisfying moments came shortly after the birth of his son: following his arrival, the *New York Sun* wrote an article suggesting that Bennett was not the child's father. Bennett sued for libel and won. The victory and surrounding publicity did little to soothe his unfortunate wife, however, and it was to be the ugly physical confrontations brought about by her husband's muck-raking that finally did for the couple.

One particularly scarring incident for Mrs Bennett took place on Broad Street in 1850. The couple were out taking a stroll when a group of men confronted them. It appeared that Bennett's *Herald* had been instrumental in ensuring that the gang's leader John Graham had failed in an attempt to get himself elected as district attorney. Now came the payback and the celebrated editor's wife – along with two apparently uninterested policemen – had to look on as Bennett received a savage horse-whipping. There were even death threats: in 1852 Bennett Sr was sent a homemade bomb by one of his enemies and only escaped with his life because the crude incendiary failed to detonate when he tried to prise the package open. In such a torrid atmosphere it is perhaps understandable that his gracious wife – now comfortably minted with her husband's hard-earned wealth – opted to relocate to Paris, where she was able to enjoy her husband's money in a city where she was not despised because of her surname. The pair separated amicably enough and Bennett was left to brood in the cloistered magnificence of his house on Washington Heights, seeing his wife only occasionally. His heart ever harder, his commitment to journalistic excellence and general skulduggery redoubled. All the while he accumulated a great wealth he had no interest in.

Bennett Jr grew up to be a handsome man, described by a contemporary as 'tall, aristocratic in bearing, haughty and beak nosed with dark, darting suspicious blue eyes'. He divided his youth between Paris, where he was doted upon by his mother, and New York, where his father terrorized him and tried to instil in him the importance of good journalistic practice. No doubt young Jimmy was a painful reminder to his father of those few golden months when his heart had melted. It didn't help that the youngster appeared a foppish, vapid and frivolous young man. Growing up in Paris had also given the youth an air of sophistication. In New York he rather lorded it over his contemporaries: a man of wealth and taste who was widely envied. True, it was often said of him that when sober he displayed the worst attributes of the Scots, and when drunk the worst of the Irish, but he still carried an air of languid cosmopolitanism that was totally beyond his rather crude father.

Bennett Sr despaired of his son; he didn't even display the first shred of ability for writing and seemed to be entranced by the very trappings of wealth and opulence that Bennett had spent years lampooning in the *Herald*. Bennett Sr was not a moral man, but he could see little to be gained from excess of any kind and once wrote: 'I eat and drink to live, not live to eat and drink. Social glasses of wine are my aversion; public dinners are my abomination; all species of gormandizing, my utter scorn and contempt. When I am hungry, I eat; when thirsty, drink. Wine or viands taken for society, or to stimulate conversation, tend only to dissipation, indolence, poverty, contempt, and death.'

His son was light years away from this ethos, a by-product of a new, wealthy elite. The question of what was to be done with young Jimmy must have been uppermost in Bennett Sr's mind for several years. Yet, for all their differences, Jimmy was his only son and, in his own dysfunctional way, he doted upon him and spared him nothing. He could afford to. The *Herald* was the highest-earning newspaper in the country, and the coming of the railways had not only benefited financiers, it had also benefited newspapers. Circulations soared as new printing presses were able to pump out thousands of newspapers cheaply. Improved communications brought unprecedented demand for news and also the means to supply it. Bennett's *Herald* rode on the crest of this wave and his paper earned him a staggering $1m annually in gross income ($15m in current values) in 1865.

A good deal of that money found its way to Jimmy, who understood better than most that the only way not to think about money is to have a great deal of it. In 1857 when he was 16 his father gave him a more significant gift than any allowance – the yacht *Rebecca*: 70 feet long and with a crew of 22. Her arrival brought out the first hint of some kind of focus in this hitherto thoroughly unpromising young man. He applied to join the New York Yacht Club, which had been formed in 1844. Initially, the yacht club had been a modest affair, but as America grew and flourished, so too did the club as the newly monied needed somewhere to pour away their wealth. There are few better ways to get rid of a small fortune than to own a yacht and by 1857, the year Jimmy Bennett applied for membership, the club was flourishing.

In 1851 the club had been given an unprecedented shot in the arm when its commodore, James Stevens, had sent his new yacht, *America*, over to England, where she had proceeded to humiliate the cream of the Royal Yacht Squadron by winning the 100 Guineas Cup. In 1857, the race for this cup had been formalized as the America's Cup, so the stock of the New York Yacht Club was extremely high. In fact, given Bennett's rather unsavoury family ties, he was fortunate to be granted consideration at all. Jay Gould, another obscenely rich parvenu, was conspicuously denied entry a few years later. However, the great and good of the club averted their gaze from this nouveau riche young thug making merry in their back yard and were gratified with the enthusiasm and energy he brought both to racing and to social events.

So the hot, lazy summer of 1857 passed pleasantly for 16-year-old James Gordon Bennett Jr; he devoted much of it to yacht racing, entering fully into the New York Yacht Club's cruising calendar. This involved meeting up for a programme of racing which, over a series of days or weeks, gradually took the competitors along the coast. Days of brisk racing were followed by languid evenings when the yachts were moored up and draped with lanterns. The harbour the contestants had chosen to descend on would be alive with rowing skiffs as owners and guests headed from yacht to yacht paying social visits. Long into the velvety night the chatter and murmur of genteel small talk and the tinkling chime of the champagne flute would drift across the waters of the sound, whispering of wealth.

The cruise generally made its way north to Martha's Vineyard and then on to Newport, where the programme ended with a banquet and a ball. Newport in those early days was not the lavish millionaires' playground we know of now. It was described by New York's Mayor, Philip Hone, as a 'tolerably dull place of sojournment', but by 1857 it was already shaping into a bolt-hole for the newly rich. The New York Yacht Club's end-of-season celebrations were often lavish, stultifying events; ballrooms and banqueting halls crammed full with the 'right sort' exchanging meaningless pleasantries.

Bennett by and large managed to curtail the exuberant side of his personality at these showily dull affairs and his first cruise was a social success. He would later make up for this lapse into socially acceptable behaviour and gain notoriety in Newport by getting himself barred from the Reading Room, Newport's prestigious gentlemen's club, after he bet his chum Augustus Candy that he, Candy, could not ride a horse through the main entrance, up the stairs and into the library. Candy took him up on the dare, Bennett lost the bet, and both lost their membership to the club, though they had the satisfaction of seeing the occupants of the club flabbergasted by the sight of the horse clopping its way into the library. Bennett's novel solution to this ban was to build the opulent Newport Casino nearby, which duly superseded the Reading Room as the gentlemen's club *par excellence*.

Although Bennett didn't win any races that first summer, he did impress sufficiently to become the youngest ever member of the club, being inducted by the members on 12 August aboard Commodore William Edgar's flagship *Widgeon*. He was only 16, but he had already been handed the gilded key to a door that was slammed and bolted shut in the face of his father.

What his father made of this is not recorded, but you can be sure it wasn't very much. To make matters worse, Bennett Jr's yachting exploits in 1858 exposed him to the ire of the old buzzard, after a minor misunderstanding on the race course. It happened like this: Bennett Jr entered his beloved *Rebecca* into a race against seven other yachts around Long Island. At the time, this was termed an 'ocean race', which seems deliciously ironic given what Bennett and his associates would get up to eight years later. Bennett was, as always, keen to win. He spotted a risky short cut through Plum Gut, while the others went the safer route to the north of Plum Island. Bennett won the race but was later disqualified for this piece of daring, which was viewed as deviating from the official course. The race was followed with intense scrutiny in the press, and the disqualification of the son of the proprietor and editor of the *New York Herald* was too priceless for Bennett's rivals, who reported the incident with barely disguised glee. The *Hudson Daily Star* wrote as follows:

THE GREAT YACHT RACE BENNETT'S BOAT AHEAD, BUT DOESN'T WIN!

In our telegraph report yesterday we stated that the yacht *Rebecca*, belonging to James Gordon Bennett of the *Herald*, had distanced all competitors and won the prize. Later accounts, however, inform us that the *Rebecca* was ruled out by the committee in consequence of unfair advantage taken. It seems that she deviated from the course and gained eight or ten miles by passing thro' 'Plum Gut', or in other words cutting cross lots. An old game of Bennett's. The *Times* talks to the 'poor old man' of the *Herald* as follows: 'If our neighbour is going into sports of this kind, he must learn to play fair. It is very difficult, we know, to teach an old dog new tricks; but Bennett must make an effort if he expects to sail his yacht. Get up another race old fellow, – and be honest, if possible.' P.S. Since the above was written, the cheating of the *Rebecca* has been accounted for. Bennett himself was on board!

You can imagine that the atmosphere in the *New York Herald* office was sulphurous when old man Bennett read editorials of this nature, and you can bet that Jimmy got a rocket for his carelessness. He remained undeterred and continued to race, with rather mixed results. What cannot be denied, however, was his enthusiasm for the sport. In 1861, shortly after the first shots at Fort Sumter confirmed the beginning of the Civil War, Bennett Sr had a new craft built for his son. This was the *Henrietta*, named after his dear mother and designed by Henry Steers, whose uncle had designed the legendary *America* and was actually aboard the vessel when she had scored her famous victory over the English fleet in 1851.

The *Henrietta* was a beautiful two-masted schooner, 107 feet in length with a beam of 22 feet. She was a typical vessel of her time, low, sleek and sylph-like to look at, with an intimidating sail area. Bennett kept a full-time crew on board to deal with her upkeep and, unless she was out of the water for repairs, she would have always looked immaculate: teak decks scrubbed and scraped until they almost glowed white, the brass gleaming, the varnish of such a deep lustre you could see your reflection in it. Down below, she barely resembled a yacht at all. Here she was more like a gentleman's drawing room, all dark panelling, tiger-skin rugs and sumptuous upholstery. What was unquestionable was that she was a beautiful if decadent symbol of a new age. She was one of the first of the big American schooners that would dominate the New York Yacht Club's racing calendar through the 1860s.

If it was easy to dismiss the *Henrietta* as frivolous, that accusation became much harder to level at either her or her flamboyant owner when he put both himself and his yacht at the disposal of the Union Army in the struggle against the Confederates. The offer was accepted and, unlikely as it may have seemed, Jimmy Bennett joined the navy – that he took the extravagant step of bringing his own ship with him was merely a sign of the times.

You can level many charges at James Gordon Bennett Junior, but one thing he didn't lack was pluck. The annals of the Civil War are littered with heroes and heroic acts, but what you will struggle to find is a single wealthy financier or shining light of the Reconstruction Era that followed it who actually took part in the war. Look among the big beasts of this brave new era – Andrew Carnegie, Jay Gould, JP Morgan, Jim Fisk – these men were money-making machines. But when you look at their active service, you will draw a blank.

There was a good reason for that. Although conscription existed, which should have meant that every able-bodied man in the Union had to fight, the Draft Act was amended so that it was possible to 'buy' a substitute to go to war in your place. The price was $300 ($4,500 in today's terms). Thus, while there was a great deal of patriotic bluster surrounding the Civil War, there was precious little action on the part of the monied classes. We have already seen the slightly questionable role that JP Morgan played in providing defective weapons, and he is certainly not alone; there are major questions over Cornelius Vanderbilt's role in profiting by providing the unseaworthy *Niagara* as a troop carrier for the Union Army's Banks Expedition – the vessel was so rotten that disgusted troops pulled her apart as they went along and would certainly have perished if the weather had not remained clement. Both Morgan and Vanderbilt were subsequently lionized as great patriots. In fairness to Vanderbilt, he did donate his mighty SS *Vanderbilt* to the Union Navy.

Perhaps the most breath-taking piece of Civil War self-delusion can be found in Andrew Carnegie's biography *Gospel of Wealth*. At the time war broke out Carnegie – who by 1901 was worth $480 million (around $100.5 billion today) – was learning his trade and working on the railroads. As the conflict began, he was assigned the role of repairing the Annapolis–Washington line, which had been damaged by Confederate sympathizers:

> Some distance from Washington I noticed that the telegraph wires
> had been pinned to the ground by wooden stakes. I stopped the engine
> and ran forward to release them, but I did not notice that the wires
> had been pulled to one side before staking. When released, in their
> spring upwards, they struck me in the face, knocked me over and cut
> a gash in my cheek which bled profusely. In this condition I entered
> the city of Washington with the first troops, so that with the exception
> of one or two soldiers, wounded a few days previously in passing
> through the streets of Baltimore, I can justly claim that I 'shed my
> blood for my country' among the first of its defenders. I gloried in
> being useful to the land that had done so much for me, and worked,
> I can truly say, night and day, to open communication to the South.

Needless to say, Carnegie had bought a substitute to fight in his place, and this man will have shed a good deal more blood than he did. Of course, it's not fair just to pick on Andrew Carnegie. He was a young man trying to make his way in the world and he was at least doing *something* to help the cause. As Jay Cooke, the man who bankrolled the Civil War and mortgaged the Union by selling high-interest government bonds during the war, noted: 'No-one loves their country more than their pockets.' It is telling that Cooke himself, the great patriot, was also the richest man in America by the time hostilities ended in 1865. Yet perhaps the last word on this matter of substitutes should go to Thomas Mellon, founder of T Mellon and Sons Bank. He wrote the following to his son during the war:

It is only greenhorns who enlist, those who are able to pay for substitutes do and no discredit attaches … In time you will understand that a man may be a patriot without risking his life or his health. There are plenty of other lives less valuable.

In 2016 the bank Thomas Mellon and his son played a part in founding is worth around $20.7 trillion.

Unsurprisingly, many working-class men were not too thrilled with the Draft Act and this was particularly true in New York where many newly arrived Irish immigrants had been delighted to be granted American citizenship, but less so when they realized this meant they were now obliged to go to war at a time when the coffins of the dead lined the wharves. In the brooding heat of July 1863 dissatisfaction erupted into three days of the most violent insurrection in the history of the United States – the Civil War itself excepted. Downtown New York burned. Up to $5m-worth of damage was inflicted on the city and at least 120 people died, with a further 2,000 injured. Most of the fury of the mob was directed at blacks, who, not being citizens, were exempted from the draft. At least ten were lynched by the mob. The wealthy men of the city who had purchased a substitute – a key factor in sparking the fury – were left largely unmolested, bringing real weight to Jay Gould's statement that he could 'hire one-half of the working class to kill the other half'. You begin to understand why the New York Yacht Club declined Gould's application for membership.

Many talked big about 'doing their bit', but that bit was often pitifully small. Bennett perhaps deserves some credit for being man enough not only to donate his boat, but also his own personal service, though this wasn't pure altruism on the part of young Jimmy Bennett. The father's shadow loomed large over the youngster and his decision to go to war owed a lot to the media.

Bennett Sr had always sought to ensure his newspaper was politically neutral. It was one of the hallmarks of the *Herald* and one of the great cornerstones of its success. In his early years as a journalist, Bennett Sr had worked for one of these politically affiliated newspapers and had quit due to a violent falling-out with his associates there. Over time he came to realize how damaging they were to the integrity of journalism, as he later recalled:

> *I found out the hollow heartedness and humbuggery of these political associations and political men; but yet I was so fascinated by them that I could not disconnect myself from it until the revulsion took place between me and my partners in Philadelphia. After that I regained my liberty completely and very fortunate thing it was for my prosperity.*

During the early months of the Civil War he retained this neutral outlook on the conflict – if anything he seemed to favour the south and continually lampooned President Abraham Lincoln as 'a third-rate Western lawyer', an 'illiterate Western boor' and a 'vulgar village politician'. He was even more scathing about his inaugural address, writing that 'it would have been almost as instructive if President Lincoln had contented himself with telling his audience yesterday a funny story'. The *Herald* was also guilty of stirring the pot of racial discord by running editorials suggesting that one day there might even be a black president if the country continued on its current slide.

Lincoln, most would now acknowledge, was smarter than Bennett made him out to be in his editorials, and he realized the importance of getting the country's most powerful paper on-side. Just as the Labour Party under Tony Blair knelt before Rupert Murdoch prior to election in 1997, so Lincoln realized how much he needed Bennett in the early days of the Civil War. He wasn't nearly as mealy-mouthed about it as Blair, but he still paid court to Bennett. At that point it is hard to imagine how beleaguered the Union was; defeat was a very real prospect and Lincoln himself noted: 'I begin to believe there is no North.'

He had first sounded out Bennett Sr in 1860 when one Joseph Medill had paid a visit to his 'satanic majesty', as he referred to him. Medill reported back to Lincoln that what the old man craved was 'social position'. The next step was to send an emissary by the name of Thurlow Weed to Bennett to request his cooperation in the war effort. Weed was chosen because of his skill in 'belling cats', as Lincoln termed it. Bennett proved much more receptive than expected and actually invited Weed to dinner at his house, where he launched into a harangue on how he and his rival New York editors had been instrumental in bringing on the war. Bennett had been particularly shaken after a mob of Confederate sympathizers had threatened his office in 1861. In the wake of this incident, Bennett proved to be receptive to Weed's proposal for throwing the weight of the *Herald* behind the war effort. Weed returned to Washington and reported to Lincoln, who was 'greatly gratified'.

Shortly afterwards Bennett sent his own emissary, the *Herald*'s Washington correspondent Henry Villard, to confirm his support. In his memoirs Villard recalled the encounter he had with both Bennetts before being sent on this mission, and also the unusual caveat to the *Herald*'s support for the Union:

I had seen Bennett only twice before, and then but for a few minutes each time, and the opportunity to learn more of this notorious character was therefore not unwelcome to me. I must say that his shameful record as a journalist, and particularly the sneaking sympathy of his paper for the Rebellion, and its vile abuse of the Republicans for their antislavery sentiments, made me share the general prejudice against him to such an extent that I had been thinking for some time of severing my connection with the Herald, *although the agreement that all I telegraphed should be printed without change or omission had been strictly kept.*

With his fine tall and slender figure, large intellectual head covered with an abundance of light curly hair, and strong regular features, his exterior would have been impressive but for his strabismus [squint], *which gave him a sinister, forbidding look. Intercourse with him, indeed, quickly revealed his hard, cold, utterly selfish nature and incapacity to appreciate high and noble aims. His residence was a good-sized frame house in park like grounds, with no great pretensions either outwardly or inwardly. On the drive and during the dinner, at which his one son – a fine-looking, intelligent youth of twenty – was the only other person present, he did nothing but ask questions bearing upon the characteristics and doings of President Lincoln and the circumstances of my acquaintance with him.*

After dinner, he disclosed his true purpose in sending for me.
First, he wanted me to carry a message from him to Mr Lincoln
that the Herald would hereafter be unconditionally for the radical
suppression of the Rebellion by force of arms, and in the shortest
possible time, and would advocate and support any 'war measures'
by the Government and Congress. I was, of course, very glad to hear
this, and promised to repeat these assurances by word of mouth to
the President. The truth was, that the Herald was obliged to make
this complete change in its attitude, there having been ominous signs
for some days in New York of danger of mob violence to the paper.
Secondly, he wanted me to offer to Secretary Chase his son's famous
sailing yacht, the Rebecca, as a gift to the Government for the
revenue service, and to secure in consideration thereof for its owner
the appointment of lieutenant in the same service. The last wish I
thought rather amusing, but I agreed to lay it before Secretary Chase,
to whom I had ready access as the representative of the Cincinnati
Commercial, his strongest supporter in Ohio.

The upshot of this was twofold. First, James Gordon Bennett Jr headed
to Washington and met with President Abraham Lincoln. Shortly
afterwards he was given a commission to serve as third lieutenant in the
US Navy. He would serve not aboard the *Rebecca*, as initially proposed,
but his new vessel the *Henrietta*. Secondly, in 1864 Lincoln offered
Bennett Senior the Paris-based position of French ambassador. You
could surmise that, despite the fact taking up this tempting sinecure
would have reunited Bennett with his wife, the old curmudgeon still
had sufficient scruples to politely decline the offer. It is more likely,
however, that he was simply too busy making money. It wasn't just

the wealthy financiers who benefited from the war, so too did the *Herald*. Bennett quickly realized that there was news in war and money behind that. During the conflict Bennett further bolstered the *Herald's* reputation for high quality, accurate reporting. To do this he used 63 correspondents in the field and invested $525,000 ($7.8 million today) on war reporting. During this period the newspaper more than doubled its circulation.

If you were thinking from reading this that Bennett Sr was going soft, witness this editorial on Lincoln from 1864. It gives a full insight into the unpredictability and savagery of Bennett Sr, and explains why he was often loathed by allies and enemies alike:

President Lincoln is a joke incarnated. His election was a very sorry joke. The idea that such a man as he should be President of such a country as this is a very ridiculous joke. The manner in which he first entered Washington – after having fled from Harrisburg in a Scotch cap, a long military cloak and a special night train – was a practical joke. His debut in Washington society was a joke; for he introduced himself and Mrs. Lincoln as 'the long and short of the Presidency'. His inaugural address was a joke, since it was a full of promises which he has never performed. His Cabinet is and always has been a standing joke. All his State papers are jokes. His letters to our generals, beginning with those to General McClellan, are very cruel jokes. His plan for abolishing slavery was a broad joke. His emancipation proclamation was a solemn joke. His recent proclamation of abolition and amnesty is another joke. His conversation is full of jokes ... His title of 'Honest' is a satirical joke. The style in which he winks at frauds in every department, is a costly joke. His intrigues to secure

a renomination and the hopes he appears to entertain of a re-election
are, however, the most laughable jokes of all.

Whatever the machinations behind Jimmy's rather unexpected entry into the navy, we can be sure he did so with his usual thirst for adventure. On 19 June 1861 *Henrietta* and her owner both entered into the United States Revenue Cutter Services – a branch of the US Navy whose principal purpose was to seek out smugglers. In wartime this obviously took in a wider role of ensuring no Confederate goods were run in or out of blockaded areas, and of sniffing out trouble. Bennett was granted a crew of ten seamen and two non-commissioned officers, and paid $353 a month. The *Henrietta* was armed and despatched to patrol Long Island and Nantucket. Bennett's orders were as follows:

> *As soon as you have received your armament and shot you will*
> *proceed with the US Revenue Yacht* Henrietta *under your command*
> *along the North Shore of Long Island to Block Island and Nantucket,*
> *touching in at all the ports (intermediate) calling on the different*
> *Collectors reporting yourself and Vessel ready to perform any duties*
> *required of you as Commander of a Revenue Cutter in the service*
> *of the United States. You will obtain all the information in your*
> *power respecting the fitting out of slavers and other illicit trade,*
> *permitting no vessel to pass having on board arms and munitions of*
> *war unless she is in the service of the United States, keeping a journal*
> *of that and all passing events. On your return you will visit all the*
> *intermediate ports on the South Shore of the Main Land of New*
> *York boarding and examining all vessels not known to be regular and*
> *honest traders.*

Altho important powers and duties are confided to you, you will
please exercise them in as pleasant and agreeable manner as possible, not
detaining an honest trader a moment longer than necessary to prevent
fraud upon the Revenue as also just to the fair and honest trader.

> *Wishing you a very pleasant cruise*
> *I am, dear sir, very respectfully*
> *Your obdt Servant*
> *W.A Howard*
> *Senior Captain*

Bennett's time in this service cannot be described as successful but, like most things he did in his life, it entertained him. His role was not a glamorous one, but the work was worthy and necessary and had enough spice to keep him going. If nothing else, the first cruise must have been a great way for Bennett to get a strong grounding in the art of seamanship and navigation.

His first cruise passed off without note until 13 August, when the *Henrietta* encountered the trader *Adelso* in Newport. This vessel was sheltering from the weather, having just run through the Union blockade at Wilmington on her way to Boston. She had recently been renamed and her captain was English. In other words, there were plenty of reasons to view her as suspicious and worthy of investigation. Bennett and his crew boarded her with the kind of polish and finesse that became his hallmark in later years. According to her captain, Thomas Kimball, Bennett was 'in martial panoply with drawn sword, several revolvers and his followers similarly accoutred'. The vessel was seized and searched and clear evidence was soon uncovered that she had run army blankets, coffee and quantities of iron into North

Carolina. Further damning evidence was found in the trunk of one of the passengers, Louis De Bebian – detailed instructions on how to run the Union blockade. De Bebian was arrested and tried but later released. He returned to Wilmington, where he gave an amusing account of Bennett, describing him as a:

> ...squint eyed bibulous youth who is the owner of a yacht he used to cruise around Newport. He tendered the yacht to the US government as a cutter or something or other on condition of him getting a commission as her commander although he hardly knew one rope from the other, having proceeded to secure the services of real seamen to work the vessel.

De Bebian had clearly been caught red-handed, and there is no doubt that this whole affair was a feather in the cap of the young Bennett, who was next despatched to Port Royal, South Carolina, to help maintain the blockade there. It didn't help that, en route, his rakish, sleek little yacht was frequently mistaken for a raider and enjoyed a number of desperate chases with Union vessels. However, once it was established that Bennett was actually on their side, he was welcomed. He entertained the officers of the blockade squadron in lavish style during his time there.

During this period Bennett began his lifelong obsession with owls. This came about during a long night watch as *Henrietta* trickled along the coast on one of her blockading missions. The night was warm and stifling. *Henrietta* stole along in the faint breeze with only the creak of her boom and the occasional chuckle of water under her forefoot for company. The atmosphere was soporific and after an hour or so Bennett was inclined towards wooziness. Presently his head nodded and he surrendered himself to blissful sleep. Unfortunately land was close and *Henrietta*'s serene progress was toward what would have been her doom had not a kindly owl intervened. It hooted with such vigour that Bennett awoke with a start and was able to save his gallant little schooner. In later life he kept a large number of both owls and small yappy dogs. The yappy dogs can only be explained away by insanity, but at least there was some rationale behind the owls.

At the end of April 1862 Bennett withdrew the *Henrietta* from active service. There is no recorded explanation for this, but it is likely that he simply tired of hanging around. It's not as if he needed the $353 that the US Navy paid him. Thus, by the summer of 1862, Bennett was back cruising and racing with the New York Yacht Club. It was back to the usual round of racing and wafting before the breezes; champagne lunches and lavish dinners with the same old set; the same carefully cut clothes and vapid gossip; the same well-fed, carefully exercised bodies, the same bored minds tired of wondering whether passion would ever come their way. Bennett was only in his twenties, but already he carried the tired but seductive ennui of a man who has seen too much of life too soon. He longed for adventure.

His brief naval service had been an escape of sorts and although it had not exactly been glorious, it had been productive, and earned him respect in the eyes of his peers. More importantly, it gained him a sniff of credibility with his father. Perhaps, just perhaps, the youth would amount to something after all. With the summer yachting season over, Bennett Sr installed a second desk in his editor's office and the pair worked side by side.

The return to the business-like anger of his father's office must have been a trial after the freedom of the open sea, but Bennett made the most of it. While Bennett Sr sat in his office preoccupied with vendetta and vengeance, young Bennett returned to the old routine: cigars in the morning and a bit of mooning around, followed by Delmonico's for lunch washed down with champagne, then back to the office for a spot more cut, puff, cut, puff, then out to the Union Club for dinner.

If the ennui got too much, he might step out with a society girl or take in a show or two. Ultimately, however, his favoured method of whiling away an evening was drinking. Champagne and brandy were both favoured tipples, but it was the discovery of a new cocktail – the Razzle Dazzle – that really put a firecracker under young Bennett's backside and helped set him up as a hell-raiser par excellence. A Razzle Dazzle is one part ginger ale, one part brandy and one part absinthe. Young gentlemen had a tendency to find this tipple extremely invigorating, and under its influence Bennett developed an exciting new hobby. This involved waiting until the young ladies of a certain girls' school walked in line past Delmonico's and then dashing outside to launch himself into their terrified midst – an early version of crowd-surfing. This pastime gained quite a following and for many years afterward was referred to as 'Bennetting'. His father took the prudent step of employing an extra member of staff to act as a chaperone for his often wayward son in order to curb his more outré moments.

For Bennett Sr the only sense in which his progeny might not be a completely lost cause was down to his exploits aboard *Henrietta*. This was the vessel that Bennett Jr surveyed when he headed down to Hoboken. Pierre Lorillard and the Osgoods viewed the *Vesta* and *Fleetwing* coldly as racing machines designed to bring them glory and kudos, but *Henrietta* was different. As Bennett surveyed her sweet lines, he felt a surge of confidence that he and his fine little yacht could go on and win this race he'd signed up to. He returned to the office with renewed determination to give himself the best possible chance of securing the prize.

3
CAPTAIN SAMUELS:
THE HIRED GUN

He turns his head, but in his ear
The steady trade winds run,
And in his eye the endless waves
Ride on into the sun.

ROBERT LAURENCE BINYON, 'JOHN WINTER'

I t is not clear when exactly Pierre Lorillard and the Osgood brothers announced that they would not be taking part in the yacht race personally. Presumably it was some time in November as the icy easterly gales howling into New York Harbor developed real bite. A quick seaward glance would convince most that their time was better spent brokering deals or even just tending to the fire of the ancestral home. Of course, their yachts would still take part, just not with them on board.

It is remarkable that this astonishing *volte face* should have been accepted largely with indifference by the press. True, there was a brief, rather sniffy comment from Lorillard stating:

I am altogether indifferent to the race. I was anyway going to send the Vesta to Europe to take part in the Universal Exposition; then I

*learnt that centreboard vessels weren't recognized. Now I shall send
her to England in the charge of my brother who will win the race for
me and sell her in Europe afterwards; and meanwhile I shall stay
here and build another yacht to put in the exposition.*

Although he was only 33, years of good living had given Lorillard a
jowly, well-upholstered look and at first glance it was easy to write him
off as a nincompoop. Without doubt he was a rather supercilious, self-
important fellow. His reputation for pomposity had been cemented when
he changed his name from Peter to Pierre, in recognition of his family's
French Huguenot lineage.

Nevertheless, he was viewed in refined circles as the sort of Dauphin
of New York – the Sun King of the old money set. He was fabulously
rich by old money standards – one of the first millionaires in the US, in
fact – although that fortune was now being dwarfed by Vanderbilt and
his ilk. But he was still a big fish in 1866. He had inherited his family's
tobacco fortune, which had underlined its rich history by celebrating
100 years in business with the launch of a centennial line of cigarettes
hand-rolled in $100 notes. The company evidently had money to burn.
William K. Vanderbilt, a contemporary of Lorillard's who also owed
much of his fortune to his father, once stated that inherited wealth was
'as certain a death to ambition as cocaine is to morality'. Yet Lorillard's
inherited millions did not seem to hold him back. He had added to the
family fortune by acquiring tracts of waterfront land from New York's
notoriously corrupt officials and reclaiming, redeveloping and selling
them on.

He was also a canny marketing man, and one of the first high-profile
millionaires to employ a publicist with the express aim of keeping his

name in the gossip columns. This eye for publicity soon brought upon him the ire of the New York Yacht Club in relation to the 1866 race. It came about following his annual celebration of obscene wealth. This yearly ritual involved Lorillard heading to the strong room where his broker held all his stocks, dividends and general wealth. Puffing luxuriantly on a cigar, the tycoon would strut around inspecting the bundles of bonds and scrip, patronizingly urging his broker to invest wisely again the following year. This ghastly ritual was followed by a lavish banquet where friends and business associates were urged to eat, drink and prostrate themselves at this great font of wealth, marvelling at the money that poured into the Lorillard coffers. Meanwhile at the head of this table lounged the gracious, all-providing host. Truly, the Sun King shone forth and all should have averted their gaze. Those who did not, however, could place the blame squarely on the rather conspicuous and eye-catching banner positioned behind his lofty perch, trumpeting forth:

TOBACCO – LORILLARD – TOBACCO

Perhaps unsurprisingly this got up the nose of some in the media and the *New York World* vented spleen as follows:

> *Self advertisement is excellent in its place, but it would seem to be singularly vulgar when entertaining one's friends. We begin to wonder whether Mr Lorillard's participation in the forthcoming Atlantic yacht race is in the nature of a further advertisement for his commerce and whether* Vesta *will perhaps carry sails emblazoned with the words* Lorillard Tobacco.

This public dressing-down rang alarm bells with the gentlemen of the New York Yacht Club. To have Lorillard using the race for his own commercial gain was their nightmare. A committee meeting was convened and the issue of self-promotion raised. After the yacht club's commodore William McVickar had said his piece, Jimmy Bennett chimed in:

> *This race we are undertaking is no ordinary yacht race where two private individuals sail their boats as friends engaged in a harmless contest. It is a race to reflect credit upon the club and it is becoming that the owners of the three yachts should proceed to Europe in their yachts as representatives of the club.*

Lorillard remained unmoved. He was considerably older than James Bennett and no doubt age brought the wisdom to tactfully withdraw from the contest. Lorillard was rich and comfortable; he had no desire to throw it all away on a trifling race. He retreated to his rich home to live his rich, full life and left the race to other men who could risk their lives on his behalf. Men whose lives were not worth as much as his.

As for the Osgoods, they did not even bother to dignify their withdrawal with any statement to the press whatsoever. They simply retreated into their stocks and shares and money, and let others get on with the arduous business of dealing with the icy North Atlantic. Perhaps it was George Osgood's previous experience of yachting across the Atlantic that had put him off. In 1853 he had been part of his father-in-law Cornelius Vanderbilt's entourage when that dog-faced old curmudgeon had taken his 270-foot steam yacht *North Star* across the Atlantic on a pleasure cruise. It hadn't been an entirely happy trip, for the huge yacht, which featured ten cabins, ornate rosewood furniture and a banqueting hall with a marble floor, succeeded in running aground twice. On arrival, Vanderbilt, who was used to adulation back home, had also found himself sneered at by the British press, who condescendingly noted that 'perhaps it is time that *parvenu* should be looked upon as a word of honour'. This dispiriting encounter with the snooty English was followed by a slightly fraught cruise through the Mediterranean, but the real catastrophe for Vanderbilt came at the conclusion of the trip when he discovered that two of his previous business associates had set up a rival shipping line in his absence. It was at this juncture in his affairs that Vanderbilt reportedly wrote:

Gentlemen:
You have undertaken to cheat me. I won't sue you, for the law is too slow. I'll ruin you.
Yours truly,
Cornelius Vanderbilt.

Vanderbilt kept his promise, ruthlessly undercutting his rivals until they went bust. Money doesn't just make your life better, it gives you the power to eviscerate your enemies. Perhaps the Osgoods just didn't quite have the stomach for this, which explains their desire to attend to their business ashore instead. It was left to the *New York Herald* – unsurprisingly – to call out these disingenuous sportsmen with a lengthy article which included the withering observation:

...people who do not intend to sail in yacht races ought not to decide whether other people shall cross the ocean in midwinter.

The *New York Times* was similarly disparaging:

> *In this Atlantic race Mr Bennett is, we believe, the only one who*
> *proposes to accompany his yacht. The others are either not going at*
> *all or will go by steamer to await the arrival of their vessels on the*
> *other side. We confess the race would have more interest and be a*
> *pluckier affair if the owners would take part of their yachts in person.*
> *They may plead, and doubtless with reason, the claims of business,*
> *the discomforts of such a voyage, and the chances of being drowned,*
> *as reasons they should not go: but all these hazards and hardships*
> *are incidental to the peculiar sport they have seen fit to patronize.*
> *The very fact that these gentlemen assume to be conspicuous and*
> *eminent, implies they have superior leisure, courage, readiness to*
> *face the hardships peculiar to their sport.*

But in general the reaction to Lorillard and the Osgoods' withdrawal was fairly muted and perhaps that is because it was far from unexpected. Jimmy Bennett's 'hands on' approach to yachting was, by 1865, already the exception rather than the rule among the kind of gentlemen who were members of the New York Yacht Club. As early as 1860 the *Herald* – probably on Bennett Jr's prompting – had noted: 'It is a singular fact that half the yachtsmen of the present day do not know how to sail the yachts themselves in a match, and seldom know where to find a good captain for them.' Many owners hired a crew and captain and then retired to the comfortable deck of their steam yacht to observe from a safe distance.

In fairness, many competent modern yachtsmen and women would struggle to handle a 100-foot schooner. These big vessels were confusing, sophisticated racing machines, often dangerously over-canvassed and unwieldy. Being aboard during a yacht race could be a chastening experience for an owner used to getting his own way. JP Morgan once said that the man who asked how much it cost to run a yacht had no business owning one, but even as early as the 1860s some were questioning this approach. Amateur English yachtsman EF Knight, a contemporary of the racers, perfectly summed up what an ordeal yachting could be to men who viewed their boats first and foremost as symbols of wealth and in the course of displaying their largesse were occasionally forced to face the inconvenience of travelling aboard:

> By many, yachting is regarded as the amusement of the rich man. It is nothing of the sort, and indeed it may be said that the richer one is, the less enjoyment one gets out of it. I can see before me one of the newly rich, for example, who has bought a palatial yacht because he thinks it is the thing to do. He is as miserable in her at sea as a convict in Portland. He has to do exactly what his officers and crew order him to do, for he knows nothing of sea ways, he has to submit to insolence; knows that he is regularly cheated and is always on the slightest provocation lying down seasick in his luxurious cabin. Now when one can dispense with paid hands, when three or four men who know something of the sea join together to go cruising, they will find this one of the cheapest amusements.

This was not an ethos that the gentlemen of the New York Yacht Club generally adhered to. As a matter of fact, skippers generally found that 'fighting' owners (as they were termed) such as Bennett were an infernal nuisance.

This is well illustrated by an exchange between Bennett and Dick Brown, a skipper he had hired for the season aboard *Henrietta*. Brown was an old pilot who had honed his sailing skills racing his pilot schooner out past Sandy Hook to intercept packet ships as they approached New York. His reputation had been sealed when he had been chosen to take *America* out to Cowes for that historic 1851 race where he had humiliated the Royal Yacht Squadron on their own turf. In other words, he was a legend.

During one particularly intense race aboard the *Henrietta*, Brown had her perfectly in the groove, slipping softly through the water. His face was picture of concentration as he crouched down to leeward, peering up at the set of the sails, one finger caressing her tiller as he painstakingly coached the last ounce of speed out of the yacht. At this point, Bennett came up from below. Approaching Brown, he said: 'Very well, skipper, I'll take her now.' Brown, never taking his eye off the sails, replied: 'Don't bother me, cain't you see I'm racing!'

Thus, racing yachts were made up of a rather uneasy mix of professional sailors – who often worked as fishermen or boatmen during the winter months – and gentlemen yachtsmen. Generally these two very different classes were marked out by uniform. Crew were clad in white ducks, while gentlemen wore white linen trousers, blazers and a club tie. These chaps often got in the way, but did occasionally help out, as one veteran of the Newport racing scene explained: 'It's quite normal for guests to pull on the sheets every now and then, but it would be absurd to ask them to clean the deck, polish the brass or handle the sails all day!'

Englishman RT McMullen, a singlehanded sailor of some note who was just hitting his prime in 1866, poured scorn on this breed of armchair sailors, noting:

> Lone Yachtsmen looked down on the Cowes aristocracy and the Newport multimillionaires and they distrusted the Solent and Long Island racing yachtsmen. They [Lone Yachtsmen] lived private lives, often alone with just their endless love for the sea and sailing for company. They chose to wear fisherman's reefer jackets rather than blazers, white trousers and club ties, and they frequented quayside bars rather than those of the sailing clubs.

Given the 'hands off' approach to yachting taken by members of the New York Yacht Club, it is understandable that few batted an eyelid when two out of the three owners withdrew, but there was no question of Jimmy Bennett passing up the opportunity for adventure on a grand scale. Besides, it wasn't as if he could claim that he had important business to attend to. Everyone knew that it was old man Bennett who ran the *Herald*, every last column inch of it. It is also quite likely that Bennett Sr applied pressure on his wayward son to take part in the race, seeing the potential for good publicity for his beloved paper. Jimmy's decision was sealed when his great friends and allies the Jerome brothers agreed to join the *Henrietta* and come along for the ride. Given that Lawrence and Leonard were 47 and 49 in 1866, this was well beyond the call of duty. It's worth recalling, too, that the paper the Jeromes largely controlled, the *New York Times*, had been one of the few to disparage the other men's decisions not to join the race.

The immediate result of Bennett and his stalwart companions' decision to race was that the *Henrietta* was picked out as the vessel that most members of the public wanted to win. She might have been the people's choice, but she was certainly not the bookmakers', and there were a number of good reasons for this. Although the vessels were of a similar size, *Henrietta*'s record in head-to-head races against the newer *Vesta* and *Fleetwing* was poor. The summer just gone had been a lively one with a busy racing calendar and it had soon shown that *Henrietta*, by now four years old, was being outclassed. Her design was more old-fashioned and she was described as being less sharp in the bow, though she certainly had good pedigree, being designed and built by Henry Steers, whose uncle had built the famous *America*. At 107 feet she was a foot longer than the *Fleetwing* and two feet longer than *Vesta*, yet she was narrower, and some argued that gave her less power to carry sail.

This had been borne out to some extent in a race she had undertaken against *Vesta* that summer. At the time, the 209-mile course between the Sandy Hook lighthouse and Cape May Light had been considered epic and the race, undertaken in boisterous conditions, had had its share of thrills and spills, with the *Vesta* carrying away a number of sails and the two racers sailing side by side early on before *Vesta* forged ahead to what was ultimately a comfortable victory. The stakes that day had been a modest $1,000 ($15,000 today), a mere nothing to both men, which was as well for Bennett, for *Vesta* had comfortably beaten *Henrietta* and narrowly beaten *Fleetwing*. In lighter airs, *Henrietta* had also been beaten by *Fleetwing* that same summer. All in all, the odds seemed stacked against the young media mogul. What he needed was a trump card, a man with true grit, and he had a suspicion he knew where to find him. He sent an emissary down to scour the waterfront in search of one man: Captain Samuel Samuels. Bennett was after the ultimate hired gun.

If Bennett was a hands-on, 'fighting' owner, he was sensible enough to see the value of hiring a experienced skipper to get the schooner across safely. His usual captain was Martin Lyons, but Bennett divined that Lyons didn't have the transatlantic pedigree for this trip and he was demoted to sailing master. Usually this would have been seen as a humiliating step-down, but Lyons took the move with good grace, and this had everything to do with his replacement. On the giant, cruel racecourse of the Atlantic, no one commanded respect like Samuel Samuels.

Captain Samuels was a man straight off the page of an Horatio Alger novel. Cut him open and he bled the American Dream. Born in 1825, he had run away to sea at the age of eleven after falling out with his stepmother. 'My step mother and I had such differences that a house the size of the Capitol at Washington could not have been large enough for the both of us,' he later recalled drolly. This falling-out was the catalyst for an endless succession of seafaring adventures. In between serving on a diverse range of seagoing craft, Samuels managed to wind up in Mobile jail for desertion, spent a short term treading the boards as part of a vaudeville act and took part in a mutiny in Manila. By 20 he was married and by 21 he had gained command of his first ship, a truly remarkable achievement for a man with limited formal education. By 1853 he reached the peak of his profession when he was given command of the transatlantic packet ship the *Dreadnought*. It was his partnership with this vessel, nicknamed 'the wild boat of the Atlantic', which sealed his reputation as one of the greatest captains of his day.

The packet ships had revolutionized communication between the United States and Europe when, in 1817, the Black Ball Line had set up a regular scheduled service between New York and Liverpool. Prior to this, ships simply departed when fully loaded, however long that took. Not so the Black Ball liners. Whether their ships were half full or empty, blow high or blow low, the service was maintained, and the Yankee skippers drove their vessels with tenacity over this cruel stretch of the North Atlantic.

Soon, there were a number of American lines competing against one another. The Dramatic, the Swallow Tail and the Red Cross Line among many others all served to keep that vital lifeline between the old world and the new intact, their ships battling with the darkened seas, icebergs, bad weather and the hateful cold to bring over a steady stream of immigrants. Germans, Irish, Italian, Scandinavians: they headed to the new world in hordes, their heads full of dreams, to stoke the industrial revolution that was taking place. In running this route with such regularity, the captains of these tough little packets gained a reputation for their skill and sea sense. There is an anecdote from a passenger on one of the packets who describes how the ship arrived off the coast of America in a thick fog. After several days of groping around with the air as thick as pea soup, the captain commented to his mate, 'I guess we must be there or tharabouts.' Within moments the vessel nosed alongside her own pier in the East River.

By the time Samuel Samuels and the *Dreadnought* entered the transatlantic trade, the stakes were higher than they had ever been, for in 1838 the steamships *Sirius* and *Great Western* had arrived in New York after transatlantic runs, while in 1840, Samuel Cunard had introduced the first steam packet line between Liverpool and Boston, and in 1848 Cunard had added a New York–Liverpool run to his schedule. The game was nearly up for the lordly tall ship. That first shrill steam whistle that had echoed across New York Harbor as the *Sirius* arrived on her inaugural crossing had sounded the death knell of the transatlantic packet ship. But for many years the sailing ship held on; its cheaper running costs and greater ultimate speed meant the more reliable steamship did not have it all her own way. This can be seen during Charles Dickens' visit to the US in 1842. He made the trip across aboard the Cunarder *Britannia*, which had plodded across the storm-tossed Atlantic at 8 and a bit knots, often less, as she butted into an unending succession of January storms. Dickens hated it and opted to return under the white wings of a transatlantic packet. The trip was far more successful and Dickens enthused that 'The noble American vessels ... have made their packet service the finest in the world'. This was high praise indeed, for Dickens didn't have too many positive things to say about America following his visit. He had arrived hoping to find some kind of democratic, liberal utopia and departed in disgust, finding that the Americans were acquisitive, brash, almost as disappointing as the English when it came to democracy but with worse table manners. 'I am disappointed,' he wrote. 'This is not the republic of my imagination.'

I digress. Dickens made his trip in 1842 and by the time Samuels and *Dreadnought* entered the trade in 1853, eleven years had passed and the efficiency of the steamship had progressed. The relentless turn of her screw and the thud of her machinery sounded out the plodding march of an inevitable utilitarian future. For a sailing ship to thrive in this tenuous trade, something special was going to have to be done. Samuels possessed the perfect ship for the job. The *Dreadnought* was not a particularly sharp-ended vessel, but she was tough and could be pushed much harder than her rivals. 'She possessed the merit of being able to bear driving as long as her spars and sails could stand it,' Samuels later fondly recalled. 'Many a time I have been told that the crews of other vessels, lying hove to, could see our keel as we skipped from sea to sea under every rag we dared to carry.'

Samuels also believed the big secret of the *Dreadnought*'s success was his willingness to push the vessel through the hours of darkness, when other skippers tended to snug their vessel down. Samuels had to push his vessel hard as he had developed a daring business plan whereby he not only guaranteed shippers that he would leave on a stipulated date, but also that he would cross the ocean within a stipulated time, not an easy thing to deliver on a vessel at the mercy of the vagaries of wind and wave. This risky business plan paid dividends, largely due to his ridiculously hard driving. In 20 passages made eastwards from New York, his ship averaged 19 days, with the quickest journey taking 13 days. No other packet could even come close to this, particularly when you bear in mind that the sailing ship record, set by the mighty clipper *James Baines*, was 12 days.

In a short space of time, he made his ship the highest-earning packet on the Atlantic circuit and his fame spread. To wring such remarkable performances out of the *Dreadnought*, Samuels was none too gentle with his crew, extracting the last ounce of work out of them and earning the nickname of 'Bully' Samuels into the bargain. This was a time of great savagery among sailors, too, and the *Dreadnought* gained further notoriety after Samuels took on a ring of sailors called the 'Bloody Forty', who had 'taken an oath to clip the wings of the bloody old *Dreadnought* and give the skipper a swim', as Samuels picturesquely recalled. Samuels put the mutiny down almost singlehanded, although he did get some vital help from his loyal dog, Wallace, and some German immigrants who had shipped aboard. Samuels, who had a reputation as a gunslinger, patrolled the afterdeck with two levelled pistols always at the ready to keep the men at bay. The mutineers yielded to his iron will after an epic running battle lasting several days.

The culmination of his adventures aboard the *Dreadnought* came after she had been overtaken by a violent storm in the mid-Atlantic. At the peak of the storm a huge sea had overwhelmed the ship, tearing off the rudder and hurling several men overboard. Samuels' leg was badly broken and three strong men were unable to set the leg back in place, not realizing that you had to bend the limb to relax the muscles. Half mad with pain, Samuels made the decision to self-amputate and prepared a knife and tourniquet. Thankfully the second mate, who had limited medical knowledge, dissuaded him and the leg was lashed up and left. In agony, and unable to turn his ship away from the breeze without a rudder, Samuels managed to sail backwards to the Azores. It was a masterful display of seamanship, but it signalled the end of his romance with the *Dreadnought*. He spent the next year or so undergoing physiotherapy to repair his mangled leg. He had followed that little adventure up with active service in the Civil War. In 1866 he was 41 years old and still in his prime: lean, moustachioed, with a steely glint in his eye. He bowed to no one.

This was the picaresque figure Bennett tentatively approached to command his little *Henrietta*: a swaggering gunslinger reeking of sea air and adventure; a roaring relic of an almost entirely different and heroic era, one that owed more to Captain Morgan than to JP Morgan. Samuels hadn't played at adventure, it had been there for real, and he hadn't needed to buy it like the poor little rich boy begging for his help. He knew of uncertain foreign lands; he knew the surge and thrum of the trade wind in the sails of a well-found tall ship. Most of all, he understood the North Atlantic and what a cruel adversary she was: he had gazed out on this foe from the poop of the *Dreadnought* on a snarling, sleet-filled 4am Atlantic, dusted the ice from his greatcoat and waited for the dawn. The Atlantic was his workplace.

Bennett wanted true grit and Samuels was chock full of that. What must he have made of the young fop, this gilt-bespangled yachting dandy who approached him proposing to gamble against a foe when only he fully understood the stakes? What could this gilded youth possibly have to offer the mighty salt-encrusted skipper? Well, I can tell you exactly what he had to offer him: $10,000 dollars. That's the equivalent of $150,000 in today's terms. I doubt Samuels hesitated for a moment. He had worked hard his whole life. Bennett casually tossed him many years' earnings in one careless gesture. To him, $10,000 was nothing. He could just as well have burnt it; something he later did. The story goes that Bennett had summoned one of the *Herald*'s correspondents to meet him in a hotel and the pair settled by the warmth and comfort of a fire to discuss business. During this chat Bennett fidgeted constantly and it was evident to the journo that he was in some discomfort. Eventually the young millionaire grappled with his back pocket and wrestled out a great wad of bank notes. He tossed the bundle irritably into the fire before settling back to his conversation. Distraught, his employee endeavoured to retrieve the flaming notes, presuming it was a mistake, but Bennett told him not to bother, he had no further use for it.

You can probably guess that Samuel Samuels did not hesitate to take up Bennett's generous offer. The old skipper had total confidence in himself. If you wanted further proof of that, the story goes that, on receiving his fee for the race, he went straight out and put $7,500 on himself to win.

While he backed himself, he might have been less certain about the *Henrietta*. After taking up the offer, Samuels headed down to where she lay off the New York Yacht Club's humble clubhouse at Elysian Fields, Hoboken, to look her over; in his mind's eye he pictured her wrestling with those mean-spirited greybeards that lay rolling and snarling out east. She was a solidly built little vessel, but her builder had set her up for inshore racing. Her sail plan was huge. Her main boom, in particular, was over 60 feet long and a massive liability – it was likely to take charge in a heavy sea where even a large, well-drilled crew might struggle to tame it. Samuels ordered 6 feet removed from the end of the main boom and the rest of the spars in proportion.

There were other factors to be considered too. Her builder had fitted her with tiller steering: ideal for inshore racing as it gave the helmsman great control and 'feel' for the ship, but on an ocean crossing another liability. It was arduous work wrestling with a tiller for long periods of time in a heavy sea. The great leverage on the tiller could wrench it from a man's hand and then you were in serious trouble. The yacht would slew sideways to the waves and be overwhelmed. Samuels deemed that it should be replaced with wheel steering. He also surveyed her deep, open oval cockpit situated right aft and recoiled in horror, imagining the dainty little schooner out there on the howling, merciless Atlantic. In her current configuration, the yacht was in grave danger of being filled up with gallons of water in this wide open cockpit. He ordered the cockpit to be covered over and had large freeing ports cut in her low bulwarks so that any seas boarding the little yacht would drain away as quickly as possible. Her ballast was also secured with extra lashings, so that if she was thrown on her side, she wouldn't destroy herself by throwing her ballast against her frames. Samuels surveyed the work as it progressed and declared himself satisfied with the result.

Similar preparations were taking place aboard the *Fleetwing* and *Vesta*. Lorillard's skipper George Dayton wasn't as high profile as Samuels. The most notable thing he had ever done was sire a remarkable 17 children, although his wife surely deserves the greater credit for that. As a seaman, he promised to be a safe pair of hands, which is what the flighty *Vesta* needed. Indeed, Dayton was especially conservative in the manner in which he prepared the centreboard schooner. You may recall that the whole argument in the Union Club that had led to this race had pivoted on *Vesta*'s centreboard. This centreboard was essentially a drop-down keel which could be raised when the schooner was running off the wind to drastically reduce drag. This meant her underwater body was much shallower and wider. The pros and cons of the centreboard in an offshore sailing yacht are still debated to this day, but the big problem that Dayton identified was that if the weather did pick up, the *Vesta* would be unable to heave to. This was a method by which a deep-keeled yacht could ride out a storm by setting a small scrap of sail and lying across the sea, drifting with the great waves like a chip of wood. The *Vesta* didn't have enough depth to do this. In a storm she would be forced to 'scud': a truly hair-raising experience in which a vessel raced down the face of giant waves. It was for this reason that many doubted that *Vesta* was suited to a transatlantic race. The best way for Pierre Lorillard to find out for sure was to send some other people over to try it out for him.

The crew aboard the *Fleetwing* approached the task of preparing the yacht with an air of confidence. The Osgoods had picked up a first-class captain in the shape of Dick Brown of *America* fame and the yacht was acknowledged as the strongest, most powerful vessel in the race. The bookies made her odds-on favourite to win. Perhaps this was why she was not quite so thoroughly storm-proofed as her two rivals. Although her mighty spars were shortened somewhat, her cockpit was left open to the elements and no freeing ports were cut into her bulwarks. If a storm was encountered, the men aboard were going to be that bit more vulnerable.

As the work progressed, the three captains must have eyed their handsome little commands with a certain fondness, but also an element of sadness. Everything about this race pointed to the fact that their livelihood, their way of life and they themselves were obsolete. Brown was a Sandy Hook pilot, who, in his prime, had raced his schooner *Harriet Lane* against his rivals to reach approaching merchant ships and drop a pilot aboard. If you lost the race, you didn't get paid. That was racing with more than honour but also food on the table that night at stake. Yet he had watched the handsome pilot schooners be replaced, one by one, by steamships.

Dayton and Samuels were deep-water sailors through and through and they had plenty to mourn. The year was 1866 and only 13 years previously the mighty American clipper *James Baines* had thundered across the Atlantic from Boston to Liverpool in the astonishing time of 12 days and 6 hours. At times on that trip she had logged 22 knots. It wouldn't be until the 1880s that commercial steamships were touching those speeds. Back then, clipper ships had been at their zenith, racing out to San Francisco laden with prospectors hungry for gold. The vision of striking it rich out there on the chaos of the California goldfields had driven commercial sail to a spectacular high-water mark. Beautiful, sleek tall ships with pure white sails had carried all before them, often humiliating rival steamships along the way. Yet it was just a final, glorious flourish for the American clippers. Since then there had been nothing but decline and slow retreat, slumping freights and hard times.

All three captains had been forced to relinquish their beloved sailing vessels, but in their ear the steady trade winds still thrummed and their eyes seemed to gaze beyond the clutter and squalor of New York City to a blue, infinite horizon. The three captains were in an almost unique position, bridging the gap between yachting as we know it today and the commercial sailing of the past. They will always be remembered as the first skippers in an offshore yachting race. Fast forward to the Volvo Ocean Race or the Vendee Globe and you can draw a line straight back to these three. Yet it was what lay behind these men that mattered more to them. Their experience of commanding commercial sailing ships, their dying trade, their knowledge distilled from two thousand years and more of sailors plying the seas in sailing ships was more vital to them. In a little over 70 years, almost all this knowledge would be destroyed by the twist of the steamship's screw. Progress has a terrible habit of taking objects of wonder or mystery and making them prosaic, as Samuels noted sadly when he looked back on his life:

> *Nowadays there are no inducements to fire a youth as there were then – no new lands to discover, no pirates to encounter, no slavers to capture. The romance of the sea departed when our white winged racers were superseded by steamers.*

Instead, young gentlemen of an adventurous disposition like Bennett went yachting. Men like Samuels must play along to their game and shrug off their loss or weigh it up against the financial gain. The world was changing and Samuels, Dayton and Brown signalled their willingness to accept this by pocketing their exorbitant signing-on fees.

If the skippers were happy with this arrangement, the same could certainly not be said of the crew. All three yachts struggled to recruit the requisite number of hands. Given that even the usually profligate Bennett was offering only $100 per head for crew, it is perhaps unsurprising. Most of the prime paid hands were fishermen and some would have sailed regularly out to the treacherous Grand Banks off the coast of Newfoundland. All knew that a trip across the Atlantic in December was a truly tough assignment. As 11 December drew nearer, reality started to bite, and the *Henrietta* was faced with a real crisis when almost the entirety of her 23-strong crew quit. The incident was explained in the *Herald* as follows:

> Some difficulty was experienced in securing seamen to cross the
> Atlantic in such vessels and in such weather. The men were willing
> enough to engage, but their mothers, wives and sweethearts all
> interfered and persuaded them not to sign articles. Moved by such
> feminine solicitations, the crew of the Henrietta deserted her a
> few days before the start and their places had to be supplied by a
> lot of landlubbers, few of whom could climb a mast. Invitations
> to prominent yachtsmen were declined for various reasons and
> the gentlemen who finally served in this capacity were almost all
> volunteers.

This didn't sound like the ideal recipe for a successful transatlantic crossing, but at least the *Henrietta* had the kind of skipper who could whip a novice crew into shape. There was also drama aboard the

Fleetwing when Captain Dick Brown quit in disgust after being demoted to the secondary role of sailing master by the Osgoods, who favoured Captain Albert Thomas, another deep-water sailing man, best known as commander of the packet ship *New York*. Given Captain Brown's excellent record as a skipper and his track record in taking the schooner yacht *America* across the Atlantic in 1851 it seems like a bewildering decision. Brown was a proud man and felt he had little choice other than to quit. This may explain why eight other members of the crew jumped ship just days before the *Fleetwing* left. They were replaced by eight hard-bitten seamen who usually plied their trade in whaling vessels. In that profession, a jaunt across the Atlantic in midwinter was probably viewed as a holiday.

So the crews of the three vessels were an odd assortment. There were a number of ex-skippers aboard, a handful of complete novices and plenty of weather-beaten old hands who knew what they were getting into and simply needed the money. These veterans would have expected nothing but hard usage. Herman Melville, a ship's hand himself, once wrote: 'There are classes of men in the world who bear more the same relation to society at large, that the wheels do to a coach: and are just as indispensable ... Now, sailors form one of these wheels.'

This may be true in most respects, but in one matter it certainly wasn't. Sailors were eminently dispensable. Collectively they were indeed a spoke in a wheel, but individually their lives were worth virtually nothing. Many men perished at sea through falling from aloft or being washed from the decks. In 1851, the clipper ship *Challenge* arrived in San Francisco after a gruelling winter passage around Cape Horn from New York with nine crew members dead, in addition to a number dying from illness and privation. At least one man was beaten to death and three men fell overboard from aloft. It was later alleged that the mate had deliberately cast loose a rope which had led to the men plunging to an icy grave. At a subsequent inquiry, both captain and mate were absolved of any blame. The life of a sailor truly was worth virtually nothing.

In addition to officers and crew, each yacht was required to carry two judges appointed by the New York Yacht Club to ensure that everything was above board. The *Vesta* carried George Lorillard, brother of the owner, and Colonel Stuart Taylor. This gave her a complement of 26 all told. The *Henrietta* carried Lawrence Jerome and Arthur Knapp as judges, and Leonard Jerome as the stake-holder, making up a complement of 30. The *Fleetwing* carried Robert Center and Ernest Staples as judges and a crew of 25.

The three crews were an unusual melting pot of men from all classes and walks of life and the circumstances of their last supper ashore on 10 December must have differed wildly. Jimmy Bennett most likely went to Delmonico's and met up with a few of his chums. Sipping on champagne and tucking into a succulent, juicy lamb chop – his favoured dish – all the while soaking up the adulation of his contemporaries, he who would also have listened to them speaking big about their own desire to join him for the trip while tactfully making their excuses. In the early hours he would have retired to his ivory tower on 5th Avenue – the Bennetts' town bolt-hole. Amid the glittering chandeliers, burnished walls, twittering servants and honeyed luxury, Bennett would have gazed about at this easy opulence with languid boredom, sipped on a glass of port and dreamt of a life richer, more visceral and fulfilling than his own.

By contrast, Captain Samuels no doubt headed back to the rustic comfort of his pleasant middle-class home and probably basked by the fire, surrounded by loved ones and the fruits of his hard-earned labour.

Then there were others, the tough Scandinavian immigrants who supplied much of the muscle aboard the racing yachts. Many of these men will have plunged into Lower Manhattan's labyrinth of cheap tenements and boarding houses for an altogether more humble meal taken amid squalling children and grinding poverty. New York was already expanding uncontrollably by 1866 and the innards of the city were a great heaving mess of filth and poverty where swine still rolled in their own dirt. (It wasn't until the following year that pigs were prohibited from the inner city.) Disease hung in the foetid air of these great human holding pens: no running water, no sanitation, sometimes no natural light. Jacob Riis, a Danish immigrant, arrived in New York in 1870. He summed up the poverty of the tenements with an eloquence borne out of first-hand experience:

> They were not intended to last. Rents were fixed high enough to cover damage and abuse from this class, from whom nothing was expected, and the most was made of them while they lasted. Neatness, order, cleanliness, were never dreamed of in connection with the tenant-house system, as it spread its localities from year to year; while redress slovenliness, discontent, privation, and ignorance were left to work out their invariable results, until the entire premises reached the level of tenant-house dilapidation, containing, but sheltering not, the miserable hordes that crowded beneath smouldering, water-rotted roofs or burrowed among the rats of clammy cellars.

Tenement-houses have no aesthetic resources. If any are to be brought to bear on them, they must come from the outside. There is the common hall with doors opening softly on every landing as the strange step is heard on the stairs, the air-shaft that seems always so busy letting out foul stenches from below that it has no time to earn its name by bringing down fresh air, the squeaking pumps that hold no water, and the rent that is never less than one week's wages out of the four, quite as often half of the family earnings. In a room not thirteen feet either-way slept twelve men and women, two or three in bunks set in a sort of alcove, the rest on the floor. A kerosene lamp burned dimly in the fearful atmosphere, probably to guide other and later arrivals to their 'beds,' for it was only just past midnight.

This was the vision of squalor that awaited the less fortunate of our bold racing crews on their last night ashore. No job security, no minimum wage, no pension. Just a world where hunger, hardship and disappointment seemed the unalterable law of life. Such men would simply have been grateful to satisfy their hunger with what fell from the rich man's table. Even as late as 1900, the average American had only received five years of schooling in their lifetime. Dearth, death and disease lurked at every turn and 1866 had seen a cholera epidemic take 1,100 lives. Life was cheap, and down in areas such as the Bowery slums and the Five Points, violence was an everyday fact of life.

People were flooding into the swirling, menacing, melting pot of New York. Gang warfare was common as tensions between the various ethnic groups flared up, with the Irish Catholics, who were arriving at a rate of hundreds per week in the wake of the potato famine, being heavily targeted. Anti-immigration groups such as the nativist Know

Nothings and Bowery Boys often engaged in bloody battles with ethnic groups such as the Dead Rabbits. Policing was in its infancy and the anonymity of this ever-changing urban landscape also gave rise to thievery and acts of savagery – which men like James Gordon Bennett Sr exploited to titillate his audience. A bold *Herald* journalist Stephen Fiske, of whom you will hear more shortly, had first risen to prominence as a reporter for his somewhat restrained portrayal of a sickening murder in the Bowery whereby the decapitated bodies of three young children were hurled into the bustling street from a tenement window. The heads of the three were later discovered impaled on iron railings surrounding the communal water pump nearby. This was the world of alienation, casual senseless violence and poverty which a large proportion of New Yorkers lived in: an unpleasant by-product of all that productivity; an inconvenient truth.

Don't think that this suffering did not prick the consciences of the wealthy. It wasn't their fault that they were good at making money – anyone could do it if they only applied themselves; their apparent success owed more to the failings and indolence of fellow men. Nevertheless, all our well-heeled contestants had 'done their bit' to help out. George Osgood owned a number of boarding houses for the needy; Leonard Jerome gave freely to benevolent funds for wounded Civil War veterans; there is even a wonderfully evocative picture of James Gordon Bennett staring balefully out with exquisite boredom as he helps out at a soup kitchen. JJ Astor was also more than happy to hand out a few crumbs from the estimated $5m he was making out of New York tenements at this time. This was the beginning of the age of the philanthropist and the wealthy were starting to realize that they had a social responsibility to help the poor. You see, money doesn't just buy you a lifestyle, it turns you into a better human being. You can give generously to the charity of your choice and suddenly all that guilt is gone. Your hands are washed clean. You can retire to your well-appointed chamber, lean back on your duck-down pillow and once more sleep with your conscience crystal clear. It feels good.

While the working class no doubt appreciated these Olympian crumbs, most of these unfortunates continued to work until they dropped. As for our sailors, some would have been fishermen, others deep-water men. Some would have plied the transatlantic run, a trade which bred a certain type of indestructible sailor known as 'packet rats'. Captain Samuels once summed this bunch up with his usual blunt pithiness: 'The packet sailors were not easily demoralized. They were the toughest class of seamen in all respects. They could stand the worst weather, food and usage, and put up with less sleep, more rum and harder knocks than any other sailors.'

These men had very little other than hopes and dreams. In the circumstances, you might think it would be a relief to head out into the fresh, clean air of the Atlantic, yet many did it purely as a financial expedient. They left their homes the next day with the desperate entreaties of loved ones echoing in their ears as they trod the frosty, crackling cobbles of South Street in the pre-dawn glow.

It was an early start, for the yachts were towed out into the stream at 7am on the morning of 11 December and anchored off Stapleton, Staten Island. The race would not get under way until later that afternoon, but this step was taken to ensure there were no further desertions. Crammed like sardines in a tin and essentially imprisoned, the crew of the three yachts gazed out on a savagely cold December dawn and awaited departure. For six men, this would be their final voyage.

4

STICK, TWIST OR BUST?

Yes, I can understand that a man might go to gambling table – when he sees that all that lies between himself and death is his last shilling.

HONORÉ DE BALZAC

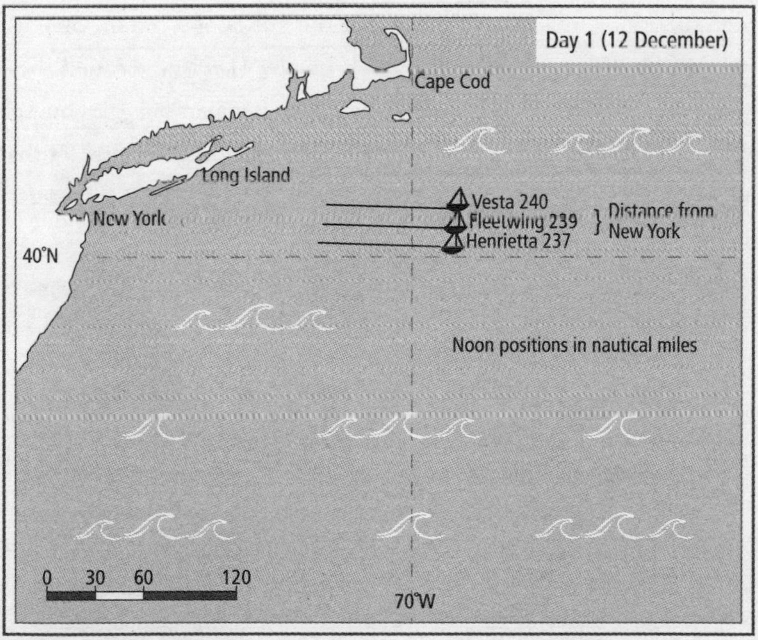
Day 1 (12 December)
Cape Cod
Long Island
New York
40°N
Vesta 240
Fleetwing 239
Henrietta 237
Distance from New York
Noon positions in nautical miles
0 30 60 120
70°W

They reckon that $1m was gambled on that race. It felt like most of the people who had placed those bets were out at the start line. There they lay, bobbing precariously in innumerable pleasure steamers and ferries chartered especially for the occasion. The scene belonged to a high summer's day, but the quality of the light and the temperature betrayed everyone. It was clear, icy-cold winter with the thermometer hovering around minus five. The squalls of merriment and gusts of music that wafted gently across to the three racers seemed incongruous in the hard, pin-sharp winter light and clashed horribly with the chill westerly wind that needled through clothes, pricked the skin and shrilled in their rigging as final preparations for departure were made. Aboard the yachts there had been the usual last-minute dramas: supplies and extra cases of champagne to be loaded for the judges, final adjustments made to the running rigging, that sort of thing, but the antics of a certain Stephen Fiske in his efforts to smuggle himself on the *Henrietta* dwarfed these minor dramas altogether. It's not every day that a man smuggles himself aboard a luxury yacht in a case of champagne and it is even rarer for that man to use the disguise of a recently assassinated president in order to do so.

Fiske was a reporter on the *Herald* and old man Bennett, ever alive to the possibility of a good story, had decided that he needed a man to cover the race from the best possible vantage point: aboard one of the yachts. Fiske was summoned into the great editor's office at his satanic majesty's request. Trembling with fear, he presented himself to his master. He described the scene memorably:

> *I went into his office with its dark red curtains and walls and the*
> *heavy mahogany furniture and the decanters of whisky and brandy*

*et al standing gleaming on the tall boy under the shaded lights. Thick
cigar smoke obscured him as he sat behind the desk, but there was
no obscuring his voice which rasped at me as if I was being given the
assignment as a punishment:*

*'This race. Yachts. One of 'em's m'son's. Cover it. No fooling
around. Fall in the sea for all I care but get the news. Properly.
Understood?'*

Fiske did understand. He was well acquainted with the methods of his
somewhat irascible boss and was a veteran of the *Herald*'s Civil War
campaign, which asked for a similar level of neglect for one's own life
in order to cover the story. This outline written by one of the *Herald*'s
reporters illustrates precisely how close to the action a journalist was
expected to be:

The instructions of the Herald *to journalists in the field were brief
but comprehensive. They were simply these: To obtain the most
accurate information by personal observation and forward it with the
utmost despatch, regardless of expense, labour or danger. Guided by
these concise instructions – with his horse, his revolver, his notebook,
blanket and haversack, the army correspondent of the* New York
Herald *set forth to share the vicissitudes and hardship of the camp,
the fatigues of the march and the perils of the battlefield.*

Others had to go even further in search of news. Many questions were
raised as to how handsome Henry Wikoff, one of the *Herald*'s
correspondents, had gained access to sections of Lincoln's first address
to Congress in December 1861, which was published almost at the

same moment Lincoln presented it. Many pointed to Wikoff's extreme closeness to Mrs Lincoln, although this was never proven. In his slightly less racy role of war correspondent, Fiske had coolly watched death march past and give a quick glance his way across the battlefields of Shiloh and Vicksburg. He had sustained a minor injury during one skirmish which he had put down to 'my own foolishness in getting too near a gun team under fire', or 'covering the story', as his boss might have put it. The prospect of a quick yacht race was small beer to such a man. He was 25 in 1866, still single and by and large excited at the prospect of a trip abroad.

The same could not be said of his friends, who were pretty convinced that the whole trip was tantamount to suicide. They very nearly thwarted his wanderlust. Fiske had been due to board the *Henrietta* on the morning of the 11th via the steamer *PC Schulz*, which was scheduled to tow the schooner out to the race course. This plan hit a snag thanks to some well-meaning friends of the young journo. It appears that Fiske had been a minor witness to an altercation in a New York street and some of his well-meaning friends had succeeded in getting him subpoenaed to appear at the trial. When word got out that he was planning to take part in the transatlantic yacht race, a couple of officers of the court headed down to the *PC Schulz* to stop him. They arrived to find Bennett, Leonard and Lawrence Jerome and other crewmembers from *Henrietta* boarding, but no sign of Fiske.

This was because Fiske had got wind of the scheme to thwart his adventure. No doubt fearing old James Gordon Bennett Sr's ire if he returned to the office having failed to cover the story, he hastily conceived a plan. Further down the wharf lay the beautiful side-wheel paddle steamer *River Queen*, which had been chartered for the start by the New York Yacht Club. The club was ultimately run by businessmen and it was inevitable that someone came up with the wheeze of selling tickets at vast expense to members of the general public. The scheme looked like a sure-fire money-spinner, but it was not perhaps as well organized as it could have been, as a rather splenetic reporter from the *Rochester Daily Union* wrote:

THE OCEAN YACHT RACE

A Hearty Adieu to the Contestants – The Yacht Club on the
River Queen

The New York Yacht Club, who are chiefly interested in the result, chartered the historic steamboat *River Queen*, and issued tickets, the fortunate holder of one being entitled to a semi official view of the departure and its details. The hour specified on the tickets for appearance at the foot of Debrosses Street where the *River Queen* lay this morning was nine o clock. Subsequent to the distribution of tickets, a change was made in the time of departure and ten o clock was the hour understood by the great majority of the club. At the former hour, however, stragglers were wandering on the dock looking for the steamboat and wondering why the programme had been deranged as the thermometer marked 22 fahrenheit but feeling much lower, made a promenade on the dock not desirable and only necessary to keep up the calorie. The boat soon appeared however and the few who were out in the cold, including some of the early rising reporters, hurried on board and comfortably seated themselves in the capacious cane bottomed arm chairs around the saloon stoves.

It is rather pleasing that editorial policy back in those days allowed reporters to vent spleen on matters of tardiness. He went on to moan about the New York Yacht Club's inability to issue invitations, which meant that only a handful of non-members were present.

I will leave the disgruntled *Union* reporter comfortably reposing in a cane chair warming his numbed toes and return to our own reporter, Mr Fiske, who seemed indifferent to the cold and was also able to put the tardy steamer to good use. The *River Queen* was one of the best-appointed steamers in New York and had been much loved by Abraham Lincoln. She was already historically noteworthy: toward the end of the Civil War, Lincoln had hosted Confederate officials aboard her in order to thrash out a peace deal. An indication of the reverence shown to the recently murdered Lincoln can be witnessed by the fact that his stateroom had been cordoned off for the trip as a slightly macabre shrine/tourist attraction in his honour.

When Fiske spotted the steamer, she was a hive of activity as porters and catering staff frantically loaded her up with supplies in anticipation of a substantial blow-out for the members of the venerable old club. A lavish banquet was being laid out: oysters, Westphalian ham, roast turkey, fillet of beef, pastries, ice creams, Californian grapes, terrapin soup and quails eggs, all washed down with Bordeaux wine. That was just the starter. Porters dashed to and fro staggering under the weight of great cow-sized slabs of beef and mounds of pastries. Then, of course, there was the band to be loaded aboard and all those helpless guests to be gently herded up the gangplank.

Fiske started out by offering to help one of the overworked porters lugging gallons of champagne aboard the boat. The offer was eagerly accepted. Having gained access without a ticket, the intrepid reporter needed somewhere to hide. Fiske made a beeline for Lincoln's stateroom where, slipping under the rope cordon, he placed himself in the recently deceased president's chair and, facing away from any observers, assumed a statesmanlike posture and hoped that any inquisitive observers would presume a rather tasteless curator had added in an impressive waxwork to give the exhibit a bit more oomph.

Up on deck, the *River Queen* shivered into life. As the last of the guests and supplies were loaded, steam was raised and lines were cast off amid an eruption of whistles, billows of smoke and a great roar of cheering from the wharf. On deck the band struck up 'Old Columbia' and all on board braced themselves against the biting wind and pretended it was summer. There was a holiday atmosphere in New York and thousands had turned out to see the brave sailing yachts head off on their magnificent adventure. The *River Queen* headed up a huge flotilla of pleasure steamers diverted from their regular trade for this special day. Pity the eighty or so passengers who paid to travel aboard the *Charles Chamberlain*, which lacked any enclosed space apart from a tiny deckhouse for the skipper. A *Herald* reporter describes their suffering:

> This was not the occasion for a display of new styles; no tiny bonnets or short dresses displaying pretty little feet were visible – but good warm cloaks, heavy woollen shawls and stout boots were the order of the day and woe to the unlucky wight who neglected providing himself with these commodities, for the cold made no distinction between elite and commoner, but froze all alike, attacking the fashionably clad with the same acerbity as those with humbler pretensions.
>
> Many of the excursion boats offered no other than deck accommodation and it was a pitiful but ludicrous sight to see the poor

*passengers jumping about, making abortive efforts to keep themselves
warm. On the* Charles Chamberlain *they seemed particularly
unsuccessful in their endeavours for everyone aboard was jumping
about, all keeping regular time but each describing a different figure,
somewhat like the traditional Indian war dances.*

The waters of New York harbour were churned white as steamers, skiffs,
punts and tugs scurried here and there. Whistles shrilled, foghorns
mooed, bells rang and there was excitement in the cold, hard westerly
wind, excitement and confusion. It was beautiful. Although it was not
yet eleven o'clock, all was madness and everyone seemed to be drunk.
Aboard the *River Queen* Pierre Lorillard headed up the orgy of excess,
glugging on champagne, wolfing down quail's eggs and generally playing
the gracious host until the yachts, lying serenely at anchor, came into
sight. Then there was an ecstasy of polite pushing and shoving to get out
of the banqueting hall and catch a glimpse of the brave little vessels.

Meanwhile, bestriding the deck of the little steamer *PC Schulz* was
James Gordon Bennett, magnum in one hand, glass in the other, cigar
in mouth. 'The very beau ideal of an English skipper, hearty and robust',
as the *Herald*'s reporter was duty-bound to write. The *Schulz* had pulled
alongside the *River Queen* so that the young tycoon could see off his
fellow club members in style. They returned his salute with cries of
'Three cheers for the only owner who goes with his boat!'

There is no indication that James Gordon Bennett Sr ventured out to
see his only son off on his magnificent adventure. It is safe to assume that
he remained in the *Herald*'s office, preoccupied with finding scurrilous
methods of irritating the very members of society with whom his son
mixed so happily and who had rejected him so cruelly. The absence of

the great editor was doubtless a relief for Stephen Fiske for, although he could see the *Henrietta*, he was still a long way from being safe aboard her. I will leave it to the man himself to explain how he achieved this:

I waited in my waxwork semblance until the presidential spectators flew up on deck when the yachts at their anchorage at Stapleton came in sight. Then I went up behind and mingled with them. The River Queen *came so closely up alongside the* PC Schulz *at one point that I had no difficulty in grasping the hand of a supposed friend aboard the* Schulz *– a man who was considerably more than three sheets to the wind and who was as ready to welcome me as if I had truly been the long lost companion of his youth. Pretending the same state myself, I clambered over the rail of the* River Queen *and made a hazardous leap to the deck of the other vessel. Staggering about a little, I managed to convey to many cheering witnesses that my athletic feat had been of the charmed kind always achieved by the drunken and I had no more than a fleeting impression – there was so much cheering, gallivanting and dancing going on and the tension was so high, that the odd appeared perfectly ordinary.*

From then on my method was clear. The cargo of wines and provisions was piled in the hold of the Schulz *with the hatches off and it was in no way difficult to persuade one of the crew detailed for the loading to accept a five dollar contribution to his welfare and prise open one of the cases and secrete myself therein in lieu of champagne. I had the greatest cricks and cramps as a result, but my object was achieved. I was swung aboard the* Henrietta *and pushed up the lid of my temporary abode to come face to face with my master cum employer for the duration of this trifling journey across the Atlantic.*

79

What Captain Samuels or Gordon Bennett made of this spectacular late arrival is sadly unrecorded. Anyway, the full complement of the *Henrietta* was finally aboard and ready to depart. The little vessel was under way a little after 11.30 and towed past great hordes of spectators on the shore at Fort Wadsworth, where the star-spangled banner was dipped out of respect for the brave three, then on past the tranquil shores of New Jersey and Long Island. The *Herald*'s reporter in the field recalled:

> *From this time to the start was decidedly the most pleasant part of the trip. The scenery on both the New Jersey and Long Island sides is so varied as to afford a perpetual feast for the eye. The picturesque villas spotted here and there on the high ground and anon thickening into villages and towns, the quiet and peaceful appearance of all surrounding them, the contrast between the restless bosom of the purple ocean and the immovable solidity of the sombre shore are but a few of the points of beauty that present themselves to the passing observer. It was pleasing to see in front of many a quiet homestead, the star spangled banner floating in honour of the day and still more pleasing to observe beneath it many a member of the fairer sex, showing her appreciation of the day's event by persistently waving her handkerchief.*

The schooners slipped on up to False Hook Sand where rough seas forced the racers to be prematurely cast loose from their tugs and sail was made. Aboard the *River Queen* the dignified and statesmanlike politician Thurlow Weed was one of the first to succumb to seasickness, 'looking as if he wished to throw a great load off his conscience', as the *Herald*'s reporter gleefully put it. Aboard the schooners the sailors must have looked back on Staten Island with great regret as their numbed hands grabbed hold of the icy halyards and sweated up the great mainsail. It was bitter out there. 'The rawest of days,' Captain Samuels later recalled.

All around bobbed the spectator fleet, disrespectfully close, and snatches of music, fights, cheers, the chink of glass and the clatter of the dice on gambling tables filtered across the water. The whole gamut of New York society was out there drinking, fighting, gambling, freezing. Thousands of infuriated drunks threw their money away with a kind of demented urgency, guzzling at drinks and missing their mouths as they swayed to the uncertain motion. They were pouring booze all over themselves and other people until the decks were sticky underfoot. Bunting fluttered, flags dipped and great signal cannon reverberated around the bay from the anchored merchant ships to mark this glorious celebration.

Almost everyone in New York had an interest in the result of the race and betting was running out of control. *Fleetwing* was odds-on favourite. *Vesta*, with her troublesome centreboard, was considered the outsider. The odds ran at roughly 2½ to 1 on *Fleetwing*, 3 to 1 on *Henrietta* and 3½ to 1 on *Vesta*. The *Herald*'s reporter, clearly terrified of his boss, maintained that *Henrietta* was the favourite, and was later rebuked in a letter to the newspaper for his 'pathetic attempts at being impartial'.

The $1m that was staked on the outcome of the race is a staggering amount, given that the population of New York City itself was only 1.2m. Gambling was technically frowned upon among more genteel sections of society, but no one paid any great heed to this. The mania for gambling gripped America. Faro and poker were the favoured card games and, even as the 1866 race went on, a pair of players down in Austin, Texas were in the depths of surely the longest gambling session ever recorded.

Major Danielson and Old Man Murphy, a pair of wealthy planters, had started a friendly game of poker in 1853 and things had got a little out of hand. In 1866, the pair were still locked in combat, and the betting continued up until 1872, when the pair died simultaneously. The cards were then handed on to their eldest sons, and the epic gambling session only ended when one of them went crazy in 1875. Even before this, gambling had a rich and colourful tradition in America. President Martin Van Buren enjoyed gambling so much that he bet $40,000 and a suit for evening wear on his chance of becoming president. President Andrew Jackson was an inveterate gambler who, after losing all the money he had brought with him to the race track, would continue, betting the clothing off his own back.

Although the organization of lotteries in New York State had been outlawed in 1833, betting went on unabated and in 1850 it was estimated there were over 6,000 gambling dens, or 'very splendid hells' as James Gordon Bennett picturesquely put it, in New York City. That was one for every 85 inhabitants. The 1860s was to oversee a fresh frenzy of betting, and control of the industry was taken by a gentleman by the name of John 'Old Smoke' Morrissey, who had risen to prominence as a champion bare-knuckle fighter and had gone on to run the gambling dens with those same iron fists. He gained his nickname during a particularly vicious bar-room brawl which upset the coals out of the stove. His adversary wrestled Morrissey to the ground and pinned him against the coals until his flesh burnt and the floor caught fire. Morrissey got out from his adversary's grip and gave him a horrible beating in return. This was the kind of shady fellow who, in collusion with Tammany Hall's 'Boss' Tweed, ran the gambling joints of New York. At his peak, Morrissey was worth $1m, and at this point he got involved in a spot of speculating on Wall Street with the 'help' of Commodore Vanderbilt. In a few short years the Commodore had fleeced him out of almost all of his fortune.

Yes, gambling was in the blood of New Yorkers from all walks of life. What was good enough for Wall Street was good enough for everyone else. It would not be until the 1880s that a moral crusade against vice got into full swing and gambling, along with alcohol, was clamped down on heavily. In the meantime, the party was allowed to go on with reckless abandon, and the 1866 race was one of the most gleefully exuberant expressions of the joy of throwing your money around in a game where the odds were never in your favour. To continue the theme and ensure that no opportunity for generating wealth was lost on this day of celebration, roulette wheels and gambling tables were set up aboard many of the pleasure steamers shadowing our three brave racing schooners and betting continued with gusto as the little flotilla cruised through New York Harbor. Not everyone was quite so taken with this great orgy of speculation. A Mormon lady terrorized the passengers aboard the steamer *Charles Chamberlain* with an impromptu blood-and-thunder denunciation of the evils of gambling, drinking and wealth until she was dragged kicking and screaming into the *Chamberlain*'s tiny deckhouse and locked up.

By 12.30 the three contestants were all set for the start, tacking to and fro under all plain sail plus flying jib, each sailing master doing his utmost not to collide with the confused mass of shipping ready to see them off. The sharp winter sunshine showed off these lovely little vessels to the very best advantage: all glowing white cotton canvas and gleaming brass. The crew of *Henrietta* and *Vesta* wore matching uniform, while the *Fleetwing*'s crew, with no owner aboard, were evidently somewhat more relaxed, and the crew were clad in 'costumes of various cuts and colours', as the *Herald* put it.

As the low black hulls of the vessels sliced silently through the water their elegance was undeniable, the graceful sheer of the schooners set off to perfection by the gilt riband running along their bulwarks, which glinted in the already westering sun. Squinting out from the warm haze of the cabin of one of the pleasure steamers it was almost possible to imagine that this was a summer frolic. Step out of the deckhouse, however, and you'd be sorely disillusioned. It was freezing out there, so cold it made your teeth ache. The fresh westerly wind made you physically hunch up against it. A conservative estimate put the temperature at minus five but with the wind chill it must have been intolerable, the sort of cold that penetrated your bones and into your heart, breaking your spirit.

Aboard the yachts there was such a blur of activity that no one had much time to feel the cold. The start was almost upon them. Back and forth the three tacked as if involved in some kind of nautical jousting match. Out past the start line lay Sandy Hook and the Atlantic Ocean. Even on this bright, crystal-clear day the ocean had an unmistakeable malevolence about it. Beyond the shelter of the harbour great frosty white rollers seemed to be piling up above the natural line of the horizon. They glowed eerie green and luminous white in the fading light, the tops blowing off them like snow, beautiful but awful. Best to look away and focus on the start; the minutes ticked away, orders were yelled, sails tweaked as the vessels prowled back and forth along the start line.

Then the countdown. Starter Mr Fearing was aboard Captain Carolus Cather's revenue cutter *Jasmine* with his rather pretentious little brass starter cannon all lined up and ready to go. At precisely 12.59pm he reached down and lit the touch paper. The three yachts hardened up their sails and began to dash for the line, now gathering momentum, now stalling to ensure they were not early over. There was a breathless silence punctuated only by the thrum of wind in the rigging and the creak of overloaded spars, then ... CRACK! the little cannon shattered the silence and unleashed the yachts, out into the wild blue yonder. 'Save for the moment I fired a gun against the rebels in sixty three, I never did have such a rich moment,' Captain Cather recalled enthusiastically.

A great cheer reverberated from the spectator fleet; a mixed out-pouring of exuberant joy and relief that they would be able to retreat to the warmth and comfort of New York. Meanwhile the three racers leant into the breeze and shouldered the first playful rollers of the mighty Atlantic.

Fleetwing, at the northern end of the start line, had decidedly the best start and was followed over by *Vesta* with *Henrietta* bringing up the rear, initially hampered by her novice crew 'They slide up and down the rigging like a blasted monkey on a blasted stick!' growled Chief Officer Jones. 'The only way to manage 'em is to climb up first and pull the lubbers after me!' Presently, however, the *Henrietta* defied her reputation as the slowest yacht in the race and drew level with the *Fleetwing* and *Vesta*. The three ran side by side, 'So close you could toss a biscuit between them,' Samuels recalled. The breeze was strong on the beam and the three were running at 12 knots and more, their white sails glowing pearlescent as the sun set over Staten Island, a glory of crimson and gold. Watching the fading city, the fading shore, from the slanting deck of the flying schooner, only a fool would not have felt a twinge of apprehension as the familiar fug and hubbub of New York City slowly receded. Over 3,000 miles of open ocean lay between them and their destination. Abeam of the racers lay the wreck of the *Scotland*, her mast a jagged stump silhouetted against the darkening sky, great icy breakers breaching her shattered hull. She had been wrecked in a collision ten days previously with the loss of 13 lives, a chilling reminder of the gravity of the game these three yachts were playing.

According to Captain Samuels, the *Fleetwing* and the *Vesta* seemed to adopt a policy of shadowing the *Henrietta* in these early stages of the race:

> We had known before the start that the captains of the other two had orders not to let us out of sight and from the way they stuck to us we could see that these orders were being obeyed. We trimmed and hauled oft shore to south'ard; they trimmed and hauled off shore to south'ard. Night set in and we put out our lights and hauled inshore. This time, they did not observe us.

They were almost out to the open sea now, running fast past the tip of the low-lying wedge of Sandy Hook, which merged with the Navesink Highlands above to form a dark, hard disc of land just discernible in the twilight. Still the *Vesta* ran alongside like a shadowy phantom until at 8pm her lights 'appeared blown out suddenly as if she was sunk' and the *Henrietta* was alone.

Slowly the land receded. There were hardly any lights except the shadowy, moving glow of the occasional ship or ferry across the Sound and the winking flash of the Sandy Hook light. As the moon rose higher the sailors looked back on New York stripped of the ugly debris of industry and houses and saw the land as it had been viewed by the first settlers from Europe: the fresh, green, unexploited breast of the new world, lavish, fertile, generous of heart, beckoning the settlers onward to discover its mystery and share its great riches. The land had already been eagerly ripped open in search of gold, silver, zinc, coal, oil. Its vanished trees had been offered up without reproach to form the timbers of these very yachts, the paper for the *Herald*, the sleepers of the railway tracks that had slashed this continent open and spilled its great bounty.

For those first settlers this great land had whispered of mystery, hope, freedom and wonder. It was a land that was fast disappearing. Soon the west would no longer be wild. In the hands of the great captains of industry this great, giving continent was bending obligingly to their will. In the process America was no longer a question mark, it was becoming a prosaic fact, and the world's collection of enchanted objects was diminished by one. Young men in search of adventure had to play at it rather than live it for real. So the yachts pressed on as the land slid below the horizon, bound with a sigh for merry England, the tired old world and all the monuments to man's achievements held therein.

Now came a crucial decision for Captain Samuels. This was the stick or twist moment, for there were several distinct routes favoured by skippers crossing the Atlantic and making the correct choice was imperative if they were going to win the race. The previous night, while others had been gawping at the receding land, Samuels had carefully noted the courses of the diverging yachts. The *Fleetwing* had melted away, ghost-like, to the north, while the *Vesta* when last sighted had seemed to be angling southward. Crossing the Atlantic was a balancing act with many different variables to factor in. Samuels had crossed the Atlantic 78 times in his career and, as Bennett pointed out, 'You would think that he knows the way by now.' He was not wrong, but there were still decisions to be made.

First there was the Gulf Stream to be considered, that great deep blue river of warm water that poured north from Cuba right up to the coast of Newfoundland before heading east, just like our adventurous yachtsmen, and surging on toward the old world. In the Florida Strait the stream can run at up to 4 knots, but this decreases as you head up the coast and, by the time you are out in the Atlantic, it has often slackened off to under a knot. Still, this can make a huge difference to the speed of a passage over 3,000 miles. Out in the Atlantic, the stream tended to be stronger to the south, but then there was a danger of getting too far south and moving out of the path of the great rambunctious low-pressure systems that swept across this area. Head too far north and you might find you got a bit more than you could handle.

Following the Gulf Stream would also potentially give the yachtsmen respite from the brutal winter cold. Close to the Newfoundland coast, this warm river of current can lead to bizarre temperature fluctuations. A passenger travelling on a packet ship in February had reported the temperature jump from minus 5 degrees Celsius to 22 degrees Celsius in a matter of minutes. In the days when navigation had been rather more approximate than in 1866, old sailors could use this temperature fluctuation as an important navigational tool. Samuels, Dayton and Thomas, all of whom understood sea lore, would certainly have employed it to some extent.

Next up was the choice of how close to stick to the most direct route across the Atlantic: the Great Circle. To adhere rigorously to the Great Circle route meant running up toward Cape Race on the south-east tip of Newfoundland and then across the shallows of the Grand Banks, those fearsome fishing grounds where the shallow waters kicked up fierce waves, great fogs billowed up and icebergs crept down from the Arctic

Circle with murderous intent. From there, it was a straightforward run across to the Scilly Isles with nothing but a few foul-tempered weather systems to play Russian roulette with.

The captains of the *Fleetwing*, *Vesta* and *Henrietta* had no satellites beaming down complex projections of what the weather was going to do. For the duration of the crossing, the three boats were in a world of their own, and all aboard were reliant on the captain to carry them to safety with the help of his sextant, barometer and plenty of old-fashioned sea sense. You played a dangerous game mixing it with these great twisting depressions. One in six of the sailing packet ships that operated on the Atlantic run between 1824 and 1847 was wrecked in service, many falling foul of the mighty winter gales. But these savage weather systems that roared down from Greenland and unleashed themselves on the north Atlantic were also one of the major trump cards of crossing the ocean east to west. In sailing-packet terminology, this direction was known as the 'downhill passage' because both current and, in particular, prevailing winds favoured the sailor. Those vicious south-westerly winds that batter the coast of Britain also hurled the sailor into its welcoming bosom. Captain Samuels in the *Dreadnought* had once made the passage in the exceptional time of 13 days 8 hours, which compared very favourably with the usual average for a transatlantic sailing packet of that time: 24 days. Contrast that with the average of 38 days going westbound and you realize how much more trying the trip to the new world could be. However, the big decision was how far north or south to deviate from the rhumb line. That night, Samuels laid out his plan of attack to his guests, as Fiske recalls:

> At dinner Captain Samuels communicated to us his plan of
> campaign. Fleetwing *had evidently taken what is called the Northern*

passage, to get all the wind possible. Vesta *had chosen the Southern passage, to avoid the Winter gales.* Henrietta *was confessedly the slowest boat, and the Captain had decided to put her on the steamer track* [the extreme northern route, shaving close to the Georges Bank and Sable Island], *and keep her there, regardless of wind or weather, because it is the shortest route. He adhered to this plan so rigidly that at one time we lay to under storm trysails for eighteen hours rather than leave our course.*

The speculation was flawed in as much as it was the *Vesta* that ended up heading north, while the *Fleetwing* stayed south. Nevertheless, *Henrietta* had her own plan and the remainder of that first night was a chance for everyone to find their place aboard the yacht and acclimatize. A few friendly snow flurries gave everyone a hint of what was to come. The crew was divided into two watches, port and starboard, and all were obliged to get into the routine of four on, four off: their four hours out on deck spent hunched against the cold, while great archipelagos of stars winked down on the icy sea. On deck, Samuels bellowed orders and sails were trimmed and trimmed some more, hurriedly furled as squalls, often laced with sleet and snow, raced through, and then loosed again with equal alacrity as the wind eased. Anything to keep the little schooner flying. For the crew, this chilly vigil was followed by four hours thawing out down below, huddled in as many blankets as was humanly possible. Samuels remained on deck.

The crewmembers' routine contrasted sharply with the new routine of Gordon Bennett and his privileged guests, who were at liberty to pad around the decks pondering sagely until it got too cold to bear it any more. After a quick cigar in the icy cockpit, they were free to head below to their quarters. Although some of the gentlemen would have had to endure the discomfort of sharing a cabin, a lit stove within minimized the hardship. As the coals clicked in the grate, the occupants would have turned in exhausted, full of fresh, icy air. Doubtless that first night they would have lain awake while listening to the unfamiliar creaks and groans of a sailing ship under way. Anyone who thinks life aboard a sailing ship is quiet should think again: there is the incessant rustle and gurgle of water against the hull, the groan of timbers, tapping of ropes, rattling of sails and the shouts from the crew. Above everything else was the restive, impatient tread on the deck of Captain Samuels. His step was uneven: a testament to that fateful Atlantic night when the *Dreadnought*, a ship twice the size of the *Henrietta*, had been overwhelmed by an Atlantic storm that had killed three of his men and left him and his beloved clipper crippled. He was no doubt thinking of the old *Dreadnought*, how he used to drive her across this barren waste of water, as he paced the deck of his new command.

His restless, uneven cadence tapped out the urgent rhythm he had set on the *Henrietta* from the moment he stepped aboard. He would not let her or the crew rest, driving the little schooner relentlessly forward. At 4am, clear of the Nantucket shoals, he gybed her across on to the port tack and on to his course to the Georges Bank and the ship's graveyard of Sable Island on the Grand Banks. In card player's parlance, this decision was calling twist, and Samuels must have hoped it was not followed by bust as he gambled with the weather.

As dawn cracked the sky, the *Henrietta* was running like a scalded cat across a great expanse of grey, hard, empty ocean; no land in sight and not another vessel. She was on her way. Her path had been decided by her doughty commander and it was just a case of rolling the dice and seeing what lay in wait out there across the darkened waters. Samuels' task was not an easy one and the weight of responsibility lay heavy on his shoulders. Yet this was exhilarating sailing and the master of the *Henrietta* was in his element, driving the crew mercilessly. 'Talk about racing,' Samuels later recalled. 'It was a race every minute with half a gale of wind to the Banks with the men standing constantly by the gaff topsail and peak halliards. It was lower away as the squalls came and hoist away as they went and with every stitch we could carry we staggered through it until the wind freshened to a full gale from the southwest and we shortened sail to meet it.'

This was the pattern set that first night at sea and it would continue without let-up for the rest of the passage as the little schooner raced on against invisible adversaries. The work for the men was mostly hoisting, lowering and trimming of the sails. This was good, solid, physical work made all the tougher by the extreme cold. The boat was flying along and leaning heavily into the waves, meaning that the lee scuppers would be constantly full of water and great sheets of spray would come flying aboard and hit the men with the force of buckshot, chilling them to the bone. If the wind freed off sufficiently, the great square sail on the foremast would have been set and this would have required a terrifying climb on icy ratlines to the swaying topmast head. Of all the tasks aboard, this would have been the most challenging for the amateur crew. As for the captain, his role was one of constant vigilance, as Fiske recalled with more than a hint of awe:

Captain Samuels jockeyed Henrietta *as if she were a racing mare.*
He fairly weighed the wind, giving the yacht all of it she could bear,
and relieving her by reefing the instant that she was overstrained.
Sails were set from the size of a handkerchief to a flowing sheet if

there was a lull in the squalls, and then taken in reluctantly if the gale increased. His was an eternal vigilance. Except one night, when we compelled him to turn in for a sound sleep, we always found him on deck, watching the weather, the sails, the compass or the crew.

This was the balancing act, the fine art. Pushing your vessel just hard enough that she carries on at maximum speed, yet never letting her get overpowered, which slowed a yacht down or, even worse, damaged her. There is no doubt that Captain Samuels was a master of it. Yet there was another aspect to the captain's job which to some was even more arduous. Each of the yachts had a number of judges and guests aboard and the captain was supposed to make these men of leisure feel welcome and like part of the team while also showing them a certain amount of respect. It was a strange dichotomy: for the captain of a boat is master and commander; his word is law. Yet in the case of the *Henrietta*, Samuels had Bennett, the owner of the yacht and his employer, aboard, which had the potential to make for a very tricky situation. Somehow the pair made it work. The young tycoon was clearly overawed by the mighty Samuels, who had the ego and also the outgoing personality to deal with any potentially troublesome young princelings.

Aboard the *Vesta*, things were not panning out quite so smoothly, however. George Lorillard had been entrusted by his older brother to ensure that his schooner got to Cowes in the quickest possible time and he was clearly taking his job extremely seriously. Captain Dayton of the *Vesta* was a very different man from the exuberant, larger-than-life Samuels: old, wise, sedulous and sure of himself but with none of the extrovert bravado of his fellow skipper. Where Samuels would have regaled his privileged guests with breezy salt-stained anecdotes of his own heroism, Dayton would have kept his own counsel, held his guests at arm's length, parrying off any friendly approach with stolid, monosyllabic answers. He was there to sail the yacht, not act as some kind of dancing bear. Where Samuels had bet $7,500 of his race fee on himself to win, Dayton had met with a lawyer and written up a will to provide for his wife and 17 children. Inevitably he clashed with young George Lorillard. George was Pierre's junior by ten years and, if anything, was the keener yachtsman of the pair. He had very strong opinions on how a yacht should be sailed. He also suffered quite badly from rheumatism, which must have been a severe trial aboard a cramped, chilly yacht slamming her way across the Atlantic. Perhaps this explains why he was irritated with Captain Dayton from day one. Whatever his reason, he did not hold back in voicing his opinion:

> The crew, certainly are a very fine lot of men, but the officers,
> without an exception are very dull. No order, no drive, no discipline.
> The result of the past twenty four hours shows the want of force and
> energy … I find but two men employed as helmsmen for the passage,
> each having two hour tricks, and but little attention is paid by the
> officers to the steering.

His rantings were later published in the *Herald* and seem to point to actual dislike of the steady old packet captain. Nevertheless, his views on the manner in which the *Vesta* was being sailed were echoed by Colonel Taylor, the other judge aboard, who noted:

> Dayton is not coming up to expectations as a captain, I feel sure. He
> is over cautious with his canvas and could have got us extra speed by

*taking an eye to the main chance. His manner is polite and he is well
liked and his crew he has chosen well. But when I see him there at the
helm or looking out over the rail to judge his next move he gives me
the feeling of slowness, a strange thing in a race but there it is. His
responses, I mean, seem to be over labored, he is stolid, firm, in a
crisis he would know and perhaps we shall need him yet to surmount
one for us. But every moment is a crisis in a race; and although as
a judge appointed I see he is scrupulous of the rules, as a judge of
a racing yachtsman I cannot enthuse. True, these are early hours.
But in racing there are no second chances! Opportunities lost are
gone forever!*

Aboard the *Fleetwing*, the absence of any connection with the elusive
Osgood brothers meant that Captain Thomas was free to go about his
business without his every action being scrutinized and, although there
is some anecdotal evidence that some of the crew resented the manner
in which Captain Dick Brown had been treated, the general atmosphere
aboard the *Fleetwing* seems to have been one of harmony and contentment
as the schooner ran on across the slate grey seas, the monotony only
broken by the rising gale and the occasional flurry of snow or sleet until
night began to bruise the sky and engulf the brave little yacht.

The positions of the yachts at noon on the first day are of particular
interest, because all the vessels ran on roughly the same course and would
therefore have experienced identical conditions. It was therefore the
best day for judging the comparative speed of the yachts. The result is
illuminating, for the *Vesta*, for all George Lorillard's grousing, was out in
the lead, having run 240 nautical miles. The *Henrietta*, a couple of miles
to the south, had run 237, and the *Fleetwing*, further south again, had run

239. This is probably a fair measure of the respective abilities of the three yachts in moderately strong breezes. *Henrietta* just that little fraction slower, with virtually nothing to choose between *Fleetwing* and *Vesta*. There were sterner tests still to come, but if you were a betting man, then the *Fleetwing* looked like a good punt once the going got tough. She was running neck and neck with the *Vesta* in fair conditions; surely she would have the better of her once the weather turned foul. One thing was for sure, the odds were stacked on heavy weather coming up before the race was out. That was the safest bet of all.

5

WILD TIMES OFF THE GRAND BANKS

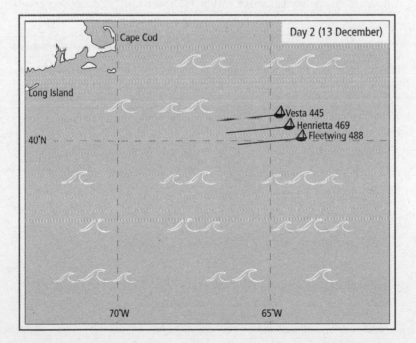

There was no talk of shortening sail by him who trod the poop and her boom with the weight of a mighty jib bent like a wooden hoop.

TRADITIONAL SEA SHANTY, 'THE BALLAD OF JOHN PAUL JONES'

Cape Cod

Long Island

40°N

Day 2 (13 December)

Vesta 445
Henrietta 469
Fleetwing 488

70°W   65°W

The morning of the second day started with a bang aboard the *Fleetwing* as her great wooden jibboom, which protruded many metres out from her bow, simply shattered under the strain of the great acres of bulging canvas it was supporting. The schooner was now to the south of her rivals and enjoying much more boisterous weather. Captain Thomas was driving her for all she was worth and the old sea shanty quoted at the top of the chapter must have rung in the ears of some of the men as the ship sizzled along, every timber shivering under the strain, her scuppers gurgling and decks running bright as great feathery sprays fizzed aboard with every scend. She was running well, but bordering on over-pressed, her figurehead bowing down into the smother, then rising and pausing before plunging down until her lee rail was almost buried, scooping great green rollers over it.

Everything has its tipping point, however, and as the *Fleetwing* stormed along, her bow took an especially deep plunge and suddenly all hell broke loose. Ernest Staples, one of the judges aboard, was just heading up on deck when the accident occurred:

I lit my pipe before going on deck. There was hail in the wind and a tattoo of shot on the deck and against the taut canvas. We were gybing and I could hear the shouts of the crew as they hauled. Captain Thomas was for'ard with them when a violent gust took us, wrenching the sail and jib quite away. At the same time a big wave set us awash. I glimpsed the jib and the torn sail on the white crest as it carried away. The thick spar might have been no more than a matchstick. The ship was firm, she rode beautifully, buoyant and steady. But we had lost our headsails and our steering became very heavy and difficult. It was bad fortune and it made the crew depressed. The negro, Massy, discouraged the others with his gloomy wailing and Captain Thomas berated him.

The mess was soon cleared up and the *Fleetwing* roared on, yet she had lost several miles to her rivals and the accident was seen as a bad omen by some aboard. None more so than Lincoln Massy, the black cook and by all accounts a bit of a Jonah. Perhaps he had the gift of foresight. While the *Fleetwing* was battling with damage and depressed crew members, the crew of the *Henrietta*, some miles to the north, was having a happier time of it. The second day was a mixture of sunshine and snow flurries and all the guests started to get into a routine and enjoy themselves, as Stephen Fiske recalls:

> Our party consisted of Messrs. Mervin and Knapp, the Yacht Club judges; Larry Jerome, the famous humorist of the Union Club, who, like Wegg, dropped into yacht racing as a friend; Captain Samuels, Mr. Bennett and myself. The table was covered with all the delicacies of the season, donated to us by friends. At the masthead swung a dozen brace of canvasback ducks, to be presented to the Queen if we succeeded in winging our way across the Atlantic. Our larder overflowed, and in 'the roaring forties' we feasted upon oysters in every style as enjoyably as if we had been in a private room on shore.
>
> Nevertheless, dining had its difficulties. The table, like the yacht, was tilted at an angle of forty-five degrees. It was as good as a game of baseball to see Jerome catch the soup tureen on the fly, amid cries of 'Not out!' 'Judgment!' or the rest of us make slides for the plates and glasses. Not a man missed a meal. During the pauses in the

conversation and laughter, the roar of wind and wave, the groaning of timbers and cordage could be heard, and as the water swashed back and forth over the skylights, we seemed like divers taking a rest in a submarine compartment.

Of course, we were supplied with playing cards and reading matter; but there seemed no spare time for games or literature. There were the chances of the race to be talked over; stories to be told; good old times to be revived; the log to be written up; and, when other occupations lacked interest, we could always try to straighten out Jerome's betting book, which he had filled so scientifically that, whatever yacht won the race, he would be a heavy loser. Poor Larry was the life of the party. His wit and humor were inexhaustible. At the slightest complaint his stentorian voice thundered, 'If you don't like your quarters, take your carpetbag and go ashore!'

The general impression was of a happy bunch aboard the *Henrietta* and there is no doubt that this owed a lot to the bonhomie of the two Jerome brothers. There is some question as to both of the Jerome brothers having been aboard. Some accounts specifically state that Leonard Jerome, as the stake-holder, was aboard, while others suggest that only Lawrence was there. Whatever the truth, Leonard was certainly deeply involved in the organization of the race and, given that his great-granddaughter and biographer maintains he took part, perhaps we should bow to her superior knowledge.

There is little doubt that the Jerome brothers were a fascinating and massively entertaining pair to have aboard. They shared a sunny disposition, huge optimism, dash, drive, dare and, of course, great wads of cash. Above all, however, the pair possessed a kind of aura that drew people in. When you were in the Jeromes' company, the sun shone. When you walked away you knew you had to be part of their wild, decadent and utterly enthralling world if life was to be worth living. The pair were perhaps the ultimate expression of the nouveau riche vulgarians, who were making New York such a crass and unrefined and breathlessly exciting playground of the parvenu. The pair had come from humble beginnings, growing up on a farm in Syracuse, western New York. Money was tight but, with the help of a wealthy uncle, both brothers were educated at Princeton and began work in this same uncle's legal practice. It is likely that the pair were simply too high-spirited for this kind of stultifying work and branched out into newspaper ownership, buying the *Daily American* in 1844 with money that Lawrence had gained through marriage to a young heiress by the name of Catherine Hall. Leonard clearly saw the sense in this and married her sister, Clara. The pair had the satisfaction of seeing circulation of the *Daily American* double, then triple, in a few short years, and they were well on their way to wealth. The next step was to head to Wall Street and apply all that energy and industry and enthusiasm into stocks and shares.

Although the pair evidently shared an awful lot in life, history has remembered Leonard Jerome because he is Winston Churchill's grandfather. Leonard also had marginally the more spectacular career. Once they descended on Wall Street it was he who ended up on the kind of hot streak that all gamblers dream of and it wasn't long before he joined New York's rapidly swelling list of millionaires. His younger brother followed him into the rich list some time later. Back then, Wall Street was one step closer to the wild west than it is today and, unlike the sedulous brokers and financiers we now encounter, whoring and debauchery were a simple fact of life among money men who needed to fully 'relax' after a day plundering and looting. As one famous proprietor of a well-known den of vice said at the time: 'American men are driven to bouts of dissipation by the relentless pressure of money making.'

But how the money poured in! For a while it seemed like the Jeromes could not put a foot wrong. Their newspaper connections allowed them to wine and dine leading editors, all the while feeding them tips on good stock. In 1860, this 'understanding' with certain newspapers was formalized when Leonard Jerome bought a 25 per cent share of the *New York Times* and used his position to control the financial editor. The Jeromes were doing well, very well, and cut quite a dash on Wall Street, particularly once they joined forces with another social butterfly, William Travers. This trio was labelled the 'three musketeers', famed for mixing frivolity with ruthlessness in a manner that infuriated the men they crossed. Just like their namesakes, they thrived during conflict.

It was to be the Civil War that launched their wealth into the stratosphere. It was money gained in questionable circumstances, for the Jeromes devised a means of communicating in code with prominent generals at the front. By this means they were able to receive information on victories and defeats well ahead of anyone else and therefore able to trade shares connected to these wins and losses with absolute certainty. Now you may consider that a flagrant example of insider trading, yet one glance from the twinkling eyes and winning smile that lit up the room and Leonard Jerome was forgiven. As he himself said, Wall Street was 'a jungle where men tear and claw' and advantage had to be gained by fair means or foul. For a short while he was the king of that jungle, the Wolf of Wall Street, if you will. In 1866 he was near his peak, with an interest in the *New York Times* and in the newly laid transatlantic telegraph cable, and was feared and revered throughout Wall Street.

Yet it was not wealth or canniness that either of the Jerome brothers is remembered for, rather it is the manner in which they enjoyed their wealth. Both Lawrence and, in particular, Leonard knew how to get through their money in style. Leonard's six-storey mansion on Madison Avenue aped the hugely elaborate French second empire school of architecture. In an era of drab, brownstone mansions, its cheerful bright red brick and white marble frontage meant the house shone out like a great glowing jewel. It took the breath away, so ostentatious was it in its magnificence. Even the stables were a thing of beauty, brand new, fitted out regardless of expense, and a wonderful imitation of the greatest creations of the European nobility. No horse was better housed than in this fabulous structure, with walnut panels, burnished silver and stained-glass windows. 'Except for the Emperor's Mews in Paris, it is doubtful that any stable is finer', the *New York Tribune* wrote in awe. Then there was the house itself, with its acres of marble; glittering chandeliers that tinkled and winked; panelling with a lustre so deep it glowed; and gold, everywhere gold. Upstairs through bedrooms awash with priceless silks and luminescent with freshly picked flowers, through dressing rooms overflowing with furs and gowns and shoes and on to gleaming bathrooms with sunken baths. Every brick, every stick of furniture spoke to the casual observer of money beyond their wildest imagination.

The parties were unforgettable. So decadent, so elaborate, so perfect. On one occasion, Jerome spent $300,000 on a single party. At another, guests were invited to dress up as biblical figures. On that occasion they got through 1,000 bottles of wine while polishing off a ten-course meal. Yet perhaps the crowning glory was the house warming. Many years after the event, New Yorkers still gushed at the memory of this, the first ever ball the Jeromes hosted at their new abode. This was one of those golden days when the great gardens had been draped with glowing bunting and in the heat of the afternoon armies of caterers had scurried to and fro preparing for an evening of debauchery. As afternoon heat turned to glowing dusk, the first guests arrived, waiters flitted about noiselessly proffering silver salvers of glistening *hors d'oeuvres*. Shimmering through into the huge ballroom, guests would gaze in delight and amazement at the pair of fountains in the centre of this room, which bubbled and splashed with a constant flow of champagne and cologne respectively.

In the banqueting hall, the tables had been loaded until they groaned under the weight of succulent sweetmeats, whole hogs roasted until they glowed deep gold, caviar, fragrant foie gras, venison that just fell off the bone. Guests gorged on these exquisite dishes until the juices ran down their chins; hunger seemed incomprehensible and they could barely taste the exquisite flavours. Still they ate and drank as if they could never be satisfied. The finest French wine, imported at vast expense from the old world, and painstakingly selected to match the rich, succulent food, was swilled down with such abandon that few noticed its delicate refinement. And the music! No reedy five-piece ensemble, but a whole legion of saxophones, viols, oboes, piccolos and cornets, sending waves of beauty and harmony pulsing into the sweet evening air.

And there, amid all these wonders, Leonard Jerome, his winning smile illuminating everything; friends and admirers flitting around him like moths around a great, gilded orb. Under his benign, reassuring gaze, the revellers immersed themselves in this orgy of pleasure, heading out into the cool, fragrant night air and dancing until the small hours. As the dawn crept up on the scene and the guests finally started to trickle away, gentlemen retreated to the seclusion of the smoking room in order to gather their thoughts. Sipping on great treacly globes of brandy, they all agreed that no one did a party like Leonard Jerome.

Leonard was a man of many passions and a great lover of music, in particular opera, so much so that he had a 600-seat private opera house attached to his mansion. It was here that he frequently indulged in another of his favourite pursuits: the wooing of women. He was a rapacious lover and it is generally said that Jennie Jerome, mother of Winston Churchill, was named after one of his great passions, the famous opera singer Jenny Lind. After Lind came the young, beautiful starlet Minnie Hauk, one of the great singers of her day. Hauk was virtually adopted by the Jerome family and many assumed that she was a kind of surrogate daughter. Others with a better knowledge of the family conceded that she had got a great deal more than just singing lessons from Leonard Jerome.

Next in his roll call of lovers came Fanny Ronalds, whom Jerome competed for with his friend and rival August Belmont, the prominent banker. At times, Mrs Ronalds' parlour would be awash with gaudy bouquets of flowers from her two exuberant, unabashed lovers, hell bent on 'attempting to satisfy her every desire', according to one friend of the family. Many years later, Belmont and Jerome were reminiscing about the vast expense of a particularly spectacular party that Ronalds had hosted. 'I should know,' commented Belmont sardonically, 'I paid for it.' 'How strange,' Leonard rejoined. 'So did I.'

Yet it was in the field of sports that the Jeromes truly excelled and, again, it was Leonard who stood out. August Belmont once commented: 'One rode better, sailed better and banqueted better when Jerome was in the party.' He first came to prominence as the parvenu *par excellence* after taking up the English sport of coaching. The cream of society watched open-mouthed with horror as this arriviste raced up Broadway, whip in hand, flowers extravagantly bursting from his buttonhole and his coach loaded with beautiful women who would shriek and giggle as he took a corner at full tilt. This eyebrow-raising hobby earned him the rather derogatory nickname of 'the bus driver' among polite society. Horse racing in America also owes a big debt to the Jeromes. Prior to their arrival on the scene, the sport had come to be viewed as rather an unsavoury pastime. The pair put it back on the road to respectability with the setting up of the Jockey Club and the opening of Jerome Park that very year of 1866.

It had been coaching that had first drawn Jimmy Bennett into their orbit. Ever a man who inadvertently seemed to have the hand of history tapping on his shoulder, Bennett had come very close to altering the whole course of world events when, on one of these high-speed coaching excursions, he had lost control of his four on a sharp bend and 'nearly killed' [her words] Jennie Jerome, Leonard's daughter and future mother of Winston Churchill. Leonard Jerome clearly forgave him this lapse and there is little doubt that Jimmy viewed the brothers with a mixture of awe, admiration and affection. In turn, they had taken to the wild-eyed youngster in an instant and under their excellent tutelage he really started to appreciate how to have a good time. The Jeromes ensured that Bennett was an integral part of New York's burgeoning 'fast set' of sportsmen and hedonists. Where his father was the eternal outsider, Bennett had already found his niche.

It helped that in social circles the Jeromes were almost as big a catastrophe as James Gordon Bennett's own father. This was not terribly evident to the gents involved, who were unquestionably one of the lads and able to rub shoulders with the likes of the Lorillards at the Union Club and the New York Yacht Club. Only a really drastic faux pas could see a wealthy fellow excluded from that clique. Yet there is no way the likes of Pierre Lorillard would invite a Bennett or a Jerome to a dinner party. That was unthinkable. While this was little loss to the men themselves, their wives endured social leprosy in their stead, smarting in the knowledge that they were little short of pariahs among the upper echelons.

The top end of New York society was a complicated and unpleasant affair in those days as the old-money families like the Astors and the Lorillards struggled to deal with the uncontrollable influx of new-money upstarts. Never mind that the Astors had made a substantial portion of their vast fortune from smuggling opium, and another handsome chunk from questionable property deals in their beloved New York. Never mind that John Jacob Astor, the founder of this dynasty, was also famed for dining habits so crass that he was frequently caught using the shirt-tail of the man seated beside him at a dinner to wipe his hands on. Ignore all of that. Put it to one side if you will; when it came to manners and gentility, the Astors set the agenda in New York, and by 1866, this was infinitely more refined than poor old JJ could ever have envisioned as he grabbed hold of that shirt-tail with his greasy paw.

To this end, a complex and utterly stultifying social framework had been put in place that was almost as hidebound as a Victorian one. As Edith Wharton, an astute observer of this era, put it, when discussing the misery of social status in *The Age of Innocence*: 'It seems stupid to have discovered America only to make it into a copy of another country.' This is exactly what had happened in high society. All had to pay court to Mrs Astor, a sour-faced bulldog who always referred to herself simply as THE Mrs Astor and, peering down from her parapet, could, with a single disdainful glance, send a young debutante's world crashing down around her slender shoulders. This fearsome battle-axe controlled the Astor 400. This term came about as the capacity of the Astors' fabulous ballroom was 400; if you weren't on her list of invitees, you were toast. Nothing else mattered in genteel society. If Mrs Astor rejected you, that was the end of any pretensions of gentility.

Of course, Bennett had no chance. It didn't help that his father had described JJ Astor in the *Herald*'s obituary as: 'A self-invented money making machine' and even had the temerity to suggest he return half his wealth to the people of New York whom he had screwed the money out of. Nope, Bennett Jr's card was forever marked. Meanwhile, the Jeromes were simply too outré in their habits and too ostentatious in their womanizing to have a hope. While this meant pariahdom for the respective Mrs Jeromes, and James Gordon Bennett Sr's wife Henrietta for that matter, the likes of Bennett Jr and the Jerome brothers cared not one jot. The men had cheerfully embraced their status and gone out there and shown the old money set that they didn't need social approval to have a damned good time.

To all three this meant doing something life-affirming and real, like this yacht race. In this respect they differed wildly from other parvenu social outcasts, such as Cornelius Vanderbilt or Jay Gould. These were tycoons to whom money, the thrill of making money, was everything. Mark Twain in a particularly searing attack on Vanderbilt had written: 'You rob yourself of restful sleep and peace of mind because you need money so badly. I always feel for a man who is so poverty ridden as you.' Bennett and the Jeromes did not belong to this breed. They threw their money around with barely a care in the world; money was important, but how you spent it was even more vital. Mammon was there to be enjoyed, not hoarded. With the wide Atlantic under the *Henrietta*'s keel and a few bottles of Chateau Margaux in the hold, the Jeromes were as happy as Larry and their easy bonhomie permeated the yacht.

Things were never quite so harmonious aboard the *Vesta*, which was slowly slipping behind the *Henrietta* and *Fleetwing*. Colonel Taylor gives a good warts-and-all account of life on board:

Anyone who has been on board her [Vesta] in port, when she is rigged and habited only for the summer sailing, would never recognize an old friend. The cabin floor is littered with all sorts of stuff – sails ropes blocks, pieces of board, marline, buckets, an anchor, spare rigging, brooms and any quantity of things that have no name or, as far as I can see, there will be no use for! Not ten minutes in the day that some infernal thing isn't wanted; and if a poor devil is getting a few winks of sleep at night, in come half a dozen or more burly sailors looking for another sail or a small piece of rope and in their haste turn the cabin upside down and you topsy turvy! Then you growl a little and smooth your ruffled feathers again, only to be awakened five minutes later by the emptying of a bucket of coal upon your head! Such are the joys of yachting out at sea! We all sleep by fits and starts – first in our state rooms then on the sails and soft sides of rope in the cabin. We eat sometimes sitting, sometimes standing and sometimes we don't eat at all. Generally our appetites are enormous! Our cook is sick and steward and mess boy do all the work. A slight trickling of water last night down my nose reminded me of the delectable fact that the deck overhead was badly caulked; and I accordingly shifted myself on to the small anchor, where I chafed my weary bones and bruised my weather beaten skin for an hour or more, when I was compelled to deposit one half of me, for the remainder of the night in a coal bucket, where by close hugging, I tried to keep the stove warm! Ah! The further we go on this grand race the more our comfort increases and – never mind – let us win and we don't care about that! Throw comfort to the dogs!

At midnight went on deck, and the spectacle was certainly a very pleasing one, the yacht flying through the water, every possible sail set and the crescent moon tinting the sea with her soft silver light. Can anything be more delightful than this! Yacht sometimes going 13 and 14 knots. Thus passed our second night at sea.

It would be interesting to know if, given the presence of James Gordon Bennett aboard the *Henrietta*, this yacht was kept better furnished than the others, which sound like they were stripped out for racing. Certainly the general ambience aboard the *Henrietta*, which filters through from the writing of Fiske, seems much more positive. A description of *Henrietta* when she lay in Cowes following the race also suggests that she was still pretty lavishly furnished. The description reads as follows:

It is some qualification of that idea of extreme hardship which everybody entertains on the subject of the late exciting race that the furniture, or let us boldly and appropriately, say the 'fixins' of all these yachts are so very comfortable, nay luxurious. Ladies are very apt to moderate their admiration and applause when they see how 'jolly' everything looks below. In one bookcase I observed that the gilt letters on the callbacks of the volumes denoted an appreciation of English nautical literature.

This suggests the *Henrietta* was at least modestly comfortable for the voyage across, while also conveying a certain incredulity that an American could be cultured enough to possess books aboard – and English ones at that. This was the era of the giant schooner and *Henrietta*, *Vesta* and *Fleetwing* were the super-yachts of their day, although that day was a relatively short one. By the mid to late 1870s they were being supplanted by the steam yacht. After that, a sailing yacht owned by one of the super-rich was generally used primarily for racing. For comfort and for entertaining the ladies, you had your steam yacht, and only a few outlandish 'enthusiasts' persisted in keeping a sailing yacht for cruising. It was for just a short period that these big schooner yachts were both racer and cruiser, and were fitted out in the most lavish manner as a result. This was an era of interior decorating where 'more is more' was the order of the day. The yachts could be cloyingly over-furnished with acres of panelling, stucco and velvet. This reached its culmination with the schooner yacht *Mohawk*, built in 1875 for textile magnate William T Garner.

It is perhaps worth retreating from the chill of the Grand Banks and heading back to New York Harbor, forward to the summer of 1876, to relate the tragic story of Garner and the *Mohawk*, not least because to some extent Jimmy Bennett was to blame. Garner had inherited a textile business from his father and built up the company into a powerhouse noted for a ruthless attitude to laying off workers in times of decline. By 1873 he was worth around $19m, a tidy sum in those days, and he felt the time was ripe to take up a sport that befitted his status as a gentleman. What better pursuit could there be to display his success than yachting? Gad! Had he not earned it? All those years of hard yards, the scrimping and screwing to turn his father's mouldy old business into a going concern? He saw his contemporaries taking to yachting and was tempted. Surely there was nothing foolish or harmful in indulging in such a refined sport. He joined the New York Yacht Club and initially dabbled with some sloops and schooners of modest proportions, but, despite racing success, he couldn't help but feel that these vessels lacked glory. He needed something that was commensurate with his wealth and status. Something that made a statement and demonstrated beyond doubt that he had arrived.

Egged on by James Gordon Bennett and his cohorts, he ordered the *Mohawk* from the drawing board of Joseph Van Deusen who, a decade previously, had built the *Fleetwing*. The *Mohawk* was a very different and more extreme vessel, however. At 140 feet long, she boasted an immense 25-foot beam yet drew only 5 feet 10, although a huge centreboard, when lowered, boosted this draft to a massive 30 feet. Her sail area was huge: 20,000 square feet, with an immense 90-foot main boom. She was a monster.

This was the ultimate development of the schooner yacht. Today the super-rich choose to flaunt their wealth through obscenely flashy super-yachts such as Roman Abramovich's *Eclipse* or Ellison's *Rising Sun*. Back then, the equivalent was the *Mohawk*, a great, gilded bauble that represented the crowning glory of all those years of cut-throat commerce and rapacity. The yacht was not a thing of pleasure, it was a powerful symbol that he, William T Garner, was a man of consequence.

Many in the press lauded this latest wonder of man but there were also dissenting voices against a vessel which, with massive beam and almost non-existent draft, owed an awful lot of her design features to a soap dish. A writer in the New York *Spirit of the Times* who evidently knew a bit about yachts noted: 'I cannot see the first line of natural beauty about her. If they ever carry her lee rail under, with all sail set, there will be some danger. It does not answer to get a wide flat boat too far over.'

She turned out to be desperately slow and was frequently defeated by yachts 30 or 40 feet shorter, including Bennett's yacht. People started to snigger and Garner was furious, turning his ire on designer Joseph Van Deusen, who took her back into his yard at the end of the 1875 season and eventually expired trying to work out what the devil was wrong with his final masterpiece.

Back in the water in 1876, Garner decided to concentrate on cruising and, on 19 July, despite rather threatening weather, he brought a party aboard for a short cruise. Her captain was ordered to get the sails up preparatory to departure, while Garner and his party made a beeline for the saloon, for there was evidently a rain squall approaching. The harbour was calm in the sultry, brooding afternoon heat, but the sky was darkening and it was evident something was brewing. All around, other shipping shortened down, but the Mohawk proceeded to set all sail as the anchor was hauled up short. Perhaps her skipper felt the great schooner was invincible; perhaps all aboard were simply too lethargic as the heat of that sticky afternoon sapped energy and purpose from their limbs. Just on the point of departure, the squall exploded upon the vessel, and Mohawk's mighty sails stirred to life with a deafening crack, hurling her over on her side and sending her lee rail underwater. Initially she seemed to recover, staggering to her feet, but then came another gust, a short, sharp blow to her sails, the sucker punch. The Mohawk was downed, settling with a sigh, gently, gracefully on her side, her great white wings resting in the sea while green water poured over her deck and gurgled into her saloon.

Garner had raced up the companionway during the first knockdown to see what the commotion was, yelling, 'She'll come back!' He was wrong and watched in horror as the second gust delivered its death blow. With the boat on her side, sofas, chairs and a grand piano fell off the edge of the vertical cabin sole and dropped on to Mrs Garner and another guest, Adele Hunter. Hearing his wife's screams, Garner swung below from the companionway and clawed at the furniture, which was quickly being covered with pigs of lead ballast pouring out of the bilge after the trapdoors fell off. Water washed into the saloon through the skylight. Two other members of the party desperately pulled a lounge chair off the moaning Mrs Garner before returning to help Garner, who was frantically tugging at his wife's arm. 'For God's sake try and help me pull her out!' Garner cried. Just then, the *Mohawk* abruptly lurched to leeward, settling deeper, and the water flooded over his wife's head. Still Garner would not let her go, and he perished along with seven other members of the party. His final great symbol of achievement had plunged him into ruin and destruction. The great yacht was towed into the shallows, where she lay half sunk and shattered. Thus passed the greatest and most magnificent schooner of the era. One wonders if Lorillard and the Osgoods' argument over the seaworthiness of centreboarders might have been settled more easily had the *Mohawk* incident occurred a few years earlier.

Let us return to the North Atlantic, where the *Henrietta*, happily still afloat, continued to head north-east, encountering the steamship *Cuba* just before night closed in on the second day. The *Henrietta* flew a blue racing flag to distinguish her from the other racers and this was duly noted by the *Cuba*. Shortly afterwards, the steamer also spotted the *Vesta*, still pushing hard but a good ten miles or so astern of the *Henrietta*. This information was quickly transmitted ashore once the *Cuba* arrived in New York and hungrily snapped up by the newspapers which were – at least briefly – able to provide some solid facts amid the snowstorm of speculation surrounding the race.

Dawn on the third day emerged cloudy and mild and the guests aboard the *Henrietta* continued to enjoy their rather novel holiday in some style, as Fiske recalls:

> *The weather being warm, some of the guests enjoyed their siesta on deck, the servants unexpectedly emerging in white trousers seemed like the ghosts of long departed summer. Nothing was in sight upon the ocean except flocks of gulls and Mother Carey's Chickens. At noon we had made 204 miles by fine observation. In the evening a moon showed silvery upon a sea as smooth as the Thames. Reclining in the comfortable cabin, the Chateau Margaux and cigars within easy reach, the guests listened to the Captain's stories of haunted ships and suicides at sea and dismal wrecks of the southern ocean. Toward midnight, however, the scene changed, and repeated squalls with rain and hail struck the tiny craft and howled her along at a rate of eleven, twelve and thirteen knots. At sunrise the next morning a snowstorm began; the sea and sky seemed one and both were a deep slate colour; the men, half white with snow, moved slowly at their work; the dark horizon was noticeably narrowed; as the snow drifted down, the Henrietta passed through the water that foamed upon the deck: to leeward a spar from some wreck lifted itself to the view like a skeleton finger indicative of ruin; all our surroundings were mournful and depressing.*

Bennett's schooner was now approaching the Georges Bank, the signpost to the Grand Banks further out to the north-east, that violent stretch of shallows hemmed in by the unfathomable Atlantic. It is here over the Grand Banks that the warm Gulf Stream meets the Labrador Current, and the result is great walls of fog that can sweep in with no warning at all. These shallow banks can also kick up a fearsome chop as the seabed shelves rapidly from 2 kilometres deep to 36 metres. It was a menacing stretch of water that lay right in the path of the worst storm tracks in the world. Low-pressure systems form over the Great Lakes or Cape Hatteras and follow the jet stream out to sea, crossing right over the fishing grounds in the process. Names like Sable Island, the Georges Bank and Flemish Cap still speak to the sailor in a simple but eloquent language of wreck and destruction. Yet for all the Banks' fearsome reputation, fishermen were beckoned back year after year because this great confluence of currents teems with fish.

Samuels and his crew would have skirted respectfully past the Georges Bank, mindful of its reputation. For 300 years, fishermen had refused to exploit this area's rich bounty, spooked by its unpredictable currents and fearsome reputation. Sailors finally broke the hoodoo in 1827, and then the floodgates opened and fishermen flocked there to plunder nature's generosity.

They paid for it in full. In February 1862, a fleet of 70 schooners was anchored off the Georges Bank when a storm blew down out of the north-west. It came on so quickly there wasn't time to heave up anchors and run for deeper water to get away from one another. So they did what they could: posted two lookouts, one on the fore gaff and another on the main, out of the way of boarding seas. Both were peering to windward – with snow and sleet driving at them, nearly blinding them, spray freezing against eyes, beards and hair – hoping to discern a vessel drifting down on them. If the boat could be seen soon enough, their anchor cable could be cut and a collision avoided. If the vessel was spotted too late, the gale-force winds would send the drifting schooner careening into the anchored vessel and both would probably sink.

Collisions happened with appalling regularity on that fateful day. Thirteen schooners and their crews disappeared. Two more were abandoned and their crews rescued by other vessels. The human toll: 120 men, leaving 70 widows and 140 fatherless children. This was just one incident among hundreds. The Banks were a place of consequence, and while our bold passengers were swilling Chateau Margaux and polishing off bucketloads of oysters, the sailors aboard, battling with the snow squalls and hauling on frozen ropes with numbed fingers, would have looked to the north-west and tipped their cap respectfully to the widowmaker that lurked just below the surface. The Grand Banks and all the horrible possibilities therein were still to come.

They pressed on, the *Henrietta* making 225 nautical miles, her best 24-hour run so far, and by the evening of that third day out she was flying, as Fiske recalls:

*As night closed in on the third day the yacht sailed faster and faster,
until as we looked over the side where the waves came cascading
over the diminutive bulwarks we seemed to be fairly flying along.
The sky cleared but the wind freshened and the light sails were
hauled down and the mainsail reefed. The yacht quivered like a
race horse over driven. Sea after sea boarded the staggering craft.
A wave came bursting through the skylight into the cabin. All night
long this heavy weather continued; but the yacht ran so easily before
the free wind that everybody slept as if the Henrietta were the
Great Eastern.*

Off the Banks of Newfoundland we raced by a clumsy brig in the
fog so quickly that we could not make out her name as we passed
under her stern. Her crew manned the rigging, but were too much
astonished to answer our hail. They had not heard of the yacht race;
they had never before seen so small a boat defying the Atlantic in
such weather; in every bulging eye could be read the question, 'Is
she the Fenian privateer or the Flying Dutchman?' If there was
any betting on board the brig the odds must have been in favor of
the latter.

In both Captain Samuels' log of the *Henrietta* and Stephen Fiske's later recollections there are a number of references to meeting sailing vessels which 'stood off' in order to avoid them, and this is probably because any ship witnessing the little racer tearing through the water, her sails black against the reddening sky, would have assumed she was up to no good. In 1866, yachting was in its infancy, but piracy and smuggling were pastimes centuries old and fast schooners were the vessel of choice in such crimes. The British and American opium smugglers operating on the Chinese coast in the 1850s and early 1860s used schooners, some converted yachts. The best thing for a captain viewing a vessel of *Henrietta*'s design and rig racing for her life across a desolate stretch of the ocean was to steer well clear. Flying the New York Yacht Club pennant probably didn't help much either, for the club also had some pedigree in this area. The scandal surrounding the club's *Wanderer* was only just subsiding.

The story of the *Wanderer* is one worth relating here, as it featured another pioneering high-stakes race across the Atlantic. We will once again leave our three protagonists leaning into the icy waves of the north Atlantic and head south, back to the heat of Newport in the year 1857, where the New York Yacht Club was winding up its summer cruise. Young Jimmy Bennett, making his debut on the yachting scene, had been one of the leading lights of that year's cruise; another was the schooner *Wanderer*, which had also made her debut. She was the biggest and arguably most beautiful vessel in the history of the club and wherever she anchored her low, sleek, glistening black hull and immense rig drew admiring glances. At Newport, over 600 guests had visited her to coo over her exquisite beauty and elegance. Yet it wasn't long before she and her owner were cast out forever after the yacht had become the centre of the biggest scandal in the yacht club's history: captured on the coast of Georgia after successfully dropping off a shipment of slaves. This was in 1858, 50 years after the importation of slaves had been prohibited, and the embarrassment was compounded because when she was captured she was flying the colours of the New York Yacht Club from her masthead.

At the end of the 1857 season, the *Wanderer* had been sold by her original owner, Colonel John Johnston, to William Corrie, a wealthy and extremely well-connected gentleman from Charleston. Corrie, all oily manners and hustler's smile, was as smooth and slick as a pat of butter left out too long in the South Carolina sun. With his soft, slow drawl, quick wit, velvet tongue and greasy smile he could charm the skin off a snake. He was known to have great influence within Congress and, when in drink, was often given to quoting the exact price at which each congressman could be purchased. Given that the *Wanderer* was the jewel in the crown of the squadron and Corrie was such a smooth and winning young gentleman, he had no difficulty attaining membership to the NYYC and his debut season had passed pleasantly. No doubt he would have rubbed shoulders with young Jimmy Bennett, as the yachtsmen whiled away the summer with the usual round of languid cruises, brisk racing and fabulous parties.

Just as things were getting into full swing, Corrie raised eyebrows by withdrawing the *Wanderer* from cruising and taking her into the shipyard at Port Jefferson for modifications. There was further puzzlement when she was fitted with several substantial water tanks, capable of carrying 15,000 gallons of water, for 'ballasting purposes', her owner said. It must be for ballasting, for 15,000 gallons was enough water to keep a crew of 12, plus eight guests, at sea for two years. In addition to this, large quantities of cutlery and plates were loaded aboard, plus a vast quantity of supplies and even weapons. Something was clearly afoot. Whispers began to circulate around New York, with the result that when the *Wanderer* departed she was immediately arrested by the revenue cutter *Harriet Lane* and unceremoniously towed back to New York for a full inspection. Although the authorities were suspicious, they could prove nothing and, besides, young Corrie was such a fine gentleman and gracious host with such an exceptionally well-stocked drinks cabinet that surely nothing could be amiss. The only logical answer was that he was simply on an extended and adventurous cruise, as the *New York Times* reported:

MYSTERY OF THE YACHT *WANDERER*

She is seized at Port Jefferson, Long Island – Brought to
New York and overhauled – curious outfit – Is it a pleasure
trip? – A slave hunt or a filibustering expedition?

Several weeks later the *Wanderer* arrived off the African coast, the elegant yacht slicing through the greasy swells and shimmering heat as she ghosted in the light airs toward the Congo river. The keen observer would have noted the New York Yacht Club's pennant flying proudly at her masthead. Corrie had one priority: to secure a cargo of slaves, and he picked up 487 at the price of $50 a head. The yacht had already been carefully fitted out for a sinister purpose and under her exquisite rugs and beautifully polished floorboards a grid of 'berths' had been laid out for the slaves: 12 inches wide, 18 inches high and 5 feet 11 inches long. Down below the heat was stifling as she made her departure from the African coast. All who were at liberty looked ahead to America, the land of the free. It didn't pay to look astern, marked as it was by the trail of the dead. A little over six weeks later the *Wanderer*, now loaded with 407 slaves, and reeking of foetid squalor and criminal activity, arrived off Jekyll Island, Georgia. Shortly afterwards her human cargo was unloaded and sold for $500 a head.

Corrie nearly got away with it, but he was collared after close inspection of his papers revealed that his departure stamp, purportedly from the island of Trinidad, was a fake. By 12 December, Bennett's *Herald*, generally first to a really juicy story, ran the following headline and leader:

IS THE SLAVE TRADE REOPENED?

Is the yacht *Wanderer* a slaver – Curious conflicting
responses concerning the *Wanderer* – rumour of the landing
of a CARGO of slaves near New Brunswick, Georgia –
Particulars of her arrest in New York in June last – prophecy
of a *Herald* reporter

Soon evidence started to emerge which demonstrated without any doubt that the *Wanderer* had indeed run a cargo of slaves into the

United States. Perhaps the most compelling evidence were the slaves themselves. Five hundred bewildered Africans, speaking no English, are not easy to conceal, and it is damning that they were dispersed and sold with minimum fuss. It turned out that smooth-talking Corrie, evidently so crooked he could have hidden behind a corkscrew, was simply a front for one Charles Lamar, a prominent Savannah cotton-plantation owner with a searing hatred for the north, the Union and the evils of abolition.

Lamar was a luminary of the 'fire-eater' movement. These fire-eaters were a group of backward-looking southern gentlemen who longed for the 'good old days' and resented the union with the north. These days, the thought of a bigoted, racist, retrograde political party having any sway might seem ridiculous, but back then the politics of ignorance had real influence. Whenever anything went wrong, the fire-eaters blamed the union and pushed hard for the southern states to leave, using a rhetoric of racism and bleary-eyed sentimentalism to whip up southern pride. They particularly loathed New York, which, as early as 1819, had been described by one southern merchant as 'that tongue that is licking up the cream of commerce and finance in this country'. The depth of this antipathy is summed up beautifully in this editorial in the *Vicksburg Daily Whig*:

> New York City like a mighty queen of commerce sits proudly upon her island throne sparkling with jewels. Waving an undisputed commercial sceptre over the South. By means of her railroads, and navigable streams she sends out her long arms to the extreme south; and with avidity rarely equalled grasps our gains and transfers them to herself – taxing us at every stop and depleting us as extensively as possible without actually destroying us.

Lamar's slaving mission under the auspices of the hated city's most prestigious sporting institution was the ultimate gesture of defiance by the south. In fairness, the issue of slavery was only one facet of the conflict between north and south. At its heart lay the death of an old gentlemanly agrarian aristocracy and the rise of a new, brash, grasping elite of financiers and businessmen who, by 1859, held the whip hand over the south and weren't afraid to flay it if needs be. The final result was, of course, the Civil War, and Lamar later noted with glee that he had 'done more than any man in the south' to promote disunion. When the New York Yacht Club – staunch unionists and abolitionists to a man – discovered the truth, they were outraged and struck the *Wanderer* and Corrie off their membership list. For many years it was taboo to even mention the name of the yacht in the club.

Despite all the outrage and mountains of evidence, no one was ever convicted of any crime connected with this notorious case. As for Lamar with his failed dreams and terminal identity crisis, justice crept up on him and shook him savagely by the lapels. He was one of the very last men to perish in the Civil War conflict, killed by a bullet in the back. His dream of the southern gentry restored to its former glory was pushed face first into the mud of Appomattox and trampled on by the victorious north. Perhaps death was better for Lamar than facing defeat, for the consequences for the south were dire, as President Andrew Johnson observed: 'An aristocracy based on nearly two billions and a half of national securities has arisen in the northern states to assume that political control which the consolidation of great financial and political interests formerly gave to the slave oligarchy.'

We have once again been blown off course and must now return to our three racers far away, cutting a dash across the Atlantic at the whim of three members of this new northern aristocracy. We will return to the deck of the *Fleetwing*, which is toiling manfully against a vicious head sea and heavy north-eastern gale as night closes in at the end of day four and the stars burn bright and clear, polished by the gale. Her decks stream as she pounds into the waves. Her whole fabric seems to tremble like a leaf as she is hurled onwards, shouldering the waves aside with a shuddering thud, which throws up great sheets of icy sprays. Each fresh wave checks her progress and the poor, hard-driven schooner pauses, shakes herself down and then plunges once more into the billows. Captain Thomas's gamble of heading south in search of more clement weather was evidently not paying off.

Further north the *Henrietta* and *Vesta* are skimming along, enjoying fresh, fair breezes and more moderate seas. Both gained on their hard-pressed rival and for the first time in the race, *Henrietta* takes the lead, edging a couple of miles ahead of *Fleetwing* by the end of day four. She is also 20 miles ahead of the *Vesta*. As ever, all is not well aboard the *Vesta* and George Lorillard continues to find endless fault with Captain Dayton, noting in his diary of the race:

> *Recommended Captain Dayton to set the large squaresail as the weather was so fine; but no go as he is so careful with his crew, not wishing to call all hands to hurry up matters, as I can see that they wouldn't like it and the captain is afraid that the big sail might carry away the yard. This place is certainly getting very hot for me and I can see that if we win this race, it will be by fluke.*
>
> [Later that same day, he again noted in exasperated tones that:] *I desired the officer of the watch to slack off the main sheet as the wind was on the quarter and the main boom at an angle of*

45 degrees with the vessel griping. The officer called the captain, who
was asleep alongside a red hot stove in the cabin to see whether he
should slack off the main sheet or not. The captain thought not.

Back in New York, the first serious snowfall of the year was swirling through the streets. One wonders if Pierre Lorillard or the Osgoods, snugly ensconced in their mansions, spared a thought for their little yachts and the men aboard them, out there racing across the icy Atlantic for the glory of their owners. If they had, then a very brief article in the *New York Times* of 17 December may have caused just a murmur of disquiet in their ordered, comfortable lives. It read as follows:

THE GALE ON THE COAST

Halifax, N.S

A heavy gale accompanied by snow is prevailing this
morning. The Bark Bismarck went ashore in the Gut
of Canso also the brig Edwin Daniel in Little River. No
particulars are received.

Whatever hit Nova Scotia would soon be bowling out into the Atlantic with malicious intent, roaring down upon the three brave little yachts still racing gamely onward to England and glory.

6
RIDERS ON THE STORM

༒

God moves in a mysterious way, His wonders to perform.

He plants His footsteps in the sea, and rides upon the storm.

WILLIAM COWPER, HYMN

Day 7 (18 December)

Henrietta 1673

Vesta 1554

45°N — Fleetwing 1512

40°W

hat first Sunday out the already boisterous conditions were showing signs of taking a turn for the worse. Aboard the *Henrietta* the wind no longer howled, it screamed, and the schooner often lurched violently, only to check and steady herself before continuing her headlong progress. Captain Samuels surprised everyone by holding a prayer service. The bluff old sailor didn't seem like the religious type, but perhaps when you have eyed death enough times at close quarters it gives you pause for thought. As the little racing yacht lurched and shuddered, the crew tried to focus on the Lord while they dodged the great wind-whipped sprays that clattered aboard. Fiske was a bemused participant: 'Captain, officers and yachtsmen assembled for divine worship while the winds whistled shrilly without,' Fiske recalled: 'The prayers for the day were repeated and a chapter from the bible was read.' On a wing and a prayer the *Henrietta* raced on before the gathering storm.

Meanwhile, aboard *Fleetwing* Ernest Staples was greatly distraught when he discovered that Captain Thomas deemed the weather too wild for prayer meetings. Clear of the Grand Banks there was nothing but open ocean all the way to England. The yachts were well into what the transatlantic veterans called the Roaring Forties (named by sailors after the 40th parallel of latitude). In winter this lonely screaming wilderness offered little but desolation, as Stephen Fiske recalled:

For days the yacht was running between walls of water, as through a tunnel. Behind the moving walls, as they rose and fell, were lovely mirages of cities of white marble or windblown veils of rain and snow. The yacht was being driven at steamer speed by a succession of squalls and gales. Now and then a huge wave, like a white-crested monster of the deep, would crawl out of the darkness and fling itself upon the deck in a roaring rage.

In six days and 14 hours we had sailed half way across the Atlantic. In the afternoon a beautiful rainbow brightened the horizon; but this 'bow of promise' proved most deceitful, and brought us renewed hail and snow squalls instead of pleasant weather. During the night the wind shifted to W.S.W. We 'jibed' ship and hoisted the squaresail, but were forced to lower it again in a few hours, as the signs of dirty weather ominously increased. The effect of 'jibing' we may explain to the uninitiated, is to change the cant of a vessel from one side to another. The weather was now exceedingly threatening. The mainsail was double reefed, for the first time, and the vessel put in order for a storm.

Still the racers tore on over darkened seas under leaden sky, reeling the miles off at a relentless pace. If anything the deteriorating conditions seemed to suit the *Henrietta* better than her supposedly faster rivals, and every day she opened up her lead over the *Vesta* and *Fleetwing*. Perhaps Samuels really was just able to get that little bit more speed out of his yacht than his rivals. On paper, the *Fleetwing* should have been the fastest in these tempestuous conditions because she was the largest and most powerful. Yet she had met with the toughest conditions early on and by day seven, with the racers over halfway across, she had dropped 119 miles behind *Henrietta*. The *Vesta* was making better pace but was still 61 miles behind the leader. Perhaps, despite her shortcomings, the *Henrietta* was simply the most suited to sustained periods of hard pressing and inspired the most confidence. Certainly, her close-knit passengers and crew were learning to love the plucky little racer, as Fiske recalls:

> *Before leaving New York none of us had cared much for Henrietta; but she was so stanch, she sailed so much faster than anyone had expected, she responded so nobly to the care lavished upon her, that all of us fell in love with her. When we patted her deck affectionately and called her 'Good old girl!' she thrilled under the caress, and appeared to increase her speed.*

It is an unfortunate fact that James Gordon Bennett never committed one word of his own memories of the race to paper. His reputation as a writer of even a basic editorial was somewhat shaky, to be fair, and I suppose if you had paid Fiske to do the writing, there didn't seem a great deal of sense in exerting yourself in that direction. Still, it certainly would have been interesting to know how actively involved he was with the sailing and Fiske seems to have rather overlooked this aspect of things. There is no question that Bennett was passionate about the sea and this was reflected in his actions when he took charge of the *Herald* on his return from the race. One reporter recollected how dreadfully pernickety he was about the shipping columns:

> *Bennett's devotion to the sea took the further form of minute supervision of nautical items printed in the* Herald. *Each day a copy of the paper was sent him with the name of the writer of each article written on it in red pencil and that of its editor in blue. Woe betide the writer who perpetrated lubberly errors in technique. The instant one caught Bennett's eye there would come a blast by cable:*

'Why was that damned fool Blank allowed to write that shipwreck story? Doesn't he know the wind and tide in that neighborhood never perform as he states it? Never let him touch a sea story again.' Mistakes in terms were equally sinful. To erect a crow's nest on ships that do not carry that form of convenience for look-outs was to be for ever excommunicated from anything pertaining to navigation.

Bennett certainly knew what he was doing on a yacht and he was also an excellent navigator. It is documented that in later years he always insisted on navigating his own yachts, even when there was a skipper running the ship. Still, one gets the feeling that Captain Samuels would have brooked no interference of this kind, and no press report suggests that anyone other than Samuels plotted their path. Unlike George Lorillard on the *Vesta*, there is no mention of any friction between owner and captain. I suspect that Bennett – budding despot that he was – remained sufficiently awed by this legendary man to keep his mouth shut. Still, it is likely that Bennett took his turn at the helm when he felt like it and generally enjoyed the racing until things became sufficiently unpleasant to induce him to retire to the comfort of the warm cabin and the crackling stove.

Conditions were still merciless and it remained bitterly cold. When the pale sun deigned to show her face, *Henrietta's* brightwork glittered with a rime of bitter frost. Most of the time, however, the sky was grey, sullen and sodden with rain or sleet, dark waves, ruffled by wind with the occasional lonely gull wheeling and dipping. Throughout it all, Samuels continued his relentless vigil: wet through and cold to the bone, his greatcoat dusted with snow like a plum pudding, his feet inside sea boots that squelched icily whenever he moved. He was in his element here. The command of a fleet little sailing ship moving at speed made him complete and happy, despite the hardship. Occasionally he would go below to the comfort of the stove for some respite and exchange a cheery word with the passengers, but he would soon hark at some shift in the wind or subtle change in the rhythm of the yacht and dash back on deck, issuing a volley of fresh orders. The watch on deck, stamping their feet and blowing through numbed lips, would rouse themselves and return to the loathsome frozen ropes, sometimes clambering up into the icy rigging to furl a sail, hanging up there silhouetted against the dark sky like great black crows.

For all the hardship, there were also rewards. The yacht was being pushed to her limit and there is a great beauty and thrill in feeling a boat – particularly a big yacht like the *Henrietta* – being driven at maximum speed. As the weather worsened, the little schooner soared dizzily over the whitecaps, leaping clear of the great rollers and rising to the sky like a bird on the wing, rebuffing the big wind before plunging, smashing into the next sea. Great sheets of white water fizzed over her bow and rapped against her headsails, her scuppers ran like brooks, and you couldn't help but laugh at the beauty of it all. At times the sheer joy of it made you forget the cold and the misery; the exhilaration and beauty was almost as much as you could bear. The schooner seemed to tremble and shiver with excitement, full of a fiery, unquiet life. She seemed inhuman, glorious, spiritual.

To be at the helm was a revelation and as the weather worsened it took real skill and nerve to handle the little yacht in the mountainous following seas. Each wave became a fear-inducing, out-of-control elevator ride that would snatch the *Henrietta*, shuddering and surging, up to its peak and then hurl her off the edge of the cliff into the abyss below at dizzying speed. When you come down the face of a wave, you're on fire: there is a pause as the wave picks you up and you teeter at the top of the precipice, then a surge and an uncontrollable rush of adrenaline. For a few moments as you wrestle with that wheel and the yacht shivers like a human being, nothing else matters, the rest of the world is an irrelevance. You are part of something bigger. All you can do is roar and scream with a great primal surge of sheer joy to be part of it.

Samuels recalled this desperate dash before the gathering storm:

With every stitch we could carry we staggered through it until the wind freshened to a full gale from the southwest and we shortened sail to meet it. There was a high sea and prudence dictated that we heave to but all we did was to take in the mainsail and under close reefed foresail and forestaysail we kept our course with two men at the wheel and the rest of the watch astride the main gaff, which had been lowered on the main boom and hoisted about six feet off the deck. They were sent there so that if a sea broke it would wash under them. This was a race and we were taking chances of the deck getting swept.

By 4pm darkness had closed in and the weather was steadily worsening. The sailors peered out at a world ruled by the unknown. Waves became dark monsters that roared and terrorized, occasionally lashing out with stinging, icy spray. The gale continued to agitate itself into a state of fury and by 8pm it was truly terrifying, with the wind blowing 64 knots. At this point a monster wave 'boarded us abreast of the fore rig, burying everything forward – bow clean underwater and stern in the air', according to Samuels' log. Then 'a terrific sea washed over her, burying her almost completely. It ripped the foresail out of the bolt ropes'. At 8.40pm another great sea boarded the yacht and carelessly smashed her lifeboat to smithereens. 'That's no loss,' Samuels roared cheerily above the gale. 'The boat couldn't live if this yacht couldn't float.'

They needed Samuels then, for the storm was like a horribly vivid nightmare. The wind howled at them out of the blackness as if it had a conscious intention of terror. Round them there was nothing but a waste of sea, a livid grey whipped up here and there to white foam, and then beyond it, like a threatening wall, the surrounding dark, the chaos and fury of the night. In the darkness the waves roared around the boat like wild beasts. Death snapped and snarled just metres away. Anyone falling overboard into that icy maelstrom would not have had a hope.

Down below the passengers cowered against this hateful foe, praying for deliverance, as Stephen Fiske recalls:

> *Larry Jerome had promised his wife to read the Bible in times of danger and distress, and in a quavering, lugubrious voice he commenced to recite the first chapter of Matthew: 'Abraham begat Isaac; and Isaac begat Jacob; and Jacob begat Judas and his brethren.' We could not help laughing at his characteristically inappropriate selection, but the laughter was somewhat forced.*

The yacht bumped and thudded down below while up on deck the continuous roar of the wind was like an express train travelling through a tunnel. The wave that stove in the lifeboat had also hurled the gallant schooner on her side for a moment, shooting the terrified passengers across the cabin.

The groaning of timbers was like the fearsome shrieks of some demented soul in the depths of the ocean. Anything that wasn't lashed down fell and rattled about the ship like dice in a box. Crockery that was not in the box smashed all around us. We ourselves were flung on our backs.

It was a nerve-shattering experience and the first man to completely lose it was the *Henrietta*'s carpenter, William Shadbolt. Shortly after this fearsome knockdown he came tearing into the main cabin yelling that the *Henrietta* was opening up forward and water was pouring in. He implored Bennett to heave the little vessel to.

Bennett remained calm and made his way as coolly as he could on deck where he informed Samuels of the development. The captain headed below where he immediately noticed the wild excitement in his carpenter's eyes. Shadbolt was an old shipmate from Samuels' days in command of the *Dreadnought*. Though there is no doubt he was a first-class carpenter, he was prone to hysteria and bouts of extreme introspection. Earlier in the trip, Fiske had overheard him muttering 'about the evils of gambling and the utter depravity of risking men's life for gold'.

'One would have thought he was God's appointed watchman,' Fiske had mused sardonically. 'It is a good thing the rest of the crew treat him as a joke.'

That joke wasn't funny any more and Samuels dressed him down in suitably salty language. Shadbolt continued to babble that they 'were all drowning for the sake of idle gold and that the sea was already flooding the forward part of the ship'. Taking a lantern, Samuels headed forward and deduced that the ship was *not* sinking. When the schooner had been knocked down by the huge sea, all the water in the bilge had run up in between her outer planking and her decorative interior panelling. The water had then found a way back out through some gap in this panelling and spurted out, giving the impression the yacht was awash down below. He turned on the carpenter with a few more choice epithets and returned on deck.

The incident had shaken Samuels more than he let on, for only a matter of minutes later, during a brief lull in the storm, he ordered the *Henrietta* hove to, lying across the waves with only small trysails set to keep her steady. It would mark an end to racing for the night, but, with the helm lashed in position, all could retreat down below and sit out the storm. There may have been other reasons why this was a prudent move; according to Fiske, the *Henrietta* had, at some point in her life, been 'lengthened at the bow' and 'the overlapping timbers were writhing and scrunching terribly'. Whatever the cause, everyone seems to have had enough for the night and there is little question that heaving to was the prudent course to take. Fiske recalls the moment of decision:

> *Captain Samuels was solemn and he took off his cap as if in the presence of death: 'We must heave to Mr Bennett' he said; 'she can stand the strain no longer,' and ordered it to be entered on the log. Then he added: 'I have been over thirty years afloat, and never saw a ship that could have carried on so long as this little plaything has.'*

*But that was cold comfort. Heave to during a race! The simile
of a death seemed not too exaggerated. It was emphasized when the
sailors lifted out the storm trysails that were stored under the cabin
floor and carried them slowly up the companion way, as the bearers
carry a corpse. Heave to, in the slowest boat, only half of the course
covered! The wind whistled at us mockingly. The waves danced
about us, rejoicing at our failure and their victory. The storm trysails
once rigged, Henrietta rocked as comfortably as a cradle*

*But could we win the race in a cradle? For eighteen hours
we endured this aquatic purgatory; then we resumed the race
determinedly, like good Americans, but we had lost all hope of
winning.*

Despite the loss of time, Samuels was generous enough to point out to his
shipmates that they must hope their rivals were enjoying better weather
than they were.

They were not. The *Vesta* was similarly clobbered by the storm.
Captain Dayton had the added complication that he did not feel the
centreboard yacht would be able to heave to. Her shallow draft meant
she would not grip the water sufficiently and she might end up sliding
sideways down the waves too quickly. If the boat was not working
in harmony with the waves when hove to, she was in a vulnerable
position. The only other sensible option was to scud before the snarling
seas. This was a far more hair-raising prospect than heaving to, but
there was no option.

All through that wicked, uncertain night, the *Vesta* swooped and
dived across the great mountains of water running north-west directly
before the storm. She hurled great sheets of icy steaming spume out

from her bow as she smoked across the ocean at a scorching pace. During this desperate roller-coaster ride she passed only a few miles astern of the *Henrietta* as the latter lay snugly hove to, riding the waves. By dawn she was only ten miles behind her but, having previously been to the south of Bennett's schooner, she was now many miles to the north. It had been a testing night, but the centreboard schooner had held her own.

Not so the *Fleetwing* which, some miles to the south, was overtaken by the same savage storm. Thomas followed exactly the same procedure as Samuels, shortening down to reefed foresail and fore staysail, and carried on racing before the mountainous seas. No doubt spirits were not quite as buoyant aboard the *Fleetwing*. She had been dogged by minor pieces of misfortune since leaving New York. Down to the south of the other racers, she had encountered rougher, less favourable conditions. Following on from her snapped jibboom, the pumps had been manned in order to drain out the troublesome cockpit.

Nevertheless, there is no sign of the kind of acute disharmony that was present aboard the *Vesta*. Captain Thomas clearly knew his work and, despite lying in last place, he was still pushing her hard. But as darkness closed in on that awful night, it was hard not to feel a deep sense of foreboding. The gathering storm had given the sea an outline of senseless violence. The fading light had shown a square mile of water with huge waves flooding in like mountains sliding down the surface of the earth; with a haze of spray and spume scudding across it continuously. Night added the terrible unknown. Isolated in the blackness, *Fleetwing* suffered every assault.

On deck the eight members of the watch huddled in the shallow cockpit and dreamed of warm fires and their homes in New York, their families

Regatta of the New York and Eastern Yacht Clubs, off Swampscott, August 14, 1871.

ABOVE: An interesting old photo of one of the New York Yacht Club's many regattas. This one dates from 1871. (Photo by John S Moulton via Wikimedia Commons)

LEFT: A bluff old mariner who bowed to no-one. Captain Samuel Samuels in his prime. (Picture © Kay Jefferson)

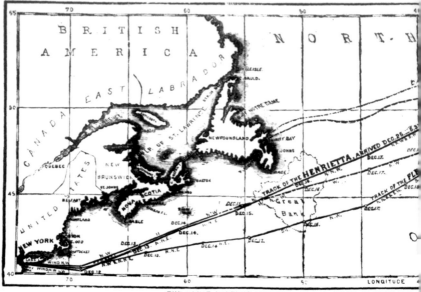

THE GREAT NAUTICAL TRIUMPHS OF 1866—CHART SHOWING THE

THE YACHT "HENRIETTA" 205 TONS.

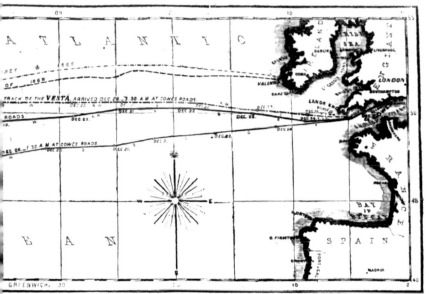

TLANTIC CABLES AND ROUTES OF THE YACHTS IN THE LATE RACE.

LEFT: The *Henrietta* under a press of sail. Built in 1860, she was beginning to show her age by the time of the race and few fancied her chances. (Lithograph by Charles Parsons, 1867, via Wikimedia Commons)

BELOW: *Henrietta* serving as a revenue cutter during the Civil War. She is alongside the famous ironclad *Monitor*. (Photo via Library of Congress)

ABOVE: A contemporary chart of the race showing the tracks of the three contestants. The artist has picked out the positions of the two transatlantic telegraph cables, laid in 1858 and 1866. (Chart from *Harper's Weekly*, 1866–1868)

James Gordon Bennett in 1860 serving as second lieutenant in the US Navy.
(Photo via Library of Congress)

James Gordon Bennett's replacement for the *Henrietta*, *Dauntless* shows the absurd sail area these schooners carried. (Photo via Library of Congress)

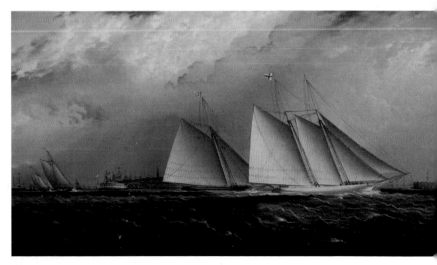

Magic and *Gracie* off Castle Garden, New York. *Magic* was the first successful defender of the America's Cup and was owned by both Osgood brothers and also George Lorillard. (Painting by James E Buttersworth, via Wikimedia Commons)

Schooners of the New York Yacht Club racing during the 1860s, or early 1870s. (Painting by Antonio Jacobsen, 1879, via Wikimedia Commons)

The *Fleetwing* survived many years after the race and was eventually converted into a sailor's mission, as a sort of floating church. (Photo by John S Johnston, 1895, via Library of Congress)

The New York Yacht Club Regatta of 1869. *Henrietta, Fleetwing* and *Vesta* are all present. (Currier & Ives lithograph, 1869, via Library of Congress)

By the 1800s, Cowes was already establishing itself as a yachting Mecca. Yet when James Gordon Bennett and his cohorts visited in 1866, it retained a sleepy air, which is perfectly captured by JMW Turner when he visited in 1827. In this painting, the Royal Yacht Squadron is preparing to start a race and East Cowes Castle is in the background. (Painting by JMW Turner, 1827, via Wikimedia Commons)

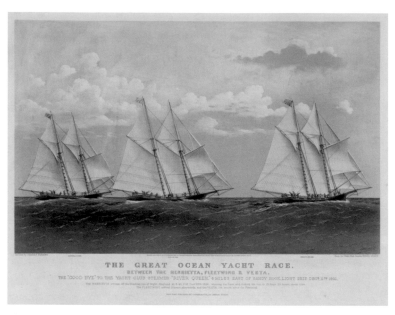

The start of the 1866 race. *Fleetwing* is to the left, *Vesta* in the middle and *Henrietta* to the right. (Currier & Ives lithograph by Charles Parsons, 1867, via Library of Congress)

Between about 1850 and 1875, the schooner ruled the roost at the New York Yacht Club. They were the super-yachts of their day. In this painting, two unidentified members of the club are locked in a fierce contest, illustrating just how heavily canvassed and hard-pressed these mighty racing machines were. (Painting by James Butterworth, 1871, via Wikimedia Commons)

preparing for Christmas. The fee for a crewmember for the crossing was $100 (about $1,500 today). On that dark night it probably didn't seem worth it. The storm seemed to reach its howling crescendo between 8pm and 10pm, and it was during this fraught period that the tragedy occurred. By now the wind had reached a monstrous force. Charged with salt water snatched from the wave crests, it roared over the little vessel, intent on destroying her. The crew was choked, deafened and blinded by its ferocity. It stunned the senses until simple thought or action became a great effort. Two men clung desperately to the spokes of the wheel and the others huddled close together seeking comfort and camaraderie.

At 9pm a huge sea thundered aboard the *Fleetwing*, a massive weight of water that threatened to crush the deck like an eggshell. The water roared aft with the force of a fire hydrant and the men, stunned, must have stared at it transfixed and braced themselves for that fearful rush of cold. Even as they gazed at that wall of water, something in them will have said they would survive it. There is always hope. They didn't stand a chance; the water poured into that open cockpit and scooped them out. A torrent of destruction overwhelmed them.

How can you convey the sensation of being washed overboard? What goes through a man's mind as he tumbles in the rush of the wave across the deck and into the open sea? For the eight men of the *Fleetwing* there was nothing to stop them: the low bulwarks of the little yacht offered no barrier to the sea. For that unlucky eight there was nothing but open ocean and perhaps the flicker of lights as the *Fleetwing* disappeared, then the jumbled, disorientating roar and shriek of wind and wave, and perhaps the muffled cry of one of your shipmates, and panic, the air forced out of your lungs by the shock of icy water, desperate thrashing around, desperate gasps for air as you are buffeted by waves charged with bucketloads of spray forcing great mouthfuls of salt water down your throat. Then perhaps a brief respite, a snatched breath, and the desolating loneliness of your own doom washes over you; the cold starts grabbing at you with icy fingers, finding your vitals and prising life from your hopeful grasp. 'Three times, 'tis said, a sinking man/Comes up to face the skies' wrote the poet Emily Dickinson. Then nothing; eternity, death reaching out his icy hand.

The North Atlantic in December has a temperature of around 3 degrees. Even in calm conditions that would give a survival time of 30 minutes to an hour for a fit, strong swimmer. With the bullying sea toying with you, and clad in heavy seaboots and oilskins, buffeted by giant waves, the end must have been mercifully quick.

Ernest Staples later recalled:

> I was below at the time lighting my pipe and talking – shouting were the better word in that great gale – to Captain Thomas. We heard and felt the great concussion caused by the striking of the sea and rushed on deck with all the speed the shuddering of the ship allowed. The sight which met our view was a most affecting one. The cockpit which, but a few minutes before we had seen filled with the watch was now clean swept of every living soul and the deck and cockpit, from the main rigging aft was completely covered with water.

The position was extremely perilous: with the helmsman washed overboard, the schooner would have slewed sideways across the waves, exposing herself to the full force of their anger. It was fortunate that Staples chose that moment to smoke his pipe on the companionway, for he was well placed to clamber up to the waterlogged cockpit and grapple with the wheel – now missing two spokes. With the cockpit full of water, the *Fleetwing* was also sluggish, but thankfully she was not totally overwhelmed. While she floated there was hope.

Captain Thomas immediately hove to with the intention, even in that hopeless, hateful sea, of finding his lost men. As they grappled and cursed and trembled with fear there came snatches of voices, eerie, chilling cries across the wind-whipped wasteland. Two men had managed to grab hold of the foresail, which had been ripped from the mast by the great wave and was dragging in the water, still attached to the yacht. By some miracle they were hauled aboard, drawn back out of deep waters, rescued from death. Shivering, almost weeping with cold, shock and relief, they were bundled down below and plied with brandy and blankets. It was the only miracle of that hateful night. For the other six, there was no deliverance, although, God knows, Captain Thomas did all he could. For five hours they scoured the desolate ocean with lanterns. They called and called for their comrades, but the only reply was the scream of the lonely wind and the roar of the angry ocean.

After five hours the storm showed signs of dying off. The sky cleared, the wind fell from a scream to a sigh and the waves were hushed. Stars winked in the heavens as Captain Thomas hove down the helm and the *Fleetwing* squared away with sighing sails to resume her course. Hope finally extinguished.

So who were these men? Contemporary accounts of the race give them incredibly short shrift, merely referring to a 'very sad accident' of the 'loss of six men'. Faceless, nameless, not worth a eulogy. Life was cheap, and the life of a sailor was cheaper still. Death was an everyday fact in 1866. Captain Samuels stared it in the face on every one of his transatlantic crossings and on that last voyage aboard his beloved

Dreadnought three men perished without anyone blinking. In 1866, the average life expectancy was about 42 years; few hung around long enough to experience old age. Still, delve deep enough and you find an inquiry held into these six drowned men, which at least puts a little flesh on their bones.

They were Peter Wood, Thomas Hazleton, Patrick McCormick, Sean Kelly, Matthew Brown and Lincoln Massy. The inquiry was only held because Wood and Hazleton were captains and their shipping line felt it was the decent thing to do. This pair were presumably among the emergency crew members the *Fleetwing* had drafted in after many of her men deserted. Mr Wood left a wife and grown-up child and Mr Hazleton a wife and two young children. Next up came Patrick McCormick and Sean Kelly, both Irishmen and ordinary seamen. McCormick was married to a Mexican woman and the pair had a young child. Kelly was married to a Irish woman and had two young children. At the inquiry Mrs Kelly stated how she had been duped by her husband into leaving her home in Queenstown (now Cobh) and coming to America in search of wealth. She observed bitterly that New York offered 'nothing but luxury to them that could afford it and nought but disgrace to them that were put to poverty'. McCormick's wife informed the inquiry that since her husband's death she had been working in a mill packing samples as this was the only place she could bring her baby to work with her. The seaman Matthew Brown was given especially short shrift at the inquiry because he was clearly an absentee husband and a drunk – at least according to his wife – who professed surprise that he had not died long before for all that she had heard from him.

The last man was Lincoln Massy, the black cook who had proven such a Jonah in the early stages of the race. He had been born Obadiah Massy and served as a slave down in Louisiana. When Civil War had brought liberation, he had changed his name – presumably in honour of the man who played a large part in gaining him emancipation – and headed to sea. On shore he left four grown-up children and his wife, Japonica, behind. According to Japonica he had chosen the sea because it offered him the ultimate form of liberty, although, as she observed with great sadness at the inquiry: 'He ain't free no more because he's dead and I's also dead most powerful.'

The sea probably was Massy's best opportunity to taste equality, for on land he was still very much a second-class citizen. True, 1866 had been a significant year as the Civil Rights Act had been passed – despite a presidential veto – which stated 'there shall be no discrimination in civil rights or immunities among the inhabitants of any State or Territory of the United States on account of race, color, or previous condition of servitude'. It would be a century and more before black and white were on a vaguely equal footing in America. At sea, all were bound equally to obey the captain and there was no discrimination in that matter. Black or white, officer, seaman or cook, the sea showed no discrimination: all were equal in the presence of death.

The mood must have been sombre as the *Fleetwing* settled back along her way. The empty bunks, the new watch rota set up, the extra labour required to handle her mighty sails – all would have been reminders of the missing men. There might have been little appetite for a race among men who had just been given a glimpse of the bigger picture, but all would have longed to get the passage over with; to flee from the ghosts out there in the lonely Atlantic. It wasn't long before they were back up to full speed; making an impressive run of 260 miles as they fled that godforsaken stretch of water.

Meanwhile, a race that *Henrietta* had looked as if she was going to win at a canter was back in the balance. For some reason, even though the storm had died off shortly after midnight, it was not until dawn when Captain Samuels finally squared away and she returned to racing in earnest. Perhaps he was exhausted and the enforced break had induced total collapse. By dawn all were refreshed and progress was resumed in much more pleasant conditions, as Fiske recalls:

> *The ship again started off briskly, as if rested and refreshed. The sun shone pleasantly, but the sea was still running high, the waves blown about like the sandhills of a desert, disclosing strange mirages of tents and sails as they revealed scraps of the horizon here and there. We made our shortest distance on this stormy day, gaining only 113 miles. At three p.m. we were going thirteen knots, and kept up this pace for several hours. In the evening we sailed calmly in the mellow moonlight that marked our track before us with its sheen.*

The upshot of this interruption in the *Henrietta*'s hitherto headlong progress was that the little schooner's lead was slashed. *Vesta*, which had run on desperately through that awful storm, was only 10 miles astern, although now some distance to the north. *Fleetwing* had also 'northed' after squaring away following her five hours hove to, and she had closed to within 86 miles of *Henrietta*. Captain Thomas had also decided it was time for that long-deferred church service, as Ernest Staples recalled:

> *No one had the heart for singing and tears stood on the cheeks of the rough and ready sailors as prayers were recited and they remembered*

absent friends. It was time well spent, for I do believe the crew put
forward more effort after their communication with their maker.

There was nothing for it but to run on to England. Like it or not, the
race was on. All turned their back on the battlefield of the Atlantic and
looked toward England and the old world for salvation.

———

7
STRANGER THAN FICTION

He who makes a beast of himself gets rid of
the pain of being a man.

SAMUEL JOHNSON, QUOTED IN *ANECDOTES OF THE REVD PERCIVAL STOCKDALE*

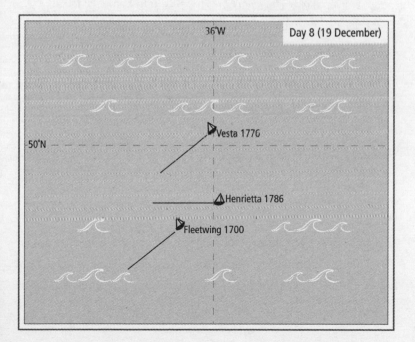

With the passing of the storm, the Atlantic decided to display a very different side of its personality. The following morning, memories of that fearful night were ushered aside by a pristine, crystal-clear day, as Stephen Fiske aboard the *Henrietta* recalls:

> As in the middle of a desert there is an oasis, so in the middle
> of the Atlantic we presently came upon a calm. In one night we
> passed from Winter cold to Summer warmth. There had been no
> sunshine; and now the sun shone brightly. The yacht, that had
> been lashed by whips of hail and sleet, rolled lazily, like a tame seal
> in the placid water. No one could realize that such a July day was
> December 21.
> ... instead of reading more prayers, [Captain Samuels] followed
> the sailor superstition and ordered all hands to change their clothing
> and whistle for a wind. Had not the stake been so weighty in honour
> as well as money, the sight of the yachtsmen, attired in clean togs and
> unsuspected finery, every man puckering his mouth to whistle would
> have been more comical than a minstrel show.

Presently a gentle breeze filled in and seemed to playfully caress the great widow-maker, affectionately ruffling her surface with the gentlest of wavelets. *Henrietta* began to steal along her way again. In the meantime, the sunshine was there to be enjoyed and presently the deckchairs were shipped and a bottle of claret was rustled up out of the bilge. Say what you want about Bennett, he kept a sensational cellar. Bathed in radiant light, the gents sipped on the rich, sweet wine, nibbled on plover's eggs, luxuriated in the sweet, golden rays of a sun that seemed to shine only for them and swapped tales of largesse and high-class debauchery.

Yes, life was sweet for our privileged friends. The past was a golden haze of excess, and the future seemed to beckon them on, as warm and inviting as that beautiful sun-infused morning. Perhaps this is an apt time to look a little more closely at James Gordon Bennett and what lay in store for him, for the conclusion of this transatlantic jaunt was to prove pivotal. Upon his return to New York, his father finally bowed to the inevitable and handed over some of his editorial power to his wayward son. Even as he crossed the Atlantic, Bennett must have had an inkling of his father's plans and been pondering the mayhem he could cause if he controlled the most popular newspaper in the world.

To get a real idea of his potential for havoc and a full insight into the psychology of the individual, we have to fast forward nigh on nine years to the morning of 9 November 1874 when the *Herald* got the exclusive on one of the greatest tragedies ever to hit the city of New York. To understand how the drama unfolded, we will head to the pleasant middle-class parlour of Mr Average of New York. It's Sunday and Mr A is tucking into a hearty breakfast and wrestling open his crisply folded, freshly delivered copy of the *New York Herald*, the world's most read paper. Proprietor, James Gordon Bennett Jr. All is well as he prepares to prong a sausage and quaff a cup of coffee. Suddenly, Mr A stops dead in his tracks, takes a deep breath and inhales a gullet full of hot coffee, which then explodes across the table. Staggering to his feet, he emits a strange gurgling sound then bolts from the room, paper in hand, gesticulating wildly at the following article:

AWFUL CALAMITY

The Wild Animals Broken Loose from Central Park.

Terrible Scenes of Mutilation – A Shocking Sabbath
Carnival of Death – Savage Brutes at Large – Awful
Combats Between the Beasts and the Citizens – The Killed
and Wounded – General Duryee's Magnificent Police
Tactics – Bravery and Panic – How the Catastrophe was
Brought About – Affrighting Incidents – Proclamation by
the Mayor – Governor Dix Shoots the Bengal Tiger in the
Streets

Another Sunday of horror has been added to those
already memorable in our city annals. The sad and appalling
catastrophe of yesterday is a further illustration of the
unforeseen perils to which large communities are exposed.
Writing even at a late hour, without full details of the
terrors of the evening and night, and with a necessarily
incomplete list of the killed and mutilated, we may pause for
a moment…

The report went into lurid detail about the death and destruction
this terrible accident had caused: men ripped apart by savage beasts,
bloodcurdling scenes of gore and terror. This gave rise to a strange mixture
of panic, horror and outrage in the reading public. Many cowered in their
houses waiting for the animals to disperse. Others took to the streets in
packs hunting down the animals vigilante-style. How could this have
been allowed to happen? There was even greater panic at the offices of
Bennett's rival papers, such as the *New York Times*, the *World* and the *Sun*.

How in the name of hell had the night shift missed such a story? Teeth were gnashed, doors slammed in fury. Editors and publishers stomped around offices in great demented herds demanding answers. Someone was going to get a bullet for this. The *New York Times* was so furious that it sent a deputation of reporters around to the police headquarters to officially complain about the favouritism shown to the *Herald*.

Then, suddenly, hysteria in the news rooms of New York was replaced by cold hard fury. If anything the language turned bluer and doors were slammed so hard they were nearly wrenched off their hinges. Out in the street panic melted away and was replaced by hilarity. People slapped each other on the back and chuckled freely. The cause? Someone had spotted the final addendum to the *Herald*'s grisly story, which read:

THE MORAL OF THE WHOLE

Of course the entire story given above is a pure fabrication.
Not one word of it is true. Not a single act or incident
described has taken place. It is a huge hoax, a wild romance,
or whatever other epithet of utter untrustworthiness our
readers may choose to apply to it. It is simply a fancy picture
which crowded upon the mind of the writer a few days ago
while he was gazing through the iron bars of the cages of
the wild animals in the menagerie at Central Park.

So it was a hoax. James Gordon Bennett had made a fool of everyone, apparently because he had drunkenly bet one of his chums that he could up the circulation of the paper dramatically overnight. While rival editors and publishers fumed, the public as a whole was inclined to chuckle indulgently at New York's weirdest son.

Bennett had taken over the running of the *Herald* day to day on his return from the 1866 race, and had gained total control of the newspaper when his father had passed away in 1872. He was not like his father, however, who had been a natural newspaperman with a nose for a grubby, scurrilous story. The style of journalism the son encouraged was different to anything that had come before or since. Basically, Bennett wanted to create the news. The first real expression of that had been seen with the 1866 yacht race. In this case, you witnessed the son of the owner of the *Herald*, the most popular newspaper in the United States, setting the news agenda by going out there and risking life and death on the ocean wave. It was a bizarre and grandiose way of making news, but it worked, and it was a theme that Bennett expanded upon readily when he got control of the newspaper from his father. Marry that with Bennett's own rather erratic personality, particularly if he had spent a few hours at Delmonico's mopping the stuff up, and you have a recipe for anarchy. The zoo hoax was really just Bennett warming up.

During the day, Bennett was generally a stern, strait-laced and sensible boss who took his work seriously and didn't take any nonsense from his employees. As he gained in confidence as a publisher he became increasingly despotic and would often remind them of how worthless they were, bellowing that he could hire all the brains he needed for $25 a day and frequently laying off great swathes of staff at a whim, only to rehire them the next day. Yet the Bennett who turned up for the day shift was an absolute saint compared to the character who prowled the corridors of the *Herald* as the evening dragged on and the deadline loomed. It was Bennett's habit as publisher to retire in the early evening to Delmonico's, where he would dine on a lamb chop and refresh the palette with a couple of glasses of champagne. This helped reinvigorate him for the tiresome work of browbeating his unfortunate editorial team. Wafting in amid a post-dinner haze of cigar smoke and champagne fumes, silk topper askew and a wild glint in his eye, Bennett would cut a markedly different figure from the cold-hearted and efficient man who turned up for the day shift. Just how lethal he was capable of being can be seen in the following anecdote, told by his secretary Sam Chamberlain, who spent a good deal of his time working as minder for the wayward media mogul. It concerns the devastating after-effects of one particularly bracing dinner session:

> *The effect of his potations was usually to evolve some out of the ordinary physical action, but sometimes it confused his head work. On one of his spells of exhilaration his father's anti-Catholicism gave through him an atavistic performance. Summoning me to his office, he remarked: 'Sam, I am tired of all this talk of the Herald being controlled by the Roman Catholic Church and of the number of Trinity College men on its staff. Now, I want you to write an editorial that will put us right before the public and show that we have no affiliations with Rome. Attack the Catholic Church, its monasteries, nunneries and schools and make it as strong as you can: Write the editorial and bring it to me this evening.*

Mr Chamberlain dutifully set about his work with a weary sigh. He had dealt with this problem many times when Bennett was in wine and had humoured his boss by pretending to have the story printed when in reality it never got near the typesetters. Bennett was always mightily relieved the following day. On this occasion Chamberlain, realizing the futility of the work in hand, aimed to give Bennett a nasty jolt, presenting him with a particularly savage evisceration of the Catholic Church and opening with the snappy headline:

TO HELL WITH THE POPE

And expanding on the theme with a searing indictment of this ancient institution with demands to, 'Tear down the Monasteries', 'Drive out the Monks', 'Let us have no politics from Rome'. So it went on. There was a real snap and vigour about his work and certainly the headline would halt even the most inattentive skim reader in his tracks. Bennett was sufficiently exhilarated to see only the positives. He found the editorial a most invigorating read and chuckled with glee over its provocative subject matter. He had but one concern. 'Now, Sam,' he observed sternly, 'you've fooled me many times before but you're not going to do it this time. We'll deliver this to-night.'

Bennett personally made sure the copy was submitted and went home highly pleased with himself, proceeding to extend his period of inebriety. Some ten days later he came to himself and dimly recalled the indiscretion. He summoned Sam to his bedside and nervously asked if something had not been sent to the *Herald* abusing the Catholic Church. The dutiful secretary replied that the article had not seemed strongly worded enough and he had recalled the article for further revision. Bennett was not an effusive man and found praise almost impossible to bestow on any employee. Nevertheless, he marched Chamberlain down to a jeweller's and purchased a costly cat's-eye ring which he placed on the secretary's finger as a reward for his judgment.

This was the temperament of the man who controlled the most powerful newspaper in America – arguably the world. Only the *Times* back in London could claim a larger revenue but even that could not rival the *Herald*'s 30,000-a-week circulation. You also have to remember just how powerful the newspaper was back then. There was no television, no radio, no internet. If you wanted the news, there was only one source: the newspaper. Many shuddered at the thought of what Bennett was capable of as proprietor of the *Herald*.

Certainly the results were often fascinating. In 1970 the journalist Hunter S Thompson coined a new phrase, 'gonzo journalism', to describe articles written without claims of objectivity, often including the reporter as part of the story via a first-person narrative. The kind of reporting was chaotic and unsustainable due to the frequent liver abuse that seemed to be a mandatory part of the creative process. Nevertheless, the results were hugely entertaining. Now, Jimmy Bennett couldn't write worth a damn by all accounts, but he did have some pretty wild ideas about how news should be shaped, and if anyone deserves the title of gonzo publisher, it is him. An example of the kind of weird quirkiness Bennett would throw into his newspaper can be seen in the case of a very dull letter to the *Herald* signed off 'Old Philadelphia Lady'. This was an odd name and, through some editorial error, the letter was published twice in a row. Bennett spotted that, but found it odd enough to decree that the letter should be run in every issue for the next couple of years, leaving readers bewildered. If Bennett was feeling particularly obtuse, he would sign off his own editorials with the same sobriquet. No wonder the *New York Times* once labelled the *Herald* 'that supremely odd publication'.

Yet combined with madness and weirdness was a sprinkling of genius and perhaps the ultimate expression of this was the case of Henry Morton Stanley and David Livingstone. Even today the expression

'Dr Livingstone, I presume' is still etched into the collective conscious of the western world. What Stanley did while searching for Livingstone is astonishing but it is only part of what he achieved; in 1874 he returned to the heart of Africa and managed to trace the course of the River Congo from near its source right down to the sea. He achieved something almost impossible and in the process, a huge section of the map of the world was filled in. For better or for worse, he changed the face of the modern world.

What has this got to do with James Gordon Bennett Jr? Absolutely everything. Neither expedition would have happened without him. The *Herald* supplied the financial muscle and Bennett supplied the inspiration and impetus to ensure it happened, as Stanley, who was working as a foreign correspondent, recalled after being summoned to Bennett's Paris office in 1869:

The summons came at Madrid, in the form of a telegram reading: 'Come to Paris on important business, J. G. Bennett.' *To read was to obey. Down come my pictures from the walls of my apartment; into my trunks go my books and souvenirs, my clothes are hastily collected, some half-washed, some from the clothes-line half-dry, and after a couple of hours of hasty hard work my portmanteaus are strapped up, and labelled for 'Paris.' The express-train leaves Madrid for Hendaye at 3pm.*

I was on my way, and being obliged to stop at Bayonne a few hours, did not arrive at Paris until the following night. I went straight to the Grand Hotel, and knocked at the door of Mr. Bennett's room.

'Come in,' I heard a voice say. Entering, I found Mr. Bennett in bed.

'Who are you?' he asked.

'My name is Stanley,' I answered.

'Ah, yes; sit down. I have important business on hand for you.'
After throwing over him his robe-de-chambre, Mr. Bennett asked
me, 'Where do you think Livingstone is?'

'I really do not know, sir.'

'Do you think he is alive?'

'He may be, and he may not be,' I answered

'Well, I think he is alive, and that he can be found, and I am
going to send you to find him.'

'What!' said I. 'Do you really think I can find Dr. Livingstone?
Do you mean me to go to Central Africa?'

'Yes, I mean that you shall go and find him wherever you may
hear that he is, and to get what news you can of him, and perhaps'
– delivering himself thoughtfully and deliberately – 'the old man may
be in want: take enough with you to help him should he require it. Of
course you will act according to your own plans, and do what you
think best – BUT FIND LIVINGSTONE!'

Said I, wondering at the cool order of sending one to Central
Africa to search for a man whom I, in common with almost all other
men, believed to be dead, 'Have you considered seriously the great
expense you are likely to incur on account of this little journey?'

'What will it cost?' he asked, abruptly.

'Burton and Speke's journey to Central Africa cost between
£3,000 and £5,000, and I fear it cannot be done under £2,500.'

'Well, I will tell you what you will do. Draw a thousand pounds
now, and when you have gone through that, draw another thousand,
and when that is spent, draw another thousand, and when you

have finished that, draw another thousand, and so on; but FIND
LIVINGSTONE.'

The reporter was a bit dazed at the size of the assignment and
a little uncertain as to his authority to invade a continent. 'I have
heard,' he said, 'that should your father die you would sell the
Herald and retire from business.'

'Whoever told you that was wrong,' came the quick rejoinder, 'for
there is not money enough in New York city to buy the New York
Herald. My father has made it a great paper but I mean to make it
greater. I mean that it shall be a newspaper in the true sense of the
word. I mean that it shall publish whatever news will be interesting to
the world at no matter what cost.'

On this occasion, history was instigated by an indolent man clad only
in a bathrobe. Of course, Stanley had a hell of a lot still to do before
history *was* made, but without Bennett nothing would have happened
at all. Even more marvellous, when Stanley finally did find Livingstone,
he asked the old man whether he had heard of the *Herald*. 'Oh yes,'
Livingstone replied. 'Who hasn't heard of that despicable rag.' There
is a mountain in Central Africa called Mount Gordon Bennett. It's not
far from the Gordon Bennett River. Can you imagine anything more
ludicrous? What would Rupert Murdoch give to have a mountain named
after him?

This was probably the crowning achievement of Bennett's remarkable
style of journalism, which owed very little to his father's tutelage. This
was journalism on a far more grandiose scale. It was something new and
startlingly original and few have had the means, or the arrogance for that
matter, to imitate it since. 'I want you fellows to remember,' he once said

to the executive staff, 'that I am the only reader of this paper. I am the only one to be pleased. If I want it to be turned upside down, it must be turned upside down. I want one feature article a day. If I say the feature is to be Black Beetles, Black Beetles it's going to be.'

Thus the biggest American newspaper of the mid to late nineteenth century was not run as a corporation, a money-making entity, but as the plaything for its lunatic owner. The results were rarely dull. Beyond making the news in addition to reporting it, Bennett also had some fairly sound ideas editorially. Shortly after taking over as publisher and managing editor, he changed the typeface to make it more readable and accessible. He employed famous and hugely talented writers such as Mark Twain and Walt Whitman and remained devoted to scooping his rivals by any means possible and at any price. It was the *Herald* that first reported Custer's catastrophic defeat at Little Big Horn in 1876, beating any other publication to the story by four full days. Rival publications were too timorous to copy the story because it sounded too fanciful for words.

This was a high-water mark for Bennett, and the very first day of the following year, 1877, brought about his nadir. New Year's Day 1877 could perhaps be placed as the beginning of the end for the *Herald*, for it was this day that brought about a catastrophe that would ensure that, henceforth, the editorial policy of the biggest American newspaper was largely dictated from Paris. The reasons for this were, unsurprisingly, down to a calamity in Bennett's private life.

New Year's Day wasn't the damp squib it is in our time. Back then old respectable New Yorkers continued with the Dutch tradition of their forefathers, paying house visits and drinking the good health of one's guest into the bargain. If you were wealthy, this meant hopping in your sleigh, muffling up in a goodly amount of furs and tootling around the neighbourhood partaking of a diverse range of noggins. It was all meant to be very civilized but, as you can imagine, Bennett was far from a shrinking violet when it came to getting stinko and on this occasion he excelled himself. His affairs were at an all-time high. The *Herald* was flourishing and his standing in society had never been better since he had introduced the sport of polo into the country the previous summer. He was the *beau ideal* of the fast-living rich set and even his drunken aberrations had abated since he had started courting beautiful young Caroline May. That's right, the rumour on the street and in the newspapers was that the untameable, irredeemable bachelor was in love, having fallen pretty heavily for the radiant Miss May; fresh as a lily and delicate as porcelain with the kind of profile that turned strong-hearted men into blancmange.

The closest Bennett had come to being in love before this was with a gorgeous showgirl named Pauline Markham. Bennett had pranced around with this beautiful young lady on his arm in the late 1860s. There was even talk of them tying the knot, but the young tycoon had eventually tired of her and cast her to one side just as he might toss away a cigar. Bennett was good at that; on one occasion he dumped one of his many lovers with the following telegram: 'My mind has been made up for some time. Let me know how much I owe you. Bennett.' Yet it really looked as if young Miss May had melted that stony heart of his and many congratulated her on snagging one of the richest bachelors in New York.

The pair had been engaged for some months that fateful New Year's Day and, although there were already some minor mutterings about trouble in paradise over wedding arrangements, the marriage was well and truly on when Bennett lurched up to the house. The problem was that, having behaved impeccably since entertaining Miss May and family at his Newport mansion that summer, Bennett was due a really good bender, and he chose this particular day to get on the Razzle Dazzles.

Good Razzle Dazzles come on slow. The first one slips down easy; it's all about the sweet ginger and the warm glow of the brandy. It feels good. By the time you get to the second you feel a warm air of bonhomie toward your fellow man but you're still in control of the situation. Then … BOOM! The absinthe kicks in. You find yourself grappling with even simple sentence constructions. You want to speak but words are hard to shape because somehow your tongue is too big for your mouth. Suddenly it all falls into place; words start to flow but too late you realize you are screaming gibberish and, if you're really unlucky, drooling. Coordination is also difficult: you ask your arm to move and there is a delay. Eventually it does, but everything goes wrong; you end up slapping the floor when you were meant to be reaching for your wallet. There are few things more disorientated and degenerate than a man in the grip of a Razzle Dazzle binge and you can bet your bottom dollar that Jimmy Bennett was eyeball deep into the rotten stuff when he rolled up at his fiancée's parents' house and fell out of his sleigh.

The Mays' party was the last port of call for young Jimmy. He had already enjoyed a number of stopovers on his way to the Mays' house and anyone who observed the man closely could see that he was tight as an owl. Nevertheless, on entering the Mays' humble abode, he displayed some impressive footwork as he barged through the throng of revellers. Anyone with even a shred of sobriety would have noted the somewhat stultifying atmosphere of the Mays' little shindig. Sure, there were drinks available, but this was a high-class bash; all absurdly expensive hors d'oeuvres, stifling manners and showily dull small talk.

The party was peopled with a selection of the great and good of New York, as florid and well upholstered as the furniture in Mrs May's well appointed parlour. They wafted around desperately seeking something of curiosity to relieve the ennui of this soirée. Jimmy Bennett's arrival provided a sharp focus for this curiosity and many gaped in horror as the tycoon made a beeline for the cocktail tray with all the purpose of a camel headed for the oasis after a hard day out tramping the dunes. Across the room, his lady-love spotted him and smiled palely. She had grown up in a family of hot-blooded young males and was willing to overlook her husband-to-be's little eccentricities. Boys will be boys after all. Still … he was swaying about in rather an alarming manner, hands gesturing wildly as he breathed fiery brandy fumes over the great and good of New York society. A few of the more prudent guests grabbed their coats, sensing there might be an ugly scene. Bennett was impersonating a man who had lost all sense of balance, basic motor skills and the ability to string a coherent sentence together.

It was at this juncture when the catastrophe occurred and I'm going to pause the narrative briefly to pre-emptively provide Bennett with a little bit of mitigation. I'm not saying that what Bennett did next wasn't his fault, but I think it's important to understand the catastrophic effect that alcohol had on him. I am, therefore, going to hand you over to an 'acquaintance' of young Jimmy – Camille Clermont, from whom we shall hear more later – to give you some insight into the transformative effect a few hours on the sauce could have on the man. On this occasion he was dining with Camille and seems to have refreshed himself with rather too much gusto:

> After dinner he suddenly began to swallow glass after glass of liqueur and the result was soon manifest in his thick and incoherent speech. He began dictating an article for the New York Herald to an imaginary secretary, wrote some telegrams which were sent off to the post office and speedily brought back as illegible.
>
> And then his drunkenness took another form when he ordered a carriage. No sooner had they started than he began to make the most horrible noises, imagining he was out hunting and the cries he made were supposed to be urging on a pack of hounds. At times he would yell out old wild indian cries, or what he imagined to be such and the cries of rowdy American students: Hoop Lah! Kazoo Kazah! Ra Ra Ri Ri! Hy-ah Hy-ah!
>
> At one time I thought he had really lost his reason. He lowered the glass window and through wonderful means managed to creep through it and seat himself beside the astonished coachman. Seizing the reins he insisted on driving the horse into a gallop with a repetition of wild cries. Finally the animal became so terrified it actually bolted, when there were a few moments swaying from one side of the road to the other and the drive was brought to an abrupt halt by contact with a lamp post.
>
> Bennett appeared quite unmoved and treated the accident as a very good joke. His clothes were covered in mud and his hat crushed in, but he was perfectly indifferent to all this. The next day he was quite calm and repentant and had only a vague recollection of what had happened but nevertheless swore it should never happen again.

Whenever he showed signs of mental excitement it was not always
from having drunk too much, for one small glass of brandy was
enough to render him irresponsible for his actions.

No question, under the influence Jimmy was definitely reckless to the point of self-destruction. Mad to live, mad for adventure, even if it came at the cost of his life. All admirable or at least interesting traits, but not ones to be displayed within the confines of his future in-laws' drawing room, where Bennett was trying to work out why his mind and spinal column no longer seemed to be on speaking terms. It was at this point that he realized he needed the toilet. There was no way he was going to make it to the bathroom. No, in the circumstances he did well to make it to the fire, which he achieved by a disturbing combination of fierce concentration mixed with apparently uncontrollable flapping of the hands. How he unzipped, no one knows, but … One moment of glorious relief later and Bennett sensed even through his drunken haze that all was not well. The room was strangely silent and it felt as though all eyes were upon him. What was happening here? He could not say, but even through the horrible absinthe-induced distortion of reality he sensed something was amiss.

Suddenly all was chaos and confusion, a jumble of screams and gesticulations, bad noise and a blur of shocked, reproachful faces, all shaking their heads as if part of some surreal nightmare. Then he was out in the cold, skimming across the snow aboard his sleigh, his servant chiding him gently as he dragged him to safety, then darkness and nothing.

He awoke the next day with a feeling of deep unease. All was not well. He was going to have a first-class hangover … yet there was more than that – why the impending sense of doom? He racked his brains and then the nightmare closed around him again. Caroline! The fire! He clutched his throbbing head and groaned. How in the name of God was he to extricate himself from this? He spent the day brooding on the subject. He should have apologized immediately, but instead he lay low, stirring only briefly when a note arrived from Caroline formally breaking off their engagement.

For all those fancy European manners he had picked up in Paris, Bennett was a savage at heart. When a moment of crisis like this emerged he felt the safest place of retreat was to the bosom of the Union Club and the company of men, the kind of men who would understand and forgive. By the morning of 3 January, when he was able to compose himself sufficiently to stand up and dress, he scuttled off to this oasis of manly virtue to seek reassurance. Stepping across the threshold of the old club, he felt instantly soothed. True, some of the members were a touch reticent, and there was a cry of alarm from some joker as he strolled past the crackling fire at the heart of the club, but all in all the general verdict seemed to be one of live and let live. After all, the men of the Union were nothing if not forgiving and had even refused to excommunicate old Judah Benjamin when he had committed the ultimate faux pas and become a member of the Confederate parliament a few years back. Yes, here was a fairly safe haven from the storm that threatened to engulf him. He lunched well and felt better.

The next step in his rehabilitation was to head to the offices of the *Herald*, and it was as he stepped out of the Union Club bound for the seclusion of his office that he received a nasty jolt. There, standing in the street, horse whip in hand and a rather nasty leer on his face, was Fred May, brother of Caroline and a fearful bruiser. His appearance was far from reassuring. He was a big, imposing man with a visage like the north face of the Eiger, great jagged tombstones for teeth. His muscular body had been poured into his tunic and someone had forgotten to stop until it was all but brimming over. Every time he flexed his shoulders his jacket groaned. He stood waiting for Bennett, an unpleasant gleam in the eyes that protruded from his huge thatched head. Darwin would have it that we are all descended from apes, but in the case of May, the evolutionary curve had clearly been a modest one.

May leered hungrily at Bennett as he saw him exit the Union Club. His leather glove creaked menacingly as he flexed his whip hand. What had happened to Caroline was a brutal, bilious insult, but there was no harm in him having enormous fun in the administering of justice. He would have enjoyed a bit of pleading from Bennett, but the tycoon was made of sterner stuff. He seemed to stand up to it pretty well as May unleashed the full force of his whip across Bennett's face with a fearful CRACK and a pleasing effusion of blood spilt crimson on the white snow. May's grin widened as he set about teaching the millionaire a lesson. The papers took almost as much pleasure re-enacting the gory scene. The *New York Times* described the incident with glee:

A STREET ENCOUNTER

James Gordon Bennett attacked

He is set upon by Frederick May and cowhided in front of the Union Clubhouse – The stories of eyewitnesses to the affray – Alleged causes of the difficulty – How the affray occurred – Another account – Mr. Bennett's marriage engagement – The affair fully described – What led to the assault – Sketch of the assailant.

The tide of pleasant gossip which has been in its way through fashionable circles in this City for some time past in regard to the nuptials of James Gordon Bennett, the proprietor of the *Herald*, and Miss May, was rudely broken into yesterday by the report of an angry encounter or fracas between Mr. Bennett and Mr. Frederick May...

The Meeting with Frederick May was not unexpected by Mr Bennett as the latter saw Mr May walking up and down Fifth Avenue evidently waiting for him. Mr Bennett thereupon lit a cigar and emerged from the entrance of the Union Club just as Mr May reached the corner of Twenty First Street. The two gentlemen walked toward each other and met midway between Fifth avenue and the club entrance without uttering a syllable. Mr May raised a large rawhide and struck Mr Bennett full in the face. Blood followed the stroke. A second and third blow followed and before Mr Bennett had time to recover his surprise at the suddenness of the attack, he had received two severe cuts on the face one on the nose and one over the left eye. On regaining his self possession, Mr Bennett struck at Mr May and the two men clinched and fell. In the struggle which followed, Mr May who is a powerful man being six feet one in height and some 40 pounds heavier than Mr Bennett had the advantage, and threw the latter twice, both men rolling in the snow. By this time, the fracas had been observed by some of the members of the club who ran out and the combatants were separated by Mr. John G Hecksher. At five o'clock Mr. Bennett, having recovered from the effects of the beating sent for his sleigh and was driven home. On reaching his residence he sent for Mr. Leonard Jerome and a few other intimate friends and a consultation was held as to what should be done in the circumstances. Mr Bennett who of course feels humiliated at his castigation insists, it is understood, on challenging Mr May to mortal combat.

So, after all that, it was Bennett who was the aggrieved party. The only sensible way for a gentleman to settle the dispute was through a pistol duel. Bennett was, of course, a man of honour. He submitted a challenge to May and it was readily accepted. As you can imagine, the press was agog with this latest development. The assault had been splashed all over the front pages of all the New York papers, barring the *Herald* of course, and news of the duel threatened to shove the news of the death of Cornelius Vanderbilt into the back pages, which would not have pleased that old self-seeker. The picturesque venue of Slaughter's Gap on the border between Maryland and Delaware was selected by the combatants as it meant they could easily skip over the state line should they be apprehended by the authorities. The terms were a pistol duel at twelve paces.

They eyeballed each other over the frozen ground and then, with a grin, May raised his arm and fired harmlessly in the air. Bennett followed suit and shot wide, although some later accounts claim that this was because he was shaking with fear. This is unlikely, however, and the chances are that the men had come to some kind of sensible arrangement prior to the duel. To have your brains blown out for urinating on a fire would be an odd way to go – although entirely in keeping with the quixotic nature of Bennett's existence. The papers, meanwhile, in the absence of any substantial fact devoted themselves to an orgy of speculation. The *New York Sun* led with:

BENNETT AND MAY'S DUEL

A hostile meeting at Slaughter station, Delaware

Contradictory Despatches – Bennett said to be uninjured –
May declared to be wounded – Talk at the clubs and hotels –
Latest news that has been received of the fight

The article itself proved to be little more than speculative interviews with members of the Union Club who clearly knew nothing. Only Larry Jerome said anything even worth repeating:

> *So far as Jim Bennett is concerned I want it understood that I am a friend of a man right or wrong, and particularly when he is wrong as that is when he needs a friend.*
>
> *Jim has a charmed life. If it were not wrong to wager about such a serious matter I would have staked a tidy sum that he would not have been hurt.*

Ultimately, the pair retired to a nearby hotel post-duel and settled their differences over a few beers. Honour had been preserved and all was well with the world. Well? Perhaps not quite *well*. Bennett realized that this time he had gone too far. He was horrified with the amount of publicity he had attracted and it was soon evident that he had managed to fully excommunicate himself from New York society. No respectable dinner party would ever be able to risk Bennett as an invitee. He had finally achieved the pariahdom his father had so revelled in. The problem was, he loathed it and, like his mother before him, he decamped to Paris. True, his three houses in Newport, Washington Heights and Fifth Avenue were all maintained with full staff awaiting his arrival home, but to all intents and purposes, henceforth, he was in self-imposed exile and the *New York Herald* was run from Paris.

His first few weeks in exile created quite a stir among Parisians, for Bennett did little to curb his excesses. No doubt he was in quite a bit of turmoil, for his life had essentially capsized, and the only thing to do in this situation was go on a bender. He returned to coaching with real gusto, roaring up and down the Champs Elysées at terrifying speed. Yet the most arresting thing for those who saw him race by was his passenger. For some bewildering reason, Bennett had chosen a donkey as his travelling companion. The poor beast was installed inside his coach where it sat in terror, head protruding out of the window with a placard around its neck stating: 'This donkey is the most sensible American in Paris.' Read what you wish into that, but it is evident that Monsieur Bennett was greatly stirred up emotionally and the results were predictably weird. Bennett soon established himself about town as the ultimate 'crazy American'.

He was not without allure to the Europeans, however, and his womanizing continued unabated. One victim of his charms was Camille Clermont, a showgirl, whom Bennett seduced during his Paris years. She describes him as follows:

> *His great wealth was not without its charm. There is always a certain halo hovering over the very rich man who can do as he likes in the world and who has nearly all mankind at his beck and call.*
>
> *Bennett, to give him his due, unlike most Americans who possess riches, was by no means a vulgar millionaire and never boasted of his*

*money or what he could do with it. It simply seemed part of himself
and he bore it, it must be admitted with a certain amount of good
taste and even unconsciousness.*

Yet Clermont was horrified by the transformative effect that drink had on the millionaire. Her ultimate conclusion of the man was fairly damning:

*He might have been a really distinguished man had he surrounded
himself with a different class of men to those who encouraged him
in his excess. He was intelligent and gifted, read much and retained
what he read. But, unfortunately, his immense fortune was a pitfall
to him. He had never known what it was to be poor; never had
to earn money and this position gave him unlimited power which
he constantly abused. His wealth enabled him to ignore the seamy
side of life and, encouraged by the class of people he frequented, he
resolutely turned his back on all sorrow and suffering and merely
lived for the pleasure of the day.*

The picture Clermont portrays is confusing and shot through with bitterness. But the impression is that, under that thin veneer of sophistry, there lurked a sort of primitive savage; yet he was a thoroughly modern Neanderthal. He was perhaps the ultimate expression of this ghastly age: burnt-out by excess until he was less than half a person, with just a few shards of empathy left to humanize him.

His excesses during the Paris years became legendary. He once tipped a railway porter 20,000 francs and was enraged when the porter's boss tried to return the majority of the money. Booze brought out the profligate streak in Bennett and a memorable example came during a prolonged stay in Monte Carlo. Bennett was a connoisseur of the lamb chop and, if he found a place that did it just right, he would return day after day. It so happened he had found just the spot up on the hill overlooking the town and pronounced himself well satisfied, until he arrived one day for lunch and found the place packed out and his favourite seat taken. The head waiter was desolate, aware that the daily promise of a disproportionately large tip was about to storm out. Bennett had no doubt already had a couple of stiff ones prior to luncheon and was feeling sufficiently invigorated to deal with this problem head on.

Hunting down the owner, who was cowering behind the counter, he said he would buy the restaurant there and then for the ludicrous fee of $40,000. It was an offer the proprietor could not refuse. The new owner of the restaurant unceremoniously booted out the party at his favourite table and tucked into his lamb chop with gusto. At the end of a very expensive meal, he handed a tip to the waiter which included the bill of sale for the restaurant. His only proviso was that a table would always be available to him and the chef who prepared such exquisite chops was to remain in place. The head waiter was a gentleman by the name of Ciro who went on to establish a chain of high-class restaurants which became legendary during the jazz age for their opulence and fine dining.

For all his generosity when in wine, Bennett was also capable of being ruthlessly cold-hearted, and nothing illustrates this better than his treatment of Camille Clermont. After several months of living in sin with the tycoon she fell pregnant. Bennett was furious and refused ever to speak of the child. He was also extremely reluctant to provide any kind of financial support for the fruit of his overactive loins and eventually settled on a measly allowance which ensured his daughter and ex-lover would scrape through life in poverty. Clermont was quite naturally disgusted by this. She wrote of Bennett:

> It could not be denied that he had given large sums to certain expeditions and charities but these generosities had brought interest in the shape of advertisement and self glorification. But to provide a moderate fortune for a child, sufficient to compensate it for having entered life by the wrong door, having been born a bastard, why should he? Alas! The conclusion is that Bennett cared only for the sensational generosity, proclaimed by the sound of trumpet, that he was in fact a vulgar Pharisee, an unworthy millionaire, all the more contemptible as his immense fortune permitted him to be generous, especially towards those who had a real claim on him. By doing his duty to his child and keeping his promises he would still have had large sums to be given to what appealed to his colossal vanity.

In between epic binges and dalliances with showgirls, Bennett stabilized his life somewhat by setting up a Paris edition of the *Herald* which, predictably, ran at a loss throughout its lengthy existence. Back in New York, the original *Herald* undoubtedly suffered from his absence, yet if anyone had expected the newspaper to drift with an absentee owner at the helm, they'd be wrong. Despite the great distance, Bennett continued to rule with a fist of iron and, if anything, his eccentricities became even more pronounced. He installed spies and moles within the *Herald*'s New York office and they reported back to him in Paris. If an employee decided to take a long lunch, Bennett knew about it. On one occasion he cabled Edward D DeWitt, his very capable advertising manager, to come to Paris by the next French steamer. Mr DeWitt sailed and in due season presented himself before his employer at his apartment in the Avenue d'Iena.

'DeWitt,' was the greeting. 'I have been receiving some anonymous letters about you. They say you are getting fat and lazy. Napoleon and his marshals won their victories when they were lean. If you have become fat you are of no use to me.' DeWitt was *not* fat and close scrutiny made this clear to Bennett. The man was sent back to New York and retained his job.

These summonses to Paris were a regular ordeal that most senior members of staff at the *Herald* had to endure. On one occasion, two senior members of the editorial team were summoned with the utmost urgency to Bennett's Paris office and, bidding their families farewell, they took the arduous Atlantic crossing with due dispatch. They arrived at the Paris office and waited outside Bennett's inner sanctum with a gathering feeling of doom. After a longish wait, they were summoned in and hovered respectfully in the doorway awaiting permission to be seated. 'What in hell are you doing here?' Bennett queried, as he raised his eyes from his work. 'You sent for us,' one stammered. 'Go back to New York.' End of interview.

Bennett also developed an obsession with hair, and neatness was everything. He hired a notable music critic by the name of Charles Meltzer, who fancied himself a bit of a dandy and wore his hair long and impeccably groomed. Back in Paris, one of Bennett's informants passed the word on to their boss and he acted quickly, sending a terse cable: 'Tell Meltzer to cut his hair.' Meltzer was duly advised. Meltzer refused. Soon came the query: 'Has Meltzer cut his hair?' 'No,' was the reply. 'Send him to St Petersburg.' The bewildered critic arrived in St Petersburg and Bennett submitted the same question to his regular St Petersburg correspondent. He was enraged to find Meltzer's flowing locks remained in place. Bennett continued this tactic, moving Meltzer around various obscure corners of Europe until, still refusing to submit to a restyle, Meltzer was shorn of his livelihood, although he later took the *Herald* to an employment tribunal and won.

There was more, much more. Further evidence that he was mad can be witnessed in the fact that he became obsessed with yappy little dogs such as the Pekingese and the terrier, and liked to surround himself with them. A job interview could be decided by these dogs. If they reacted unfavourably to a candidate, he didn't stand a chance. One such candidate got wind of this and secreted about his person a number of veal chops. Predictably, the dogs reacted positively to his arrival and he was hired on the spot.

Years later when war broke out, Paris was besieged and the very existence of the French nation was in serious doubt, the depth of this obsession with dogs was perfectly illustrated when he ran the following story as his lead:

ROUTINE OF CANINE LIFE IN PARIS UPSET BY THE WAR

Many dogs leave the city – others left at barrack gates and fed by soldiers

Out on the front, less than 100 miles away from Bennett and his precious dogs, men died in their thousands until the bodies piled up and rotted. Amid this carnival of destruction, Bennett wrote about dogs.

We have dealt almost long enough with James Gordon Bennett and are about ready to return to the sea and the bold *Henrietta*, where Captain Samuels' demented whistling for a wind seems to have worked a charm, for the breeze is filling in and the deckchairs are about to be stowed away. Bennett and his friends must concentrate once more on racing.

What I want you to understand, however, is that this race was in many ways the start of it all. This was the moment when Bennett first came up with the concept of creating the very news his paper reported on. The Atlantic crossing saw the birth of the gonzo publisher. On his return, Bennett Sr realized that his son had enough about him to make a go of it as managing editor of his beloved newspaper, and Bennett Jr realized the potential the newspaper held for him. The *Herald* was set on its weird course of hoaxes and sponsor of grandiose world-changing expeditions. As his shipmate Stephen Fiske later observed: 'This ocean race was the turning point in James Gordon Bennett's career. It made a man of him and showed what good he could do the *Herald* and what the *Herald* could do for him.' So we return to the wintry Atlantic and the storm-tossed race course. The gonzo publisher was plunging toward a newsworthy denouement to his jaunt.

8
A STAB IN THE BACK

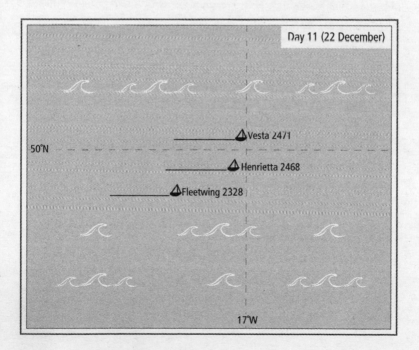

We are indeed drifting toward the iron bound coast of
England. I too have seen for some time that we shall inevitably
clash with that power. We cannot stand any more *Alabamas*.

THURLOW WEED, REPUBLICAN POLITICIAN FOR
THE LINCOLN ADMINISTRATION, SPEAKING IN 1863

Day 11 (22 December)

Vesta 2471

Henrietta 2468

Fleetwing 2328

50°N

17°W

B y 20 December land was close at hand: Ireland, Mizen Head and Cape Clear. Through the sea fret and misty grey air you could sense the British Isles, almost smell it in the damp, which seemed to find a way through any amount of layers of clothing and settle upon the skin like a cold, clammy hand. Despite the chill in the breeze, temperatures aboard the *Vesta* were running red hot. The bad blood that had been bubbling under for the whole trip erupted. George Lorillard simply could not accept that Captain Dayton was doing his job properly and continued to attack him at every opportunity. Given that Dayton had just nursed the schooner through a fairly severe storm with no damage and a very impressive run to her credit, it is possible that the stolid old captain's nerves were frayed. It may explain this run-in, which Lorillard related:

> *Morning, steady breeze NW; desired Captain Dayton to set mainsail but no go. 9am no more sail made; the captain and officers having their usual debate about my wanting more sail set. This sort of thing getting too tough for me. I sent for Captain Dayton to come into the cabin that I might try him on some other tack. He came. I told him I thought it very desirous that he should take my advice occasionally about making sail, and make his officers hurry the men, as it was much to his benefit; but the same obstinacy was shown and he left for the deck remarking that the yacht might go to Hell when she got to Cowes. After losing ten hours the mainsail was set and still we ran 277 miles.*

If you picture this meeting between George Lorillard and Captain Dayton you have to remember that the former was 23 years old and the latter well into his fifties, a grizzled veteran of the transatlantic run, and a man who unquestionably knew more about ships and the sea than Lorillard. Perhaps there was more; it is possible that quiet, diligent old Dayton couldn't fully hide his distaste for this privileged youth. To echo Edith Wharton, it is just possible that Dayton saw, beneath the glitter of Lorillard's opportunities, the poverty of his achievements.

Aboard any vessel, the captain's word is law. To take this continual browbeating from a youngster must have been intolerable, and this could only have the effect of discouraging Dayton. He had, after all, already been paid. Indeed, Leonard Jerome later observed: 'Pierre Lorillard's played his hand wrong in handing over the entire fee win or lose; there should have been an incentive to win.' Colonel Taylor, who sailed aboard the *Vesta*, seemed to corroborate that by stating that he never felt the *Vesta* was being 'driven'.

Be all this as it may, 277 miles is a magnificent run. A vessel pushed so hard that you have to wrestle with the helm will not achieve her maximum speed. It is highly likely that Dayton simply knew how to keep the yacht in perfect trim and sailing well without over pressing her. And the fact was that while captain and owner's brother squabbled, the *Vesta* wrested the lead from the *Henrietta* for the first time in the race. This is perhaps the best vindication possible for the much-maligned Dayton and his crew. By now the race was over three-quarters run; with the three schooners jockeying for position, *Vesta*'s timing in taking the lead seemed propitious. Southern Ireland lay to the north and out west England, Cowes, glory.

At that time to arrive on the shores of Britain was a sort of homecoming for many Americans. It was only a few decades since America had gained its independence and many could quite comfortably trace their roots back to the old country. James Gordon Bennett Jr is a good case in point, for his father had been born and raised in Scotland. Despite this close tie with the old country, relations between the two were, shall we say, somewhat strained. This had a lot to do with the CSS *Alabama* affair, which Britain had handled with all the sensitivity and finesse of a sledgehammer.

Back in 1866 Britain was the world's superpower. Her empire was unrivalled, and her talent for meddling in world affairs unparalleled. It was her dominance of maritime trade that truly made Britain great. America, only released from the colonial yoke a few decades before, was largely viewed as an upstart irritant. Its republican tenets of liberty and freedom were seen as dangerous and outlandish by the British, while its developing economy and social structure were generally viewed with patronizing condescension. Few in Britain would have imagined that a handful of decades later it would be America calling the shots on the world stage. Yet Britain had been given fair warning, and nowhere clearer than at sea. After all, in the War of Independence of 1812, the British Navy had witnessed the first inklings that they were not invincible after being handed a fairly sound thrashing by their American counterparts. Post independence, American transatlantic packets had also shown their superiority to the point where the passenger trade was almost exclusively in the hands of Americans by the 1840s.

The next shock had come in 1849 when Britain had opened up its ports to free trade. It had quickly become obvious that American clipper ships – hitherto excluded from many lines of trade by protectionist policies – were faster and more efficient than their British rivals. The Americans were suddenly the prime threat to Britannia ruling the waves, and there was a real fear that the Americans were going to destroy this vital power base. The New York Yacht Club had further deepened the gloom when it had sent the yacht *America* to Cowes and humiliated its British rivals in that famous race. For a time, British merchants genuinely feared that the game was up and American dominance of the waves was near at hand.

By 1866, however, Britain was once more unquestionably and unassailably the ruler of the waves. The cause? Well, the biggest factor had to be the Civil War. Union shipping had been decimated by Confederate raiders, in particular the CSS *Alabama*, which between 1862 and 1864 captured and destroyed 52 Union merchant vessels. It was a trail of havoc that crippled the American mercantile marine, setting them back many years and all but ensuring that British sea power remained dominant. You might think that convenient for the British, but many saw it as more than that. The *Alabama* had been built in Britain, crammed with British supplies and manned by British sailors. For many Americans the *Alabama* remained a powerful emblem of British treachery for years to come.

The fact was that when the war broke out, many in Britain didn't have the faintest clue which side to support. Even without the benefit of hindsight, it should have been the Union. Just as nowadays the West beats other nations repeatedly with the stick of democracy, prior to the Civil War, the British had constantly taunted America for its slave trading, a practice abolished in Britain in 1807. There was a belief that it was the outlawing of this practice that made Britain civilized and Americans barbaric hoodlums. Dickens in his *American Notes* observed with disgust:

> *when they [Americans] speak of Freedom, they mean the Freedom*
> *to oppress their kind, and to be savage, merciless, and cruel; and of*

whom every man on his own ground, in Republican America, is a more exacting, and a sterner, and a less responsible despot than the Caliph Haroun Alraschid in his angry robe of scarlet.

Hard words, yet indicative of the British view at the time. Yet once conflict arose between north and south, which was at least in part over the issue of slavery, many in Britain found themselves either smugly enjoying the chaos across the Atlantic or even drawn toward the southern cause. They were, after all, the plucky underdog. Dickens, for all his strong views on slavery, aligned himself with the Confederates, noting:

Union means so many millions a year lost to the South; secession means the loss of the same millions to the North. The love of money is the root of this as of many other evils ... the quarrel between North and South is, as it stands, solely a fiscal quarrel.

In the heat of war some Britons went further than just sympathizing with the south and felt strongly enough about it to help out the Confederate cause. One of the most interesting examples of this was the case of the mysterious English gentleman Henry Decie, a suave, affable con merchant who seems to have specialized in being all things to all men. When the Civil War broke out, Decie evidently felt the Confederates deserved his support and purchased the yacht *America*. The schooner had never returned to America after her famous victory of 1851 and was now under English ownership and gently decaying in some Cowes backwater. In 1861, Decie tidied her up and sailed her across the Atlantic to Jacksonville where he sold her to the Confederates. The erstwhile pride of the New York Yacht Club became a rebel blockade runner with Decie contracted as her skipper. Her ownership during this shady time was claimed by one Gazaway Lamar, whose son, Charles, you may remember had caused such acute embarrassment to the New York Yacht Club with his slave trading on the yacht *Wanderer*.

This is just one isolated example of the kind of help the British were covertly providing to the Confederates. Even at a governmental level many British MPs felt the south deserved a helping hand. On the one side was the abolition of slavery, on the other the importance of a steady cotton supply from the south to keep the mills of the north-west of England rumbling away. Britain therefore declared neutrality in the conflict, but at times it was clear that favour swayed first one way and then the other. It didn't help that in November 1861 the British mail steamer *Trent* was stopped at sea by the USS *San Jacinto* after word got out that two Confederate diplomats were on board bound for England. The pair were removed, but Britain was enraged at this infringement of sovereignty and disregard for protocol. For a time war between Britain and the US seemed like a very real prospect and as Henry Adams, son and secretary to Charles Adams, the American ambassador in London at the time, noted: 'I consider that we are dished and our position hopeless. This nation [Britain] means to make war. Do not doubt it.'

Following the *Trent* affair, there was serious political debate as to whether Britain should recognize the Confederate States, which would essentially have meant war. Ultimately the Prime Minister, the ancient, doddering Lord Palmerston, vetoed that, but perhaps subconsciously the kickback for the Confederates was the *Alabama*. This ship was built as a fast cruiser by Laird of Birkenhead to the order of a southern gentleman by the name of James D Bulloch. There was no direct reference to the confederacy, but all knew of her purpose early on. The British government was made well aware of the situation by the American ambassador Charles Adams, who produced nine sworn affidavits stating that she was a Confederate raider from sources including a Laird shipwright and a crewmember signed up by Bulloch for the voyage. Here was legal proof that if Britain supplied her to the Confederates, she would be breaking her neutrality. Yet just as orders to impound the ship were about to be presented to the Attorney General by the Queen's advocate, John Harding, this man rather conveniently took a detour on his way to the Attorney General's office on Victoria Street and ended up checking himself into a lunatic asylum, taking the precious documents with him.

While this unfolded, the *Alabama*, operating under the name *Enerica*, slipped out of the Mersey, ostensibly on sea trials. The Lairds, a Liverpool family who could remember when their own fair city had prospered through the slave trade, unquestionably colluded with Bulloch throughout. They were aboard for this 'trial' trip and later returned to Liverpool aboard a tug which had accompanied the *Alabama* out to sea. Oddly for a trial trip, the ship featured a full crew of 75 British sailors. Except, of course, that it wasn't a trial trip; the cruiser never returned, heading instead for Terceira in the Azores, where she was taken over by her infamous skipper, Raphael Semmes. He oversaw her fitting out as a warship and persuaded many of the hired hands to stay, with the promise of plentiful prize money. Fully stocked, fitted out and crewed courtesy of the British, *Alabama* embarked on a two-year cruise which left a trail of devastation in her wake.

British tolerance for the *Alabama* faded after Semmes mistakenly destroyed the British ship *Martaban*. A request for a badly needed refit in Britain was curtly refused. *Alabama* was finally hunted down and destroyed in 1864 by the USS *Kearsage* in a dramatic battle off Cherbourg.

Yet the damage was done, both to the US mercantile marine and also to Anglo-American relations. I will leave it to Captain Samuels to sum up the dim view of British actions taken by the average American:

At the time of which I write [1850], the American flag predominated in the docks of Liverpool. American shipping furnished the city with food supplies and with cotton for her factories. The impetus given her by American industry has made her the second, if not the first and greatest, seaport in the world. The packet services between Europe and America were entirely performed under our flag. There was not one English line of packets on the Atlantic Ocean. Our packet-ships were the wonder of the world, and so were our transient ships. We had the confidence of the travelling public and the patronage of the shipping merchants. For speed, safety, and beauty our packets surpassed any ships in the world until the California gold-fever broke out. Then our clipper-ships took precedence in speed. In such high favor were our vessels held that Bremen and Hamburg drew their supply from us, and James Baines & Co, of Liverpool, contracted with Donald McKay, of Boston, to build them a line of clippers for the Australian trade.

Alas! what has become of our ships? and why is our flag so rarely seen in Liverpool or elsewhere now? What has become of this lost industry? and why is this once strong arm on the ocean now so paralyzed that the weakest nations look in pity at our fallen greatness?

Our Rebellion, in which England lent aid to the South with money, and through letting loose from her shipyards Alabamas to destroy our shipping, is the prime cause. England took advantage

*of our internal strife to regain her supremacy on the sea, which in a
great measure we had wrested from her. She saw the advantage, and
took it; and will retain it until our legislators rise to the occasion, and
give aid to our marine interests.*

Samuels wrote this in his memoirs of his life at sea. It is a book filled with
good-humoured yarns and it says something about his depth of feeling on
the *Alabama* affair that he felt compelled to write about it so forthrightly.
If nothing else, there was a feeling that Britain had sat back and watched
with a modicum of satisfaction as America tore itself to pieces. The
Henrietta, Vesta and *Fleetwing* were approaching the treacherous coast
of Britain just one year after the conclusion of the Civil War and the
wounds inflicted by the *Alabama* affair were red raw. The general belief
was that Britain had delivered America a savage stab in the back.

James Gordon Bennett himself was no great admirer of the British and
his sometime lover Camille Clermont recalled:

*Bennett's favourite topic of conversation was foreign politics. He was
always against England and generally concluded such diatribes with
'one of these days we will give the Englishmen a damned good licking
and may I be there to see it'.*

This attitude was often evident in the pages of the *Herald*, which
frequently beat an Anglophobic drum. But the relationship between
America and Britain has always been subtle and multi-faceted, not one
of pure antipathy. For all the American idealism regarding their new
egalitarian republic, there was a strong residual awe and admiration
for the old British elite, in particular the royal family. Nothing

demonstrated this better than the visit of Albert, Prince of Wales to America in 1860. Given the troubled recent history between the two countries, he could have expected a rough ride from the Americans. Instead, he was treated to one of the greatest outpourings of adoration imaginable. The 19-year-old prince, used to the somewhat more stand-offish English attitudes, was absolutely blown away by the warmth and enthusiasm of the American public.

Few could have predicted the trip would go so well. Prince Albert, or 'Bertie' as he was generally known, was the eldest son of Queen Victoria and considered by his deeply moral parents to be shaping up to be a huge disappointment. They had hoped to produce an heir, who would become an exemplar of modern monarchy, and he had been schooled at home in an effort to shelter him from the wayward influence of the aristocracy. He was far from a model pupil, and frequently felt the lash of his father's cane (none other than the royal patriarch could possibly besmirch the royal buttocks).

All in all, Victoria and Albert looked upon their eldest son with a jaundiced eye. There was a definite suspicion that he was turning out to be an idle, feckless, sensualist who 'lived only for pleasure', as his mother put it. He required careful watching and stomping down upon regularly. All of this must have been pretty tough on young Bertie. True, he didn't seem to have a lot going on up top and it didn't help that he wasn't terribly well endowed in the looks department either, with goggly eyes, prematurely balding pate, pudgy physique and weak chin. On top of that, he measured in at a little over 5 feet 4.

Yet what he lacked in looks he made up for in style and bonhomie. He didn't know much about art or literature, but he could pick out a stylish shirt and natty tie at 100 paces and quaff a pink gin with the best of them. He was an ardent yachtsman and adored horse racing, eating, drinking and many other sensual delights besides.

As soon as he was allowed to, Bertie fled the censorious tedium and spent a year studying nothing in particular at Cambridge. In the process he established a particular template of student life, still followed by many to this day: a regime consisting of studiously avoiding work while simultaneously seeking out a good time with money borrowed from the state. Inevitably he fell in with a bad crowd, a raffish, somewhat mentally negligent bunch of idlers. The sort of chaps who understand that to get anywhere in life one needs a generous allowance, a complete aversion to any serious toil, breathtaking arrogance and an appreciation that to throw a bun at a chum's head while dining is the height of wit.

This was the nature of the young hound who in 1860 was packed off to America as part of the first royal visit since the country had gained independence. Given the somewhat fraught recent history between the two countries, it was not clear how Bertie would be received.

Any anxiety was soon cleared up. For 19-year-old Bertie this was a prime opportunity to cut loose, and he did so in a manner that beguiled the American public. It's easy to portray the prince as a chump, but at least he was an affable one and he proved that he had a natural knack for diplomacy. He was not cold or haughty like his mother and he had a natural disregard for rank which meant he could enjoy himself in diverse company and also build bridges with many of Britain's neighbours.

It helped that Bertie also had a splendid time in America. It was here that his first lustful stirrings were awoken and although there is no record of any sexual conquests (he was very closely chaperoned by the Earl of Newcastle) there was plenty of opportunity for endless flirtation. Bertie was unquestionably very taken with the American ladies. At home he was ceaselessly being introduced to 'suitable' girls who bored him to tears. In America he met girls with better teeth and real sex appeal. Bertie cared nothing for the arts or literature, nor the niceties of the English noblewomen, who could sometimes come across as a little glacial. The young prince preferred good straight-talking and these beautiful American girls were bang on his wavelength, and more than happy to engage in a bright, racy, uninhibited chinwag. It was balm to Bertie; from then on he always held a candle for American beauties.

Americans took Bertie to their hearts, and 30,000 of them greeted him rapturously when he first arrived from Canada. From the moment he stepped off the Detroit and Milwaukee ferry, he was constantly mobbed. The crowning glory of the tour came in New York where the Astor 400 was at work laying on the ball to end all balls in his honour. This was held at the academy of music and tickets were restricted to 2,000 of the most socially eligible people of New York, who paid obscene amounts of money for the honour of meeting the prince. This plan was dished when 3,000 people gatecrashed the party. It was probably this that caused the specially constructed ballroom floor to collapse. Thirty carpenters set about repairing it as the ball proceeded. The job completed in record time, it soon became obvious that one of the carpenters had been sealed in underneath the floor in the general panic. Further work was required to release him. Despite this hitch, the prince dutifully danced with as many blushing debutantes as one man could handle in a night and the whole thing was considered a triumph.

The upshot of the Royal visit was a great surge of good feeling between the two countries. Old grievances were forgotten and a great feeling of bonhomie spread across the Atlantic. As the *New York Independent* put it:

> *An embodiment in boy's form of a glorious related nation. The England of Shakespeare and Milton has come modestly walking by our doors in the form of a boy just in the fresh morning of his days.*

A handful of years on from that royal visit and all that goodwill had been thrown away in the heat of war. Things looked bleak. But as the yachts forged their way across the great barren stretch of the North Atlantic, there was something that lay many miles beneath their keels that many felt offered hope of restoring harmony between the two countries: the transatlantic telegraph. It was just under 30 years since the painter and inventor Samuel Morse had tapped out the fateful message *WHAT HATH GOD WROUGHT* in Washington and it had been successfully received in Baltimore. That message had ushered in a new era in communication, which promised to make the world a far smaller place. The telegraph was just as revolutionary in its time as the internet, and soon cables criss-crossed America. In Europe, a cable was laid across the English Channel connecting England and France as early as 1851. But the thought of a cable traversing the Atlantic still just seemed too far-fetched for words. Only a madman would dream that it was possible to stretch a cable across that great expanse of ocean and succeed.

Step forward Cyrus W Field, a successful New York businessman who had made a tidy sum out of his paper mill and was frankly bored and looking for a new challenge. He settled on the building of a transatlantic telegraph, his imagination fired after his company successfully laid a telegraph between St John's, Newfoundland and Nova Scotia.

The laying of this cable significantly reduced the time it took for news to be received from Europe and the next logical step for Field was to lay a cable between the two continents. This was a project he first mooted in 1857, although few believed it was possible. However, consultation with the famed oceanographer Lieutenant Maury gave Field hope, for the seabed was relatively flat and comparatively shallow with a depth between 1,500 and 2,000 fathoms. As Maury observed:

> From Newfoundland to Ireland, the distance between the nearest points is about sixteen hundred miles; and the bottom of the sea between the two places is a plateau, which seems to have been placed there especially for the purpose of holding the wires of a submarine telegraph, and of keeping them out of harm's way. It is neither too deep nor too shallow; yet it is so deep that the wires but once landed, will remain for ever beyond the reach of vessels' anchors, icebergs, and drifts of any kind, and so shallow, that the wires may be readily lodged upon the bottom.

Field then tried his hand at diplomacy and wheeler dealing, using his sales acumen honed in the paper-milling business to peddle shares in the Atlantic Telegraph Company on both sides of the pond, and also securing funding and goodwill from both the British government and the US Senate. But with all the goodwill and funding in the world, this was still an epic project, one that would need a cable 1,600 miles long. This cable consisted of seven strands of copper wire encased in gutta percha, a natural form of latex made from the sap of the palaquium family of trees found in Malaysia. This provided the waterproof sheath, which was then parcelled up with tarred hemp and rounded off with a layer of iron wires. The whole thing was ¾ inch thick and weighed about a ton for each mile. A cable of that length would be inordinately heavy and in 1857 there was no one ship that could safely carry the entire reel. The decision was taken to use two ships, which would travel in convoy. Once the first ship had uncoiled its reel, the cable would be spliced and the second ship would continue with the remainder. In the general spirit of bonhomie, the British government provided the HMS *Agamemnon* and the US government laid on the *Niagara* to work together.

The initial attempt was fraught. The pair of ships set off from Valentia on the extreme western tip of the Irish coast and it soon became obvious that the winch used to lower the cable painstakingly down to the seabed was struggling with the immense load. After 380 miles, there was an almighty bang as one end of the cable departed over the side, taking with it the hopes of Cyrus Field and his shareholders. At the subsequent post-mortem, the need for a beefed-up winch was addressed, and the decision was also taken to steam out into the middle of the Atlantic, splice the cable and then send off the *Agamemnon* and *Niagara* in opposite directions.

This second attempt was in 1858. It, too, failed. Bad weather was at least partly to blame, but it was also the sheer magnitude of the undertaking that weighed against the entrepreneurs. There were simply too many things that could go wrong. After the second failure, many started to question whether this was a serious business venture or a flight of fancy. By that time over £300,000 had been spent to no great effect.

Field and his band of men remained undeterred. Two further attempts were made and finally it all went to plan. America and Europe were connected. The world was not just a much smaller place, but there was also a feeling that it was going to be a more peaceful one too, with the first message reading: 'Europe and America are united by telegraphic communication. Glory to God in the highest, on earth peace, goodwill to men.' A leader in the *Times* put things even more optimistically, noting that it was 'one in the eye for conflicts and despotism'. If only it were that simple! What no one had mentioned in the midst of all the celebrations is that it had taken over an hour to transmit that first message and within a matter of weeks the cable was operating so slowly it was unusable. Ultimately the cable was burnt out by engineer Walter Whitehouse who tried to speed up transmission by sending higher voltage messages. Cyrus Field was at a banquet in his honour when he discovered that the cable was broken. As toast after toast was raised in his honour, he must have had an inkling that his project was indeed toast. Adulation turned to revulsion and many were convinced that the entire scheme had been an elaborate fraud.

Field knew better, but his cable was useless and any dreams of world peace had to remain on hold. This proved to be very much the case, because the Civil War erupted in 1860, curtailing the ever hustling Field's plans. By 1864, however, he was back, and just as adamant that the cable could and would be laid. This time Field had more reason to be confident. For a start, the manufacture of telegraph cable had come on in leaps and bounds since 1858, but the biggest trump card up his sleeve was a new ship capable of carrying all the cable in one go.

This great ship was the SS *Great Eastern*. She had been launched in the Thames in 1857, around the time Cyrus Field was making his initial fumbling attempts to lay that wretched cable. Designed by Isambard Kingdom Brunel, she was a monstrous iron ship, at 692 foot easily double the size of next largest vessel afloat. Brunel intended her for the Australian or Far East passenger run. Her immense size was required to carry enough coal to make the trip down under without the need for a costly and time-consuming top-up of the bunkers.

The problem was that Brunel's leviathan was that bit too far ahead of her time and – like the transatlantic telegraph – she was dogged by teething problems. First up, her builder went bankrupt. Then, on the day she was meant to be launched, she jammed on the slipway and remained there for weeks while all scratched their heads trying to work out how the hell to shift this monster. Finally she was launched. During her trial trip one of her boilers exploded, killing several men. Prior to her maiden voyage you could add her designer to that list of casualties, for Brunel had succumbed to a stroke that many felt had been brought on by the worry and aggravation of the project.

The *Great Eastern* had been intended for the Far East run, but there were not enough passengers to fill her massive decks, so the 'Great Ship', as she was generally known, was put into the transatlantic trade. Misfortune seemed to follow this great white elephant around as she plodded her way to and fro, narrowly escaping disaster at every turn. She was also slower than many of her smaller rivals on the transatlantic run and rarely turned a decent profit for her investors. It seemed there was nothing useful this weird prototype could do. That was until Cyrus Field and his cronies clapped eyes on her. Finally here was a ship huge enough to lay all the cable in one go.

In 1864, the Anglo American Telegraph Company was formed and Field, now almost entirely backed by British financial muscle, set about laying yet another cable on the soft bed of the Atlantic. The first attempt nearly succeeded but failed two-thirds of the way across when the cable snapped. Undeterred, a second attempt was made and this time there was no hitch. The cable was completed and brought ashore at the picturesquely named Newfoundland fishing village of Heart's Content. This time around, the cable worked perfectly. America and Europe were now attached by a great copper umbilical cord. That July day in 1866 marked the birth of a new age, one that rivals, if not surpasses, the introduction of the internet. Forget dot com, this was the dot dash that meant the world would never be the same again. This time the message from Queen Victoria to President Andrew Johnson had far greater prescience:

> *The Queen congratulates the President on the successful completion of an undertaking which she hopes may serve as an additional bond of Union between the United States and England.*

Now all the money that Cyrus Field and his cohorts had dreamt of started to pour in. Rates were set phenomenally high at $10 (about $150 today) per word. Initially business was slow, but the potential of the telegraph meant it was always going to succeed. And if the long-hoped-for world peace didn't quite come off, there was certainly a new closeness between the US and Britain. The area where this closeness arguably had the greatest impact was the money markets. Here the cable really came into its own. These days you hear of traders gaining an advantage on the market with fibre optic cables that shave milliseconds off communication times. The 1866 cable took over a week off. By 1870, Wall Street was spending a million dollars a year on transatlantic cables and the London merchants somewhere near the same. The markets began to work with far greater synchronicity. If something was cheap in Britain and expensive in America, you could buy in London and simultaneously sell in New York; you could play the exchange rate, bet on future price rises. Field's great gamble created a gamblers' paradise. The potential for making money out of speculating went into the stratosphere and, like a sickly infant, the initial framework of our global economy slithered into being, kicking and screaming.

The cable also had great significance for James Gordon Bennett and his media cohorts. When Abraham Lincoln was assassinated, the news had taken 12 days to filter across to Europe. Suddenly, it was a question of minutes. The cable was far too expensive for your average layman, so newspapers became the conduit to this new form of communication. There was almost limitless scope to the amount of news that could be reported on and how much money could be lavished on getting hold of that news. Most believed it would change the world, but some were less convinced of its value than others. As the poet and sometime philosopher Henry David Thoreau noted rather wryly:

We are eager to tunnel under the Atlantic and bring the old world some weeks nearer to the new. But perchance the first news that will leak through into the broad, flapping American ear will be that Princess Adelaide has whooping cough.

This was the cable that pulsed and clicked to its own strange cadence many fathoms beneath the keels of our three little schooners as they themselves thrummed ever closer to the old world. Whether you were a newspaper mogul or a financier, the cable was poised to change everything. After all, this cable had been one of the reasons Leonard Jerome had instigated the race in the first place. He was a stake-holder in the *New York Times* and had shares in the Newfoundland and Atlantic Telegraph Cable company. He cared enough about the success of the cable to send his steam yacht, *Clara Clarita*, out to repair the Newfoundland to

New York section of the cable following a breakage just at the moment the *Great Eastern* was expected to arrive at Heart's Content and complete the transatlantic section. At the time he was lauded for this selfless act of philanthropy, but there was more to it than that. He cared all right, and he and brother Larry were astute enough to forget about the perceived treachery of the British during the Civil War and concentrate on the positives; most of all, the potential to generate great heaps of cash.

Meanwhile, back in New York, James Gordon Bennett Senior, Pierre Lorillard, the Osgoods and the American public waited anxiously for the cable to crackle into life and deliver up the results of this race. They were greeted with nothing but silence. Bets were now up to $1.25m in total, but no miracle of communication could convey the thrilling truth that, with England only a stone's throw away, the distance between the *Henrietta* and *Vesta* was little more than 10 miles. What is more, for all the unrest aboard *Vesta*, it was that yacht that held the lead as the coast of England hove into view: a dirty, drizzly charcoal smear on the north-eastern horizon.

9
THE RACE IS WON

♔

The first man gets the oyster, the second man gets the shell.

ANDREW CARNEGIE, *GOSPEL OF WEALTH*

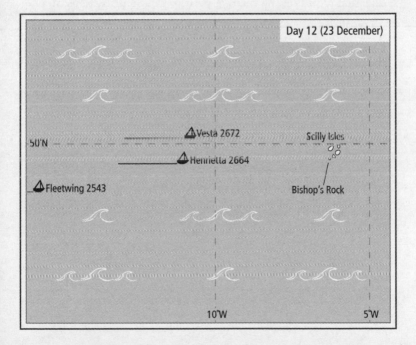

199

The day before Christmas Eve, 1866. As evening fell a great moon rose, blood red against the hazy English sky, lending an apocalyptic air to the brooding ocean. The three yachts raced on, logging 12 knots and more. Every nerve and sinew focused on what lay to the east, just below the horizon. You could almost smell the land and feel the presence of the rival yachts, noiseless, out of sight, yet tangible. The race was reaching its denouement. While the *Vesta* still clung on to her lead, it was a tenuous one. She was now only 6 miles ahead of the *Henrietta*. All the crews were on edge and indulged in a frenzy of speculation regarding the relative positions of their rivals, as Stephen Fiske recalled:

> *The excitement in regard to the race now reached fever heat. All jokes and stories became stale, and nothing was talked of but yachts and wind and the probabilities and possibilities of the contest. In every distant vessel we saw the* Fleetwing; *every star near the horizon was the* Vesta's *signal light. At 8pm we were off soundings, by midnight, off Cape Clear. Thus the next morning found us in the chops of the channel and hoping to eat our Christmas dinner at Cowes. It was a murky, damp disagreeable morning and even at noon it was impossible to take a solar observation. The carpenter, who had already given us one sensation by discovering a spurious leak, now treated us to another by announcing that the* Fleetwing *was in sight. Everybody clambered on deck. Binocular glasses, eye glasses, spectacles and telescopes were all brought to bear upon the imaginary yacht, which was soon made out to be an English topsail schooner bound the other way. Indignation followed excitement and both quickly merged into a hearty laugh.*

They need not have worried, for at that particular moment *Fleetwing* was labouring some 100 miles off the pace and seemingly out of the race. Her position appeared hopeless, but the luckless schooner did hold a trump card of sorts, for right spang in the path of the three racers lay the Scilly Isles: a glorious tangle of islands, all golden sands and jagged rocks. They sat impassive, rugged sentinels marking the entrance to the English Channel, yet they had real bite. Get in among these beautiful but treacherous islands and you would find yourself snarled up in a labyrinth of reefs and great sharp fangs of rock. Those unforgiving isles had claimed many a gallant vessel within touching distance of its destination.

The wind blew steadily from the south-east as the three racers closed with the land and this meant that if you passed to the north of the Scillies you would struggle to weather the Lizard peninsula on the Cornish coast and could end up ensnared by the Seven Stones Reef or even Wolf Rock. The only sensible way to get past was to go to the south past Bishop Rock at the southern tip of the Scillies. You may remember that the *Vesta* had northed many miles when she had run before the great storm, so she was poorly placed to get past this immoveable obstacle. By noon on Christmas Eve she was close to land but also hard on the wind, punching into the waves to get past the wretched rock, as Colonel Taylor noted:

This is the first head sea we have encountered since New York and it hurts our chances of making the passage in less than fourteen days which we had every chance of doing three days ago and this is a sore disappointment. Can it be possible that our antagonists have endured such splendid, such unparalleled luck? We cannot endure the thought! Even with the bad fortune we have just met, we may make the run in 14 days. All hands in a state of feverish excitement!

As the *Vesta* pinned her sails in and all aboard held their breath, *Henrietta* slightly to the north held the middle path and with a spot of judicious sail trim she should tickle past Bishop Rock nicely. *Fleetwing*, meanwhile, was many miles to the south and this meant that the breeze favoured her. She could romp straight up the channel with a fair following breeze without having even to consider those awkwardly placed sentinels at the entrance to the English Channel. The race was far from over yet!

Later that day, the *Henrietta* received a very welcome boost, following an encounter with the American packet ship *Philadelphia*, as Fiske recalls:

> The genial Captain nearly tumbled over the taffrail in his haste to assure us that no yacht had as yet passed up the English Channel. Hurrah! But the news seemed too good to be true. This was on Christmas Eve, and here's to the health of the losers and the loved ones at home! Nearing the land of Christmas carols and Dickens it was impossible to go to rest. After a very late dinner we had our Christmas stories and songs; amongst the former was a ditty composed in honour of Henrietta and sung to the familiar air of 'Sweet Evelina'. While these festivities were in progress we had made the Scilly islands lights at 7.45pm. The current drifting us to leeward, we steered southeast for an offing and passed the islands handsomely having made no tack since we left New York and having varied only eleven miles between the two points. So admirable a landfall reflected great credit upon Captain Samuels.

This may well have been the case, and there is little doubt that the exuberant crew had much to celebrate during their Christmas Eve carousal, but the songs would have died upon their lips and the food turned to ashes in their mouths had they known that the *Vesta* had sighted the Scilly Isles a good hour ahead of them. With the race nearly run, the centreboard schooner that all had written off was within touching distance of victory as they turned into the final straight.

Aboard the *Vesta*, Captain Dayton eyed Bishop Rock light apprehensively as it winked mockingly at them in the December night. It was clear that the *Vesta* was still too far to the north and he felt there was no alternative other than to rattle the helm up and tack away in order to get a bit more southing. Land was the enemy of the deep-water sailor and the more offing available the better as far as Dayton was concerned. Not all agreed, and Colonel Taylor and George Lorillard looked on in disgust as the *Vesta* flopped through a tack and turned away from the rock, heading south. The largely affable Taylor recalled his emotions sometime afterwards:.

Some of the officers were very nervous thinking that we were running in too close [to Bishop Rock] *and one cried out that we had struck! How could such a thing be possible in ten fathom of water? Here we tacked and stood off to southward for a long time for no good reason that I could see and as it afterward appeared. The sails were pinned in so tight that we made little headway, and the yacht bobbing up and down most uncomfortably. We should have stood straight on our course without tacking or stood but one and a half the time we did to the southward (the running ashore was all nonsense). Then we should have run closer to the land and made more rapid time had our sheets been eased off a little, instead of bobbing about to southward for an hour and a half! A fearful mistake, it seemed to me.*

How bad a mistake this was is impossible to verify without hearing from Captain Dayton, who carried his thoughts on this matter to the grave. Given that all of this fumbling around went on under cover of darkness, it is hard to know how Colonel Taylor knew for certain that they were far enough off the rock. Lights and distances can play tricks with you in the dark at sea and only Dayton would have known exactly how close he was to piling the schooner up on the rocks. What is beyond doubt, however, is that at 10pm, while the *Vesta* was desperately clawing her way around the Scillies, the *Henrietta* came bowling past on a close reach with every sail drawing to perfection and crossed her rival's bows with a good few miles to spare. Neither vessel saw the other, but once again *Henrietta* had wrested the lead from a yacht that was technically faster.

While the *Henrietta* and *Vesta* jousted for the lead, the *Fleetwing*, out to the south and untroubled by the Scillies, was making the best speed of all. Her demoralized crew had roused themselves from their gloomy torpor and the little schooner seemed to respond to the urgency of the situation tumbling before the great rollers of the chops of the channel and almost falling over herself as her crew sought to get the last ounce of speed from that fair breeze. She was five hours behind the *Henrietta* when she passed Bishop Rock, but she was flying. All the yachts were on course to finish within the fourteen days, give or take a couple of hours, and, given that this was far faster than any yacht had managed before, all must have believed that they were on course for victory.

This was to be the second great race up the English Channel witnessed that year. In September the British public had been amazed and enthralled as the China tea clippers the *Ariel*, *Taeping* and *Serica* had raced neck and neck up the English coast, leaning into the channel chop purposefully, elegantly, illuminating an early autumn day with their haunting beauty. Unlike American clippers, which had been largely killed off by the Civil War, English clipper ships reached their zenith in the 1860s and the 1866 race from China to London was their high-water mark.

The three racers had left Foochow on the same tide. Ninety-nine days and 16,000 miles of ocean later, nothing had separated the three rivals. Large sums had been wagered on that contest, too, and victory ensured a big financial bonus for the crews involved, just as it did for our three brave schooners. The difference was that the China clipper race had been a final glorious celebration of deep-water racing between merchant ships, races that meant more than pride or vanity, but also food on the plates of working men and their families. These were ships that raced with real purpose. *Ariel*, *Taeping* and *Serica* had warped into London Docks resplendent, glorious anachronisms, their flags and sails gorgeous funeral robes. The victorious captains and crews collected their bonuses of a few hundred pounds and departed once again out to the battlefield of the oceans. By 1869 the Suez Canal would kill off their glorious race once and for all and the shadows hanging over commercial sail would deepen. Everything after 1866 was a slow retreat until the last commercial windjammers shuffled apologetically off the oceans in the 1930s and the world lost one more object of wonder and beauty.

The three schooners were a different breed altogether, harbingers of a new age of leisure; the first trickle of a great flood tide for offshore yacht racing. They were just as beautiful as those magnificent clippers as they stormed up the channel under bellying canvas, yet they shared little with the merchant vessels. With their cargo of millionaires, they breezed up channel with prescient haste; their long, slender jibbooms pointing mercilessly onward into the future where thrills had to be sought out.

All through that dark winter night the three yachts reeled off the knots. By 3am the *Henrietta* was abeam the Lizard and the great light shone across to them reassuringly. To the east the softer, more muted lights of the village of Coverack twinkled. They were strangers approaching a strange land but those soft lights gleaming like jewels in the depths of the Christmas night spoke to the sailors of warmth and comfort after the savagery of the North Atlantic. An occasional whiff of wood smoke or the soft mulchy decaying scent of English winter beckoned them on and the little schooner tore past the slumbering coast running a steady 13 knots. 'Like a well-jockeyed race horse, reserving her best pace for the finish,' Fiske recalled.

As dawn reluctantly eased its way across the eastern sky that Christmas Eve morning, the coast of England unfurled before them. The lights that marked the path to safety still flashed, though subdued by the grey, weepy dawn: astern the Lizard light, fast disappearing in their frothy wake; ahead Start Point, Portland Bill and, beyond that, still out of sight, was the Needles light, gateway to the Solent, the Isle of Wight, Cowes and the finishing line. Presently low, damp clouds gave way, tattered to pieces by a boisterous, icy cold front roaring up from the south-west. The day was transformed into sudden bullying, buffeting squalls, bright piercing spears of sunlight and hurrying high clouds.

All through that bright, icy day the racers pressed on toward their goal, each one hidden just below the horizon but still closing up on one another. Anyone looking out to sea would have rubbed their eyes in wonder as these vessels foamed by in a welter of spray, smashing through the chop with joyous abandon, great rainbows of glistening spume refracting and cascading, spent, into the gleaming scuppers. The dying shards of light from that brief day illuminated the *Henrietta* until every sail she wore glowed with a soft luminescence in the hard winter light. Her fiery white sails lit up the ink dark sea as evening faded into night.

The *Fleetwing*, at the back of the group, continued to make the best time, bringing a gale up behind her. As night began to bruise the sky, the gale that pursued her overtook the schooner and she rode on the wings of the storm at greater and greater pace, reefing down as the wind gathered strength, hunting down the leaders, her topmasts bending like reeds in the wind.

Yet there was to be no catching the *Henrietta*. That afternoon the great white chalk cliffs that marked the entrance to the Needles Channel shimmered before them, glowing alien against the dying luminescence of the foreshortened day. It was time to pick up a pilot and finally discover who had won. With all crew in a state of extreme tension, the schooner hove to and the pilot was bundled aboard, as Fiske recalls:

A Cowes pilot was dragged on board so quickly that he could not speak. But his eyes and the grip of his hand spoke for him. At last he put his good news into words: 'No other boat ahead of you! What yacht is this?' You might have heard on both sides of the Atlantic the unanimous shout: ' The Henrietta! God bless her!' Then everybody cheered, and embraced, and assured everybody else that he had always said that Henrietta would win. Why, there never was the slightest doubt about it! The slowest boat? No, sir; the fastest boat that ever floated. Had to lay to eighteen hours? Why, she could lay to for a week, and then win easily! Then more cheering. Meanwhile, Captain Samuels bedecked the yacht with all her sails and flags, and, as if appreciating the compliment, Henrietta sailed faster and faster up the Channel and suddenly turned to pass the Needles,

*the winning post. Then, coquettishly promenading, like a belle
after a waltz, she slackened speed as the rocks shielded her from the
wind and sauntered leisurely into Cowes harbor, as though she had
been out for a brief pleasure trip instead of a racking race across the
Atlantic in December.*

The lights of Cowes glowed like embers, beckoning the crew ashore in a
land strange yet familiar. As the *Henrietta* wafted toward her anchorage,
the quiet little town lay peaceful as families prepared for a festive
dinner, fires roaring in the grate. The low black schooner stole in and
shattered the peace with a crackle of rockets and the boom of signal
guns. Families roused from their torpor tumbled out into the street to
see what the hullabaloo was and perceived the shadowy outline of the
sleek schooner, charcoal black against the dark night, then suddenly
blindingly revealed as blue lights and flares were burned on deck by
her jubilant crew, their cold light glittering icily in the dark water. The
race was won, the *Henrietta* had crossed from New York to Cowes in the
time of 13 days, 22 hours and 43 minutes – truly an impressive time,
particularly when you remember that she was hove to for a number of
hours. The English were ready for the arrival of their Yankee cousins,
as Fiske recalls:

*As soon as our colors were made out, salutes were fired from
HMS Hector, an ironclad, and from the Royal Yacht Squadron's
battery. A few moments after a midshipman from the Hector came
on board to offer Henrietta the hospitalities of the dockyard at
Portsmouth. That midshipman is a Post-Captain now, but he does
not forget his first experience of Yankee hospitality and retells the*

story over the walnuts and the wine. It was, indeed, a proud moment
when Mr. Bennett told him that not a sail or spar was injured; that
no repairs of any kind were needed, and that, in as fine trim as she
left New York, Henrietta *would have the honor of being paraded for*
the inspection of the Queen.

Cowes today remains much as it did back in 1866. It's an unremarkable, sleepy, provincial little town, cut off from the mainland, where life moves along at its own pace. It seems rather incongruous that this somnolent spot is often referred to as the home of yachting, a Mecca for lovers of fun and frivolity. Certainly, viewing it on a bleak winter night such as the one our fine adventurers arrived upon, it closely resembles a coastal town that someone had forgotten to close down. Only a few chandleries and the tracery of a few lofty spars whistling their mournful tune in the chill breeze betrayed the fact that, as the winter desolation passes and England awakes from its grey, desolate hibernation and becomes a land of rolling verdant fields and luminous hedgerows fragrant with wild garlic and alive with birdsong, Cowes throws off its torpor and explodes into life. In summer it becomes a hive of activity, all centred around the waterfront, with the Royal Yacht Squadron's well-appointed club building as the focal point.

In the summer months, no self-respecting gentleman would dream of not being seen among the great and good who throw themselves eagerly into the hubbub of a town alive. Through the winter months the town retreats again into the isolation of the Isle of Wight, cut off from the mainland, returning to the old rhythms of a time when the town was a simple fishing village. Only the presence of Osborne House, the royal residence, hints at the decadent summer.

The arrival of the *Henrietta* shattered the peace. Raucous celebrations began even as her anchor rattled down and kissed the mud just a few hundred metres from Queen Victoria's residence. Her crew celebrated and Captain Samuels breathed a heavy sight of relief. Now he could sleep, his work complete, his employer satisfied. Be it the *Henrietta*, the *Dreadnought* or any other vessel, he always pushed himself and his command to the limit, and now he could rest easy. Celebrations, banquets, Christmas itself could wait until morning. Dawn would reveal all.

And there was much yet to be revealed. What of her rivals? Their ghostly outlines had haunted them all across the Atlantic. So many times their sails had been imagined on the horizon. Now, somewhere out there, both of the schooners continued their desperate race. There shouldn't have been long to wait; you will recall that the *Vesta* had led until the vessels were in striking distance of the finishing line. What the devil had become of Lorillard's centreboard schooner? The truth was a comedy of errors. After her grope past Bishop Rock had seen her relinquish the lead to *Henrietta*, she too had streaked up the coast but had not been able to make up the ground on her rival. At 4pm she was off Portland Bill where she had endeavoured to pick up a pilot to take her into Cowes, but the pilot boat made a terrible hash of getting their man aboard. Precious time was spent waiting around until the whole operation was given up and the *Vesta* stormed off again. It wasn't until five hours later that a pilot stepped aboard. Colonel Taylor relates what happened next:

> The first question we asked him was 'are either of the other yachts
> in?' I think I could have assisted old Oberon in rowing his rotund
> corpse across the muddy waters of the Styx when the answer left the

old sea dog's lips. 'Yes' came the answer, the one with the blue flag. We knew from these words that cut like a knife that the Henrietta was the victress in our battle of the sea. Our surprise and grief cannot be pictured! The Henrietta had gone up the Needles only three hours before us. Only one thought we had to console us, we were not badly whipped and would not be last. We clung to that like grim death to an Ethiopian. We had fully made up our minds that ours was the winning yacht and the imparting of the news to us by the burly English pilot completely crushed us and with drooping heads we quietly slunk away into our cabin to hold sad converse over our blighted hopes.

We were ten miles from the Needles Channel. At 10.15pm the owner [by owner he means George Lorillard] and myself went on deck presuming we had passed the light and the race was over. To our horror and amazement the pilot told us he had committed the blunder of going up the passage by St Catherine's light instead of taking us through the Needles. Orders were given to 'wear yacht' and we stood down the passage, a beat of 12 miles. It was slow work; at 12.15 the Needles bore south and the race so far as we were concerned was over. Over in sadness and sorrow. The breeze had lightened and under easy canvas we ran up to Cowes. Even the dear old yacht that had borne us over wintry sea seemed to sense our grief and moved sluggishly. As we reached the little town of Cowes and drifted to our anchor we descried the Henrietta and 'horrible disbelief' there too was the Fleetwing. Like a thief in the night she had crept in while we were blundering around St Catherine's light and when we were a fair winner of second place. All hands were wretched. Fain yet unmistakeable shouts of laughter came to us across the water from

where our rivals were floating. There were shouts of exultation.
We ascertained that the Fleetwing had passed the Needles forty
minutes ahead of us so it was apparent that if our pilot had not been
at fault we would have beaten her by two hours.

Quite how the feckless pilot had succeeded in mistaking the light at St Katherine's Point at the southerly tip of the Isle of Wight for the Needles light, which marked the western end of the island, is a mystery. Bear in mind that he was a trained professional whose sole aim was to guide vessels safely and accurately into port. To commit such a howler is almost beyond comprehension. According to the *Field*, an English sporting paper, his explanation was that he mistook the red sector of the Needles light for the sidelight of a ship, the weather being misty. At best, this is a dreadfully weak excuse.

Nevertheless, the following day was for post-mortems into the race. The trip was chewed over and digested over Christmas dinner, after which Cowes roused itself in order to make the yachtsmen welcome. Stephen Fiske:

It was Christmas Day, and you can imagine the talk of the
yachtsmen over the Christmas dinner. Captain Thomas, of the
Fleetwing, explained that if he had not gone so far north and lost so
many men he would have won the race. The Vesta's Captain made it
equally clear that if he had not gone so far south and then missed his
way in the Channel he could not have lost. We modestly agreed with
them, although now and then a wink or a chuckle was irrepressible.
No matter; we were all together again, and victors and vanquished
could take part in the inevitable festivities.

These began an hour after our arrival, when White, a famous yacht builder, had us rowed to his residence and showed us his models, while the ladies of his family gathered roses for us in the garden in the Christmas sunshine. The Queen sent a couple of lords-in-waiting with the royal congratulations and an invitation to Osborne House. The Royal Yacht Squadron tendered us a banquet at Cowes, as did the Royal Albert Yacht Club at London. England loves sailormen, and we were the heroes of a minute. To cap the climax, the amusement manager of the Crystal Palace proposed to exhibit us and Henrietta as a side show, and inquired our lowest terms.

The yachtsmen were clearly given a hearty welcome, with the English papers suitably impressed by the tenacity of the American yachtsmen. *The Times* noted:

We would not say that Englishmen could not have accomplished such a race, but the idea would perhaps hardly have occurred to them. Its novelty and boldness are eminently characteristic of Americans.

While the *Review* noted slightly more sardonically:

The Yankees, who can boast that they have made the largest national debt ever made in the same time, that have carried on the biggest civil war, received the biggest thrashing, and crushed the biggest rebellion ever known can now claim the glory of having had the biggest yacht race.

Over the next century, Cowes was to witness the arrival of many offshore racers, until such occurrences were almost humdrum, but this was the first and therefore deserved the biggest reception. The sleepy port obliged. It helped that Queen Victoria was spending the festive period at Osborne House. On the twenty-ninth the three yachts were invited to sail past Osborne House and Queen Victoria watched from the beach as they tacked, gybed, pirouetted and performed for her pleasure. As the *Henrietta* departed, she saluted her, as winner of the race, with a flourish of her handkerchief.

Two days later, Queen Victoria also had the dubious pleasure of a visit from James Gordon Bennett Jr, who was accompanied by Commodore McVickar of the New York Yacht Club. McVickar, you may recall, had grudgingly sanctioned the race and had hot-footed it over to Cowes from New York aboard the steamship *Scotia*. The intention had been to arrive before the racers and prepare the ground for their arrival, but due to the speed of the three yachts he arrived the day after. Anyway, he was still in good time to enjoy tea with Queen Victoria, despite long, loud protestations from Lawrence Jerome who couldn't for the life of him see why McVickar should enjoy this privilege when he hadn't undertaken any of the racing.

The visit to Osborne House must have been a suitably surreal, austere experience for Bennett. The Queen was still deep in mourning for her husband Albert who had died five years before, and she remained so for the remaining 35 years of her life. Many visitors to the Queen's court noted how stultifying it was. The Queen was naturally shy and utterly hidebound. She was a stickler for rank and believed that she could never be truly intimate with someone who was not of royal blood. She stuck to the tradition that only her courtiers, who had noble blood coursing through their veins, could provide her with personal service. Thus if a door needed opening, a letter writing, even an umbrella carrying, it must be done by her long-suffering courtiers. Despite this rigid belief in the value of rank, Queen Victoria was often deeply dismissive of the nobility. She and Albert had never had any time for the fripperies and nonsense of the wilder elements of the aristocracy. The Queen had once damningly described them as: 'Wretched, ignorant high-born beings who live only to kill time.'

With all the trappings of playboy aristocracy apart from that precious noble blood, Bennett was doubly damned, and quite how this little tête-à-tête went has sadly never been recorded. At least Bennett had stayed off the Razzle Dazzles on this occasion and his brief visit went off without a hitch. The only upshot was a royal invitation to race the *Henrietta* against the Duke of Edinburgh's yacht, *Viking*, that summer.

You may be wondering how the American public and press had reacted to the *Henrietta*'s victory and the simple answer is, not at all. With delicious irony the race that was intended to showcase the capabilities of the transatlantic telegraph merely served to highlight its shortcomings when a break in the cable between Newfoundland and the mainland meant that all the news the eager American public got on the race was deafening silence. In the meantime the newspapers endeavoured to maintain interest in the story with wild speculation and supposition, the *New York Times* running an editorial from some wizened old seadog suggesting that the *Fleetwing* was most likely to win the race. The proprietor of the *Herald* might actually have been starting to worry about his wayward son and an editorial of

December 26, two days after the *Henrietta* had arrived in, has a faintly plaintive air:

THE OCEAN YACHT RACE

No news of the yachts

The three contestants for the great ocean sweepstakes have now been at sea nearly fifteen days, yet nothing definite or satisfactory has been heard of them. Before the close of the present week we expect to hear of the arrival at Cowes of at least one of them, or an announcement that they have been spoken by some of the outward bound steamships.

Later editorials took a slightly more exasperated tone and it would not be until 30 December that the New York newspapers could blare out triumphant headlines relating to the heroic arrival of the little vessels. James Gordon Bennett Sr in his personal editorial was understandably effusive, writing as follows:

This great race marks the commencement of a new era in yachting and in the construction of sailing vessels. Henceforth we may expect annually to see American yachts on the Atlantic race course, and the yachts of the British squadron arriving in our harbour on similar trials of speed. The three pioneer adventurers have braved the dangers of an ocean race in the roughest most threatening season and future races will create no excitement equal to that attendant upon their gallant contest. It is said that the victorious yacht was received with much enthusiasm by the British clubs and doubtless the presence, in person, of the owner on board contributed not a little to the éclat of his success.

> *The event has made a European sensation. The London journals*
> *are full of it. On Thursday last the Royal Yacht Club gave a banquet*
> *to the officers of the American squadron; on Friday, in pursuance*
> *of an invitation from the queen, the Royal Yacht Club were to*
> *present their American guests to her Majesty at Osborne House and*
> *yesterday the municipal authorities of Cowes were to give them a*
> *dinner. We hope that the young gentlemen concerned have borne and*
> *will throughout bear themselves in a manner worthy of all praise.*

It is rather pleasing to read among all that hyperbole and fatherly pride the unmistakable undertone of parental concern at the thought of the chaos his wayward son could cause given free rein among the English aristocracy. Indeed, it would not be long before his young son made a prize ass of himself in a very public manner, for shortly before departing for the US he offered the *Henrietta* as a gift to Prince Albert. At the time this was considered an extremely indelicate thing to do and the prince politely declined. The incident was largely ignored in the British press but caused an absolute snowstorm of fury in America from those who already disliked Bennett.

In the meantime, the main embarrassment was to shareholders in the Anglo-American Transatlantic Cable Company, and given that Leonard Jerome had a significant interest in both the Newfoundland cable and the *New York Times* it is unsurprising that this paper took a slightly embarrassed, conciliatory approach to the matter, reporting:

> *It is unfortunate that the Atlantic Telegraph land lines should have*
> *given out just as our English cousins were greeting with a hearty*
> *Christmas welcome the gallant winner of the ocean yacht race.*

> *The fitness of things would have been better illustrated if the cable*
> *and its connections had been in such working order as to give us the*
> *news on the auspicious day when it was due. It came five days late –*
> *a delay probably caused by the derangement of the wires consequent*
> *of the storm last week.*

Despite these communication problems, the general atmosphere seems to have been one of bonhomie and goodwill between British and Americans. This was the first signpost to the entente between the countries that remains to this day. Which, given the parlous state of diplomatic relations over the *Alabama* affair, is much to the credit of the participants of the race. When the *America* had arrived off Cowes in 1851, she had confronted the British with their own shortcomings and terrified them. When Vanderbilt had come over in his absurdly lavish yacht/ship *North Star* in 1853, there was an unmistakable feeling that the yacht was almost a challenge to the British. As the *Herald* had put it:

> *The sovereigns of Europe have looked upon our increasing power*
> *with surprise and alarm – surprise at our progress and alarm lest*
> *the lessons which it silently inculcates might be learned by their own*
> *oppressed subjects.*

Here was a country built on the sacred tenets of liberty and equal opportunity getting right in the face of the hierarchical English, threatening their sacred institutions. Vanderbilt's rough character and the nature of his great steamship almost seemed designed to rub the English nobility up the wrong way. As the *Scientific American* wrote at the time of the *North Star*: 'The yachts of the English nobility are like fishing cobles to a seventy four gun ship.' And, of course, there had been Vanderbilt himself: semi-illiterate, rough, coarse and distinctly no-nonsense. He possessed none of the good-humoured suavity of the Jeromes, nor the languid ennui of Gordon Bennett (provided he stayed off the booze). The English had treated Vanderbilt in very English style: marvelling at his yacht, flattering the multimillionaire, then savaging him once he had departed.

Yet the three racing schooners and their crew set an altogether different tone. It was as if there was a glimpse of recognition; a realization that John Bull and Brother Jonathan were not so different after all. There was a definite feeling throughout the editorials that a long period of mistrust and misunderstanding had now come to an end. There had been a time when the English had viewed Americans and their outlandish views on feudalism with a certain measure of misgiving. Misunderstandings had naturally prevailed as this strange new republic found its feet. It had been felt that the existence of a country without a sovereign and vassals was abnormal and liable to have an unsettling effect. Too many Englishmen had assumed, without due enquiry, that in such an outlandish thing as a republic a spirit of licence and indiscipline would prevail. They had been nervous about the effects on their own people. The natural reaction had been to crush, undermine and destroy, and the ultimate expression of that had probably been the *Alabama* affair and the whiff of collusion with the Confederates. But the 1866 race occurred at a turning point in the way the two countries interacted and no doubt the race itself helped to usher in a new outlook. Now the British saw America for what it truly was: the future. They looked across at their American friends with their burgeoning wealth and elite of millionaires and saw much to admire, even imitate. The two cousins looked across at each other, their eyes locked in recognition and each inwardly thought: 'We're not so different, you and I.' From here on, the two countries headed down the road toward the special relationship so cherished today. The arrival of Bennett and his friends was an early signpost.

The culmination of this Anglo-American love-in was the race reception held on New Year's Eve. One hundred and ten people were present at this banquet, during the course of which there were no less than eight speeches, and innumerable toasts. I will leave it to the journalist of the London *Times* to describe the scene:

> The extraordinary yet very natural excitement under which Cowes
> has laboured during the past week and in which, indeed every
> town and hamlet in the kingdom have in a certain lesser degree
> participated, reached the culminating point in the banquet given by
> the inhabitants of Cowes to the officers and gentlemen amateurs
> of the New York Yacht Club squadron now anchored in Cowes
> roadstead and comprising the three beautiful schooners, Henrietta,
> Fleetwing and Vesta. The Banquet was given in the dining hall
> of the Gloster Hotel, the old quarters of the Royal Yacht Squadron
> which was tastefully decorated for the occasion, floral wreaths
> and festoons running round the cornice over trophies of flags and
> emblematic devices. Among the most noticeable of the mottoes on
> the walls were 'god save the queen and the president', 'separated not
> divided' and 'NYYC and RYS'.

The paper then went on to narrate all the speeches at some length and, without the accompanying booze, it becomes rather a wearing read. Lawrence Jerome's speech during the latter stages captures much of the atmosphere of verbose bonhomie that seems to have prevailed, however:

> I did expect to be able upon this occasion to make an apology for coming to Cowes in December instead of waiting for the regular yachting season but even that subject has been taken from me. [Cheers] There is no necessity for an apology. I find December is just the time to come to Cowes [Cheers]. Hereafter I shall advise all American friends who want to go to Europe to go in a yacht in the month of December and arrive at Cowes. They will be perfectly content to stop here. [Cheers] Here we are and very glad we are to be here [Cheers]. In conclusion let me say, let us bring our yachts into friendly competition, meet together in a social way, and keep them aloof from all the politicians and there can never be any difficulty between England and America. With our flags hanging together as we see them tonight our national mottoes side by side and our hands united in the cordial grasp of sincere friendship, the two countries will go on together in their career of glory, the envy the admiration and the rulers of the world. [Loud and continued cheers]

This was the climax of the celebrations. Bennett, the Jerome brothers and George Lorillard basked in the glory, recognition and validation of what they had achieved. Leonard Jerome in his role as stake-holder was able to present Bennett with his $60,000 prize, which Bennett no doubt kept for pocket money. Jerome himself was feeling pretty flush, having won a cool $100,000 by betting heavily on the *Henrietta* to win. He was quick to share the wealth, too, going so far as to buy Captain

Samuels a brand new home in Brooklyn, estimated to cost $25,000. It was a princely gift.

Later, over cigars and cognac, the gentlemen of the party gambled at cards with their hosts. The landed gentry of England and the newly minted gentry of the new world eyed each other with interest and realized how agreeable it was to be among men with whom they shared so much in common.

There were, however, six spectres at this feast and they were the six men who had so inconveniently died. Even as the party went on they lay rocking in icy purgatory somewhere between the old world and new. These men who had laid down their lives in the name of leisure were rarely given anything more than a fleeting mention in the press reports and were never named. They were incidental to the glorious race; an inconvenient truth that wasn't quite buried amid the excitement. They were not totally forgotten, for $5,800 was raised, mostly donated by the gentlemen connected with the race, and this was split between the six widows. The golden era of the philanthropist was, after all, only in its infancy in 1866.

10
WHAT HAPPENED AFTERWARDS

☙

An aristocracy based on nearly two billions and a half of
national securities has arisen in the northern states to assume
that political control which the consolidation of great financial
and political interests formerly gave to the slave oligarchy. The
war of finance is the next war we have to fight.

PRESIDENT ANDREW JOHNSON SPEAKING IN 1866

This is an impressive crowd: the Haves and Have-mores.
Some people call you the elites. I call you my base.

GEORGE W BUSH AT THE ALFRED SMITH MEMORIAL DINNER IN 2006

The year is 1870, four years after the first great ocean race, and
another is about to start. This time the course is east to west and
two schooners, the American *Dauntless* and the English *Cambria*, are
competing for honours. The start line is eight miles off Queenstown,
southern Ireland and, in the heat of a July day, the hills and moorland of
County Cork shimmer purple and emerald against the sea. It's a languid
afternoon, all cloying heat and unsettling stuffy gloom, yet the schooners
are alive with activity as they circle cagily off the start line like a pair of
boxers bouncing around the ring, feeling each other out preparatory to

laying the first blow. One sharp crack from the starting gun and the pair of yachts sheet in their sail and punch their way through the lazy swell toward the Old Head of Kinsale, bound for New York and glory.

The *Cambria's* owner, Sir James Ashbury, paces the deck of his yacht uneasily, glaring defiantly at the *Dauntless*, which is already weathering on his beloved vessel. He's a spiky, rather supercilious Englishman, and *Cambria* he hopes is on her way to reclaim the 100 Guineas Cup – or America's Cup as it is now known – so carelessly lost in 1851. This transatlantic jaunt is merely a warm-up and so far it's not going well; even in the early stages it's clear the *Dauntless* is the quicker boat. In fact, even before the race starts few give Ashbury much hope. This has nothing to do with the innate superiority of *Dauntless*; it's because of her crew. Training his telescope upon the offending vessel, Ashbury's querulous glass picks out her captain, a bluff moustachioed old sea dog who bestrides the deck with an unmistakable air of authority, bellowing orders to his crew as his vessel slips away from the Englishman. Even at this distance there is no mistaking Samuel Samuels, flanked by the steadfast Martin Lyons, both veterans of the 1866 race. There are more old friends here too: drifting around the deck, Bollinger in hand, wreathed in a halo of cigar smoke, is the yacht's owner, recently made commodore of the prestigious New York Yacht Club and proprietor of the most read newspaper in the world: James Gordon Bennett. He's flanked by a pair of his staunchest chums; Larry and Leonard Jerome. It's the return of the dream team. What hope did the Englishman have against this bunch? None.

Having been overhauled by *Dauntless*, *Cambria* tacked in toward the coast in an effort to wriggle away from the American schooner. *Dauntless* tacked to cover just as cat plays with mouse. Again she drew ahead of her prey. Another tack out from *Cambria* was covered and once again *Cambria* tried to wriggle free, tacking in toward the Old Head of Kinsale. This time, *Dauntless* let her be. Why cover a boat patently slower than their own? So they let her go off to the north and shaped their own course home. You can imagine that night Bennett and both Jeromes drank heartily to the success of their voyage. A nice way to round off the 1866 jaunt.

Much had changed for all three of them since 1866. In fact, America as a nation had much to reflect on. If 1866 had been the year when the world had shrunk considerably with the laying of the transatlantic telegraph cable, the intervening years had also seen the very heart of America ripped open, for in 1869 the transcontinental railroad was completed. The gangs of Irish labourers coming from the east were united with the Chinese labourers from the west and the rails were connected at Promontory, Utah. In all, 1,776 miles of track had been laid at a cost of $50,000,000. It was a mighty achievement; a great vein of commerce running through the continent. For the first time you could travel uninterrupted from New York to San Francisco. Yet this incredible achievement was almost overshadowed by the scandal that surrounded the directors behind the great railroad.

This corruption stemmed from the brain of one Thomas Durant, the executive of the Union Pacific Railway Company, which was responsible for overseeing the construction of the westbound section of the railroad. When Union Pacific set about finding a suitable contractor to undertake this mighty project, Durant paid his perennial stooge, Herbert Hoxie, to bid for it. The fact that this massive construction project had been put out to tender was hushed up and – perhaps unsurprisingly – Hoxie's was the only bid, one that was rapidly accepted by Durant. Durant had effectively hired himself to do the work, which was going to be paid for through government lending and private investors.

Given that this was Durant's starting premise, it's no surprise that corruption was rampant. Construction costs were grossly inflated and the profit was siphoned off to Durant and his cronies, who kept the money safe in a limited liability company named Credit Mobilier. At times Durant's madness for money was such that the track would arc in great demented parabolas across the Midwest in order to jack up costs (the US government was loaning between $16,000 and $48,000 for every mile of track laid). By the time the railway was completed, Durant had siphoned off a cool $18m for himself and his associates. When President Ulysses Grant drove in his last 'golden spike' on 10 May 1869, east and west were finally connected and America would never be quite the same. It was a mighty achievement that had come at a certain price, one that would only be fully revealed by federal investigations in 1872. Those investigations would implicate, among others, Grant's vice president Schuyler Colfax and future president James Garfield, although these high-profile figures were later exonerated.

Yes, much had changed since the 1866 race, both for America itself and also for James Gordon Bennett, who, as he stared absently from the deck of the *Cambria* while the Irish coastline slipped on by, could reflect on how much his own circumstances had altered since 1866. That great race had made a man of him in his father's eyes. Bennett Sr had begun to hand over the reins of power at the *Herald* almost as soon as his son returned. We have already discussed the weirdness of his antics as a publisher, but there is little doubt that those first years as Publisher and Editor-in-Chief of the *Herald* were a triumph. Even as he bobbed across the Atlantic, one of his reporters, Henry Morton Stanley, was making his way to Central Africa where his search for that great wandering missionary David Livingstone would provide the *Herald* with perhaps its greatest ever coup. As an editor, Bennett was certainly erratic, but his star still seemed to be on the rise as he sallied forth across the Atlantic that July day.

The same could not really be said of the Jerome brothers, who had both seen their power and influence on Wall Street diminish considerably, as had their substantial fortunes. Oh they were still fabulously wealthy, for sure, but the intervening years had given them one hell of a scare. By 1870 the world as James Gordon Bennett and his cohorts understood it was starting to bend and twist into the mould set at the end of the Civil War. Easy money, almost unlimited credit and a lamentable lack of financial regulation were beginning to take their toll. The results, particularly in that tiny, insular financial world occupied by the Jerome brothers, were often alarming. The first warning sign was the gold panic of 1869, and given that Bennett and the Jeromes were all closely involved in an incident that threatened to destroy the very foundations of the US economy, it's probably worth explaining.

Jay Gould had instigated and masterminded the panic. That sly, rapacious tycoon was looking for a new method of making an honest dollar. He settled upon manipulating the gold market, which worked as an unofficial currency exchange. Merchants would use it to cash in greenbacks and pay foreign traders in gold, and vice versa. Corner the gold market and you could drive up the price of greenbacks and make US exports cheaper, theoretically stimulating trade. It was harvest time and grain would pour out of the Midwest bound for Europe. This in turn would create wealth for his extensive railroad network that ran from the great grain fields of the west to New York. It was a bizarre, not to mention audacious experiment with people's livelihoods, which today might strike us as extraordinary. (It's not as if anyone nowadays would ever dream of rigging the foreign exchange mechanism.) Working alongside his partner in crime Jim Fisk, the pair set about distorting the market to their benefit. At the time there was about $15,000,000 worth of gold in circulation in the United States and Gould set about buying up every last bar, driving the price up and up. The only problem was that the United States treasury held another $100,000,000 in its reserves, which could be released should the price of gold rise too high. The only way to guarantee this did not happen was to control the treasury, and Gould managed to do this by cultivating the friendship of one Abel R Corbin, who was President Ulysses S Grant's brother-in-law. Corbin was offered a share of the wealth provided he used his influence over Grant to prevent the release of the Treasury's gold reserves crashing the market.

Day after day the price of gold rose higher and higher, and it was evident to all in the treasury that something must be done. Yet Grant refused to release the gold reserves. On 24 September 1869, the price had soared to an unprecedented level and still Jim Fisk bestrode the gold room, bidding up the price. Yet something had changed. Gould, tense, nervous, sweating in the shadows, began to surreptitiously dump his own substantial reserves. He didn't tell his partner, Fisk, what was going on, but he had got a tip from Butterfield that President Grant had lost his nerve. Shortly afterwards, the treasury reserves were also released and the market plunged as Black Friday wiped out businesses and destroyed fortunes with all the arbitrary might of a financial tsunami.

Eventually Commodore Vanderbilt was wheeled in to use his immense financial muscle to pump money into the collapsing stock exchange in order, as Vanderbilt himself stated, 'to protect ourselves'. Over time he was able to stabilize the value of his own stock and the market rallied. As for Gould, he had failed in his primary goal, but he made $11m (roughly $156m today) out of his little experiment. He also did more than that. He showed the world exactly how unregulated, untrammelled speculation had the potential to bring the entire country to its knees. Historian TJ Stiles's summary of the debacle:

> Black Friday suddenly illuminated, like a flash of lightning on a midnight floodplain, the way in which the new corporate and financial reality inundated the national landscape. The bankers and brokers of New York were no longer an oddity — an isolated batch of men who seemingly produced nothing but merely juggled bewilderingly abstract securities. Now, because of railroads, corporations began to overshadow farmers, artisans and merchants. Now, because of the increasing financial integration of the country, the fears and hopes of a few hundred men on Wall Street could shake the nation. More than any other man, the Commodore frightened or excited those few hundred driving them as he willed. With the wave of one hand he created tens of millions in new wealth; with the wave of the other he crushed his enemies; with cold eyed calculation, he gambled with the lives of millions.

Although the economy recovered relatively quickly from this piece of economic vandalism, something was clearly wrong. In the wake of the crash, most Americans were able to pick themselves up, dust themselves down and get back to enjoying all that easy credit that seemed to be sloshing around at the time. For the likes of Bennett and the Jeromes, they could get back to the serious business of racing across the Atlantic.

Still, even as the bold schooner sliced away from Ireland, a stiff breeze crisping the waves, there was unease about the future, and none felt it more acutely than the Jerome brothers. Four years on from the triumph of the *Henrietta*, they trod the decks of the *Dauntless* with all their old bravado and jollity; yet there had been a sea change in their outlook. Both had been shaken by the crash and increasingly they found themselves cut adrift on a ocean of financial uncertainty. They now seemed to bob queasily across the great Atlantic rollers, eyeing the horizon nervously, as if they knew there were storm clouds up ahead. Sharks like Gould and Fisk had overtaken them and in their willingness to exercise a policy of rip, tear and lacerate against friend and enemy alike, illustrated again and again that the Jeromes' powers were waning. From 1870 onward it was a story of slow retreat.

Yet Black Friday had even greater direct significance for James Gordon Bennett. The crisis presented him with one of the toughest and most significant editorial decisions of his career. Jim Fisk, enraged at being double-crossed by Gould, was prepared to spill the beans on the whole affair and he went to the *Herald* to do so. This is what he said:

> *Members of the President's family were in with us. The President himself was interested with us in the [gold] corner. We risked our millions on the assurance the government would not interfere.*

Basically, Fisk was stating that Black Friday was the ultimate inside job. This little peacock of a man was certainly in the know, for he was unquestionably Jay Gould's right-hand man. It was an incendiary allegation from a man at the heart of the conspiracy. If true, the President could, nay, should have been impeached. Bennett didn't know what to do with the information and ultimately ran a much vaguer piece which watered down Fisk's allegations and shied away from implicating the President or potentially destroying Jay Gould. Just for a moment, Bennett had the chance to do something truly earth-shaking. Instead, he backed off. Faced with genuine hard news, he had shied away. He preferred to stick to yacht racing and sporting pursuits like presiding over this little Anglo-American yachting face-off. Sure, the *Herald* sneered at the corruption of the likes of Gould, Fisk, Vanderbilt and, most pertinently, 'Boss' Tweed of Tammany Hall, but it didn't ever hit these people where it hurt.

The *Herald's* failure to deal with Tweed was an excellent case in point. In his role as Senator for New York State and leader of Tammany Hall, which was the New York arm of the Democrat party, he abused his position flagrantly, using corruption to control the city. He had a hand on the courts, the legislature, the ballot box and the treasury. Bribery was institutionalized. Money flowed through Tweed's hands: millions and millions of dirty dollars were siphoned off and laundered until they came back daisy fresh. Jay Gould was a favoured cohort and Tweed used his political muscle to Gould's (and his own) gain. By 1870, Tweed and his cronies at Tammany Hall did not even feel the need to pretend they were anything other than utterly corrupt. They rarely covered their tracks and were quite blatant in their abuse of power. All it needed was someone, some journalist, to pull the rug from under these scurvy shysters' feet. The *Herald* sneered, but refused to engage directly with Tweed.

Ultimately it was the *New York Times* and *Harper's Weekly* that did it for Tweed. *Harper's* cartoonist Thomas Nast began putting together a wickedly funny series of cartoons lampooning Tweed and his cohorts. Even the illiterate working class got the joke and, combined with a number of exposés by the *New York Times*, there was sufficient public pressure to merit an investigation into his affairs in 1871. A committee made up of six prominent New York luminaries, including JJ Astor III, undertook the report, which turned out to be another inside job, the committee filing a report stating that Tweed was squeaky clean.

Yet the trail of wanton corruption was simply too flagrant to hide and when the *Times* also obtained and published the accounts of the recently deceased James Watson, who was the Tweed ring's bookkeeper, the true corruption at the heart of Tammany Hall was exposed. Tweed was apprehended in 1871. No one ever worked out exactly how much he embezzled from the State of New York but estimates range from $46m to $200m. He was imprisoned awaiting trial and $1m bail was slapped upon him for his release – Jay Gould coughed up.

Anyway, that is another story. If Bennett had missed out on the biggest scoops of the decade, his paper still ruled the sporting columns, and Bennett's latest madcap scheme was a great diversion. Here was another chance to show the British who really ruled the waves. In fact, the transatlantic race was incidental; Sir James Ashbury was off to New York to retrieve the America's Cup from the Yankees. The only way to get his yacht across was to sail it, and Bennett was on hand to sportingly offer some competition. As with the 1866 race, interest was intense, and this time patriotic fervour was at fever pitch thanks to the added spice of American being pitted against Briton. As previously noted, the *Dauntless* was clearly the faster yacht and with the wealth of experience aboard her should have won easily.

Yet Samuels and his collection of experts made a grave miscalculation in allowing the *Cambria* to glide away from them that first night before ascertaining exactly what course she was planning on taking. If they had stuck with her that little bit longer, they would have noted that she favoured a more northerly route to *Dauntless*. Almost from the moment the yachts diverged, things seemed to go awry aboard the American schooner. The old bonhomie and camaraderie so marked in 1866 was gone. This time Samuels and his 'professionals' struggled to hide their impatience with the amateurs. Likewise Bennett, buoyed by several years of browbeating and getting his own way, was far more willing to interfere and contradict Samuels. Things reached a head with the old clipper captain shouting down and threatening to 'clap Bennett in irons' if he continued to contradict. Martin Lyons later recalled that there was 'too much amateur talent aboard', a veiled swipe at Bennett and his friends. The atmosphere sounds as poisonous as the acrimonious fug Captain Dayton and George Lorillard fomented aboard the *Vesta* in 1866.

All the while the schooner butted into persistent head seas and unfavourable winds. On the third day out she ran right on the nose into a full-blown gale. The schooner pounded gamely into the great rollers with great slamming thuds: the kind that dislodge fillings, rattle the very ribs of a yacht and jangle nerves. It was at this point that tragedy struck: two men, Charles Scot and Albert Demar, were sent out to the end of her jibboom to furl her flying jib. The pair scrambled out to the very end of this ponderous great spar, which protruded a good 20 feet over the bow of the *Dauntless*, which was performing the most dizzying seesaw ride at the time. Just as they began to grapple with the immense jib, the schooner curtsied extra graciously to one of the mighty seas rolling toward her and almost playfully buried her bow into the great green swell. When she recovered from her dousing, shook herself free and plunged onward, the two men on her jibboom were gone. Several hours' search revealed nothing and the doomed pair were left behind in the *Dauntless*'s frothy wake.

Despite the acrimony and dreadful misfortune, American pride was at stake, and you can bet that Samuels pushed the schooner as hard as he possibly could. On 27 July, Sandy Hook and home were close at hand. With the honour of American yachting at stake, the eyes of the media were closely focused on the result, many going so far as to spend the day aboard the Sandy Hook lightship awaiting the arrival of the first yacht. As the sultry day wore on, the afternoon heat made the ocean shimmer and dance with glancing sunbeams and distorted heat. Myriad phantom yachts seemed to flicker across the horizon, only to vanish before the gaze of the reporters. Around 3pm, however, the clear, hard outline of a racing schooner materialized. Let *New York Times* narrate the denouement:

> The speck rapidly approached and assumed plainer proportions until it was discovered to be the sails and spars of a schooner. Nothing was visible of her hull, which seemed to be part of the sea upon which it floated. Exactly 41 minutes elapsed before she passed the lightship seven miles outside of Sandy Hook. The wind was blowing off her port quarter and she scudded along under full sail. The flags which she carried at ensign, together with her private pennant contained the letter 'C' in the centre. She was at once pronounced to be the Cambria. A sigh of disappointment swept over America.

The *Dauntless* wasn't far behind, arriving a shade under two hours later. It was a massive disappointment but revenge was thoroughly exacted during the actual America's Cup race in September when *Cambria* finished tenth out of a fleet of 17. Franklin Osgood's *Magic* won the cup and Bennett's *Dauntless* placed fifth just behind the *America*, winner of the 1851 race and now restored after her adventures as a Confederate raider. Ashbury proved to be an ungracious loser and eventually fell out with Bennett and the New York Yacht Club.

Fortunately Anglo-American relations were not in quite such a parlous state as they had been in 1866. In fact, Britain was poised to sign the *Alabama* settlement: a payout of $15m and a covert admission of both guilt and contrition for its collusion in the *Alabama* affair. The special relationship between the two countries was cemented. In the meantime Bennett returned to the *Herald* and the Jeromes to Wall Street, reasonably content. Perhaps 'content' is the wrong word in the case of the Jerome brothers. Both had weathered their share of financial storms, but the one that was rumbling away on the horizon would pretty much finish them off.

The trouble began, as it so often does, in France and Germany (or Prussia as it was back then). In 1870, lending rules in these countries were relaxed to the extent that it was much easier for people to get mortgages. A building boom resulted, with the associated economic benefits. Living was easy and credit even easier. Life seemed rosy. The problem was that economic confidence hadn't taken into account the huge explosion in productivity of the US. With its new railroads and improved farming and manufacturing techniques, America was the China of the era, undercutting and often destroying European competitors, particularly on grain exports. Boom in central Europe rapidly turned to bust and by mid-1873, Europe was already mired in a serious recession.

It was at this point that America – another country bloated with cheap credit, in this case fuelled by the railroad boom – started to feel the pinch. It all began with the fall of the banking house of Jay Cooke following a tussle with burgeoning banking titan JP Morgan. You may remember that Cooke was the genius who had bankrolled the Civil War with his issue of bonds. In addition to being one of the richest men in America, he was an intensely serious, religious man who referred to himself in his role as banker as 'God's chosen instrument'. If that was the case, the instrument was about to go badly out of tune. In 1873 Jay Cooke and Company remained one of the largest banks in the US; their only serious rival being JP Morgan. Cooke had diversified by investing heavily in the New Northern Pacific Railway. This was to be the second transcontinental railway, cutting another great swathe across the plains and connecting the Great Lakes in the east with Puget Sound in the west.

The problem was that confidence in the value of railroad bonds was starting to flag in a market saturated with stock. A staggering 30,000 miles of track had been laid in the US in the five years between 1868 and 1873, much of it funded by government lending and those greenbacks that were still sloshing around. A lot of bonds out there were underwritten by money that did not exist. If enough people called in their debts at the same time, the whole house would come crashing down. The Credit Mobilier scandal had certainly not helped the buoyancy of the stock market and excitement and over-speculation in the railroads turned to apathy and stagnation. Cornelius Vanderbilt noted, 'I am a friend of the iron road, but building railroads from nowhere to nowhere at public expense is not a legitimate undertaking.'

In the face of waning enthusiasm in his new stocks in America, Cooke had relied heavily on stock sold overseas, particularly in Prussia, to finance the operation. One town on the northern Pacific route in North Dakota was even named Bismarck in order to drum up Teutonic interests. In 1873 he needed his stocks to sell more than ever before. In the past Cooke's banking house had enjoyed sole selling rights over treasury-issued bonds, but by 1873, the banking firm of JP Morgan was powerful enough to demand a 50 per cent share in the latest $600m sell-off of government bonds. The agreement was that the two banks would share the commission on bonds sold, which would amount to $150m once the sell-off was concluded – and, by God, Cooke needed it to go well, for he was in dire financial straits.

Unfortunately, while his own brokers were selling his half of the bonds relatively quickly, mostly to the European market, JP Morgan's brokers were specifically told to hold back and sell slowly. There is a fair argument that he did it deliberately to destroy his main rival – we will never know for sure, although he did have the temerity to call his yacht *Corsair*, which gives a decent insight into the psychology of the individual. What we do know for sure is that Cooke was under immense pressure, and when Prussia's financial house came crashing down in summer 1873, money became incredibly tight.

That transatlantic telegraph, so handy for so many years, was now a huge problem, for the markets of Europe and America were too closely attached for comfort. Previously Cooke would have had a buffer zone of some weeks. Now a debt could be called in within minutes. Jay Gould's shenanigans during 1869 had also created a situation where gold remained in short supply, meaning that there was very little to underwrite the bad debts of the millions of greenbacks issued since the Civil War. Thus, when Europe called in its debts, Cooke soon found he had no 'real' money to pay them with. In September 1873 Jay Cooke and Co closed its doors for the last time. The result was catastrophe. It made the collapse of Lehman Brothers in 2008 look like a picnic. Banking houses collapsed like dominoes. The *Nation* described the scene with great eloquence:

> *Anyone who stood on Wall Street and saw the mad terror, we might almost say the brute terror with which great crowds of men rushed to and fro trying to get rid of their property, almost begging people to take it from them at any price could hardly avoid the feeling that a new plague had been sent among men, that there was an impalpable, invisible force in the air, robbing them of their wits, of which philosophy had not yet dreamt.*

If the likes of Jay Gould and Cornelius Vanderbilt playing games with the stock exchange were able to wipe out livelihoods on a whim, Cooke and Morgan held the power to paralyse a country and send shockwaves across the world. The result was that Wall Street stock exchange was closed for ten days straight. Many financiers were ruined – George Osgood of *Fleetwing* fame was one of hundreds. He even suffered the indignity of being booted out of his beloved Union Club for being bankrupt. Infuriated financiers and depositors alike thronged the banks demanding their assets. Men raged and frothed at the mouth in fury, tearing at the foundations of the institutions that had betrayed them. Not for the first or the last time, an assumption had been made that bankers knew what they were doing, and when it came to the crunch, they had been found wanting.

What followed was 65 months of recession – still the longest sustained period of financial contraction in the economic history of the United States. Another factor that made the crisis even worse was that the new telegraph and railway network meant that the ripples of a run on

Wall Street were felt with horrible rapidity thousands of miles from the epicentre. Many pioneers out west suffered more rapidly and more severely than they previously would have done. Europe also suffered dreadfully.

For working people, the ramifications were awful. Unemployment in New York alone rose to 25 per cent as small businesses fell by the wayside with sickening regularity. Many Americans were forced on to the road; it was this era that coined the terms 'tramp' and 'bum'. Up until 1929, this period, which extended right through to the end of the 1870s, was known as the 'Great Depression'.

The big fish of American industry at the time, the Goulds, Vanderbilts and Carnegies, generally profited from this depression. These were men who had their own very substantial financial reserves and were able to ride out the initial storm. Having done this, they were also able to buy up at fire-sale prices smaller businesses who relied on credit. JP Morgan, having destroyed Cooke, was the biggest winner of all. Inequality grew and the rise of the big corporations continued with merciless inevitability.

Wall Street men like the Jerome brothers were also wounded by the depression. Of course, the shrewd speculators still had their assets, but there was far less potential to make easy money in these lean years. As the swashbuckling Jeromes stepped off the *Dauntless* after that chastening defeat at the hands of the *Cambria*, one wonders if the pair had an inkling of what was coming. They had always been happy-go-lucky and the concept of 'live by the sword, die by the sword' was probably a fair summary of their attitude to life. So it was to be for Leonard Jerome; he battled on in Wall Street until the panic hit, but then he got truly walloped, with most of his stocks wiped out in a matter of hours.

He received the news while hosting a dinner party and took it with his usual *sangfroid*, simply announcing: 'Gentlemen, I am a ruined man, but please continue eating and enjoying yourselves. Dinner is paid for.'

That was pretty much the end of Jerome on Wall Street. He retreated into family life and finally began to appreciate his wife and daughters. As with so many 'ruined' men from the financial elite, Jerome still had adequate means to live extremely comfortably. He opted to turn his back on America for the foreseeable future and set the family up in Cowes. This hub of yachting was a familiar spot for him with good memories. It seemed like a fairly safe haven from his financial storms. Yet no sooner had he escaped the financial turmoil of New York than another catastrophe came rumbling into view. It soon transpired that Jennie, his beautiful first daughter, was in love with a fish-faced bounder of an English aristocrat going by the name of Lord Randolph Churchill.

Jennie was 19 in 1873 and in full bloom. Many belles of the Victorian era do not fit into the modern-day template of beauty. Jennie was different. One glance at a photograph of this dark-eyed, curvaceous, vivacious young lady and you can see her physical appeal. The same cannot be said of Randolph, the third son of the Duke of Marlborough. Although a meteoric and sometimes brilliant man, Randolph bore a strong resemblance to a fish crossed with a stuffed frog. He was 24 in 1873 and had graduated from Oxford with a second-class degree in 1871. Since then he had been dripping around the great draughty halls of the magnificent family pile of Blenheim Palace making a nuisance of himself and making his perennially cash-strapped father wonder what the devil to do with him.

Everyone at Blenheim doubtless breathed a sigh of relief when, in 1873, he headed off to Cowes for the summer season. He met Jennie at a ball held aboard the HMS *Ariadne* in honour of the future Tsar of Russia. One glance at Jennie, hands glistening cold with jewels, all dark hair, carmine lips and high, lovely colour, and Randolph's heart lurched. Before he knew it, he was spinning and tumbling in the glorious turmoil of infatuation. He sought an introduction to this mysterious belle and the sparks immediately flew. It was August and through the cool of the late summer evening, fiery passions were stoked as the pair flirted mercilessly with each other. Randolph was no dancer, so the pair retreated into the pools of darkness of that velvet night, gazed at the stars, talked of this and that, and fell wildly in love. By the end of the evening Randolph assured one of his chums that he would marry 'the dark one'. As the two parted, the dewy night air sodden with desire, they agreed to meet the following night. Shortly after Randolph's arrival at the Jerome residence that following evening, he and Jennie opted to take a turn around the garden. When they returned they announced to an astonished Leonard and Clara that they were engaged.

The Jeromes were slightly nonplussed and didn't know what to make of this, but Randolph's father, the Duke of Marlborough, was disgusted, the more so when he did his homework on Leonard Jerome, whom he dismissed in a letter to his headstrong son as follows: 'This Mr J seems to be a sporting and I should think vulgar kind of man. I hear he rides six and eight horses in New York and one may take this as an indication of what kind of a man he is.' Given that this was the dim view he took on Jerome, it is unsurprising that he did his utmost to discourage the match. As is so often the case, however, love thwarted only made passions burn even more fiercely. Leonard Jerome knew all about passion, thwarted and otherwise, and he had plenty of sympathy for his daughter, writing to her: 'I always thought if you ever did fall in love it would be a dangerous affair.

You were never born to love lightly.' Ultimately, both sets of parents saw that this love was not something that could be crushed.

Negotiations began between the two families, and now Jerome and Marlborough almost came to blows over money. Marlborough needed lots of it to keep his enormous property from becoming dilapidated. The perception was that Jerome had wads of the stuff, which he did not. Jerome also wanted to settle a large portion of the cash he did have on Jennie herself – this was the norm in America, but not in England – and Marlborough was infuriated. The result was a protracted wrangle over the dowry that nearly saw the marriage scrapped altogether. At this point Bertie – Prince Albert to you and me – stepped in. He had met the star-crossed lovers in Cowes and had been most taken with Jennie. He was more than happy to vouch for Jennie's many striking assets to her prospective father-in-law. Yet perhaps the thing that really swung the deal was the fact that, in all likelihood, Jennie was already pregnant with the couple's first child, Winston. The pair were duly married in April 1874 and their son, Winston Churchill, was born that November.

The marriage was moderately successful, particularly given that many believe Randolph suffered from syphilis. Others have argued that it was a rare form of brain tumour – which might explain why Jennie was never affected. Whatever it was, it didn't hold back Randolph's brilliant political career and he went on to become Chancellor of the Exchequer and Leader of the House of Commons, but he died prematurely in 1895. Jennie consoled herself by embarking on an extraordinarily pioneering bout of sexual tourism, racking up scores of lovers. Among them was almost certainly good old Bertie, Prince of Wales, who had always held a candle to Lady Randy. Now she was back on the open market, the pair indulged in a vigorous relationship that seems to have been almost entirely physical, although there was clearly a frisson of affection. Jennie coined the nickname 'Tum-tum' for the increasingly porky prince.

Jennie married twice more – both times to men 20 years her junior. By the time of her third marriage in 1918 to Montagu Phippen-Porch she was 67, but her nephew, Sunny, maintained there was ample evidence that, despite the age gap, this final marriage was a lively and physically gratifying union.

Anyway, that was all in the future and, perhaps thankfully for Leonard's sanity, he would not be around to witness much of it, although doubtless he would have understood. She was, after all, very much her father's daughter. The upshot of Jennie laying down roots in England was that she also set a pattern for the Jerome family, and that was a slow emigration to Europe. Jennie was one of the first of a group of wealthy American heiresses, characterized as 'the buccaneers', who courted the English nobility in search of the respectability that the Astor 400 and social mores in America had locked them out of. In England they had a clean slate. The British structure of nobility was so entrenched that no one really felt any need to be defensive about arrivistes; they would never truly belong, but they were, if nothing else, an amusing diversion.

This band of beautiful, young American heiresses found their interest heartily reciprocated by a British nobility fretting over how to pay for the upkeep of their crumbling mansions. Jennie Jerome's match was clearly one of love, but later ones were sometimes more cynical, cold affairs, with money the only real consideration. Lord Randolph Churchill's brother George's match to Lilian 'Rhymes with a Million' Hammersley was a classic example of some serious gold-digging.

George was the oldest son and therefore responsible for the upkeep of the magnificent but crumbling Blenheim Palace. On inheriting the family pile in 1883, George realized that unless something was done, the whole place was going to fall down around his ears. Initially he set about making up the shortfall on the property by selling off the odd Rembrandt or Rubens, but by 1888 George had decided to take drastic measures. He turned to his sister-in-law's father, Leonard Jerome, for a spot of advice. Leonard wasted no time in setting George up with Lilian. 'I hope it comes off,' Leonard wrote to his wife, 'she certainly has a lot of tin.' The good news was that Lilian, a forty-something divorcee hailing from New York, was rather keen on entering into the British nobility. She was getting on a bit in years and, as Lord Randolph once observed, had a real problem with facial hair, but George was happy to ignore all that and one of the most cynical matches ever conceived was sealed in a New York registry office in 1883.

For Leonard Jerome, the consequence of this rise of the 'buccaneer' heiresses was that all three of his girls ended up married into the British nobility, with the result that he was obliged to commute between New York, in order to drum up some cash from the flagging stock exchange, London, and Paris, where Clara had settled happily. For Clara, too, it was a relief to be free from the stifling snobbery of New York society.

They were soon joined by another pair of exiles. Lawrence Jerome also chose Paris as his preferred haven from the financial tsunami that was enveloping New York, and in 1877 there was another new arrival – James Gordon Bennett, fresh from his spectacular mistake of using a fire as a urinal. Bennett was soon happily ensconced in self-imposed exile with his two chums. Paris, after all, had been his childhood home and was much more indulgent of his general weirdness than New York.

Unlike the Jeromes, the years between 1870 and his exile to Paris had been golden for Bennett. This period was when he focused most intensely on raising the *Herald* to even greater heights – with considerable success. Bennett wasn't going to go down his father's route of taking pot shots at the elite and generally getting up everyone's noses. He adopted a new strategy: to open up the horizons of the *Herald*. Bennett exploited the transatlantic telegraph to bring European news to the American people. Foreign correspondents were hired and thousands were spent on cabling back and forth across the Atlantic. The *Herald* was one of the first newspapers with a bona fide foreign news section, while expensive, globally significant stunts such as sending Stanley off to find Livingstone sent the newspaper's profile into the stratosphere. Not that Bennett was terribly thrilled with just how successful that trip he had lined up for Stanley had become. Instead he became wildly jealous of his Africa correspondent. When Stanley returned from Africa, lauded by one and all as a hero, the only message his employer sent him was a snappy and slightly menacing:

STOP TALKING. BENNETT.

Bennett was incensed by the lack of credit he was given for the whole expedition. "'Who was Stanley before I found him?" Bennett would rant: "Who thought of looking for Livingstone? Who paid the bills?"'

In the 1870s, Jay Gould continued with his policy of essentially taking whatever he wanted to and laying it all to waste. One of his acquisitions during this period was the Western Union telegraph company. Control of this meant control of the transatlantic telegraph and Gould duly jacked up the rates to exorbitant levels. This outraged Bennett, to whom it was paramount that rates were reasonable. This became even more important once he moved permanently to Paris in 1877.

After many years of tolerating Gould's extortionate rates, Bennett decided something must be done. He allied himself with multimillionaire John McKay, himself an expatriate American, and the pair set about destroying Gould's stranglehold on the market by laying their own cable across the Atlantic in 1884. Gould was furious and engaged in a cut-throat price war that saw the rates for transatlantic communications slashed by over half. At the same time Gould sought to cripple the new cable's viability by shutting down the overland part of the telegraph from Newfoundland to New York through a bamboozling set of injunctions bribed out of crooked officials. Even worse, Gould was backed up in his shenanigans by Cyrus Field, the originator of the 1866 cable, and also none other than Fred May, that hulking horsewhip-happy bully boy Bennett remained understandably terrified of. (His sometime lover, Camille Clermont, relates how in one of her trysts with Bennett, she was bewildered to find on undressing him that he seemed to be wearing some kind of chainmail undershirt. Bennett reluctantly explained that this was because he had heard a rumour that Fred May was in town.)

Bennett was rattled by the tycoon's chicanery, but remained outwardly cool, retaliating by exposing one of Gould's many crooked schemes in the *Herald*. Gould was a cold, calculating customer but Bennett managed to strike a nerve so deeply that Gould went off the rails. The tycoon, who controlled both the *New York Tribune* and *New York World*, in addition to the *Evening Mail* and *Express*, used these publications to publish an open letter which sought to expose Bennett for what, of course, he was: a wild eyed, morally bankrupt playboy. Highlights included:

Let me see. I have known you over 30 years, and during all that time your life has been one of shame. Your private life has been a succession of debauches and scandals, so that your name is associated: on every tongue is Bennett the libertine, and however gentlemen might greet you at clubs and hotels, not a gentlemen at New York, as you well know, would allow you to cross the threshold of his residence where virtue and family honor are held sacred. Your very touch in the social circle is contaminating.

Unfortunately for Gould, the world of newspapers was as small back then as it is now. Bennett got wind of this letter's publication and, even better, managed to get hold of a copy. He calmly directed his editorial staff to run it in his own paper with a selection of gleeful subheadings, which ran as follows:

> The Corsair Raves – The Pirate, Maddened with Malice, Adopts the Weapons of Coarse Vituperation – A Brutal Open Letter – The Red handed Buccaneer Himself Signs an Infamous Personal Onslaught on the *Herald*'s Proprietor – Honored by his Abuse – He, not his Enemy, must finally Walk the Plank – Attack of a Sneak and a Coward – While addressed to the Editor of the *Herald*, the letter is refused us for Publication – But we secure it and Print it in Full to Show What Kind of an Animal Gould is – Isn't He a skunk?

Bennett's only personal retaliation came at the bottom of the letter when he wrote simply:

The proprietor of the Herald *lost his reputation long before Mr Gould was even heard of.*

It was a triumph for Bennett. Gould was already widely hated and now he had made a fool of himself. Shortly afterwards, he was compelled to back down over the transatlantic cable and accept there was room for his rival. Not long after that, Gould double-crossed Cyrus Field over the Western Union and Field was ruined, never to fully recover. Bennett's victory was one of the only times Gould was outwitted or outmanoeuvred by anyone, and one of the few times the media ever took on the muscle of one of the great robber barons.

It was something of a pyrrhic victory, for while Bennett put his resources and his focus into destroying Jay Gould, he took his eye off what was going on in the world of newspapers. When he finally looked up, he discovered that the *New York World*, edited by Joseph Pulitzer, was cutting the kind of dash in journalistic circles not seen since his father had turned up in New York with the *Herald* and rattled everyone's cages. Prior to 1883, the *World* had been owned by Jay Gould and used by him as another unpleasant tool to manipulate markets – and issue bizarre personal attacks on his enemies. Unsurprisingly, given the character of its proprietor and the nature of the content he demanded, the *World* wasn't massively popular and Gould eventually sold it on to Pulitzer. Suddenly the newspaper found its voice.

Unlike Bennett, Pulitzer had absolutely no regard for the establishment. Hungarian born, he had come to America to fight as a substitute for some wealthy citizen during the Civil War. After the war he worked in a number of menial jobs. As his English improved, he was able to establish himself as a journalist and later an editor of rare skill and vision. By the time he took over the *World* in 1883, he was a battle-hardened campaigner and embarked on a circulation war with rivals that made use of in-depth investigative journalism and a fair amount of sensationalist or what came to be labelled 'yellow' journalism. Yet his secret weapon was a natural empathy with the man on the street, including newly arrived immigrants. Back when James Gordon Bennett Sr had set up the *Herald* in the 1830s, his paper had been just like the *World*: stuck firmly on the outside of society looking in. It had openly mocked the aristocracy and lampooned establishment figures mercilessly. This had made the paper hugely popular with the general public. Bennett the younger *was* an integral part of the very group of society his outcast father had mocked so vociferously. Even after his excommunication to Paris, Bennett continued to treat the establishment figures perhaps with more respect than they deserved. As Pulitzer himself observed:

> *They* [the newspapers] *cannot help it. It is only human nature. Man*
> *is greatly controlled by his environment ... there is one* [newspaper]
> *not controlled or in any way swayed by capital ... that is the*
> New York World.

Bennett, with his haughty airs and vast wealth could never hope to compete. By the late 1880s, his *Herald* had been knocked off its perch. Bennett retreated to Paris and his yachts and sporting fads. He was a pioneer of motor racing in Europe and even set up a hot-air-balloon race. His yacht-racing days were over, however, and he switched to steam yachts, first purchasing the *Namouna*, nicknamed *Pneumonia* by members of staff at the *Herald*, who feared above all else the sight of this vessel steaming over the horizon into New York Harbor for one of Bennett's little visits to the newspaper, which generally meant a fresh round of sackings. After the *Namouna*, Bennett went one bigger and better with the *Lysistrata*, launched in 1901. This monster vessel came in at 95.7 metres, a three-decked giant boasting an average speed of 19½ knots. She had a crew of 100, and featured Turkish baths, steam rooms, theatres, and a specially padded stall for an Alderney cow to ensure an adequate supply of fresh milk at sea. Not that Bennett was especially fond of milk, but freshly churned butter was a must, plus he needed a drop of the stuff to go in the brandy milk punch that he enjoyed over breakfast. In the tropics an electric fan wafted cooling air over this pampered bovine, while in cooler climes it was clad in the finest woollens. A number of *Herald* correspondents related tales of being handed an urgent assignment to find an Alderney cow and bring it immediately to some outpost on the *Lysistrata's* cruising itinerary, suggesting the poor beasts never fared too well on the boat.

As owner of the *Lysistrata*, Bennett was a terror, dictating that none aboard but himself could sport facial hair and outlawing card games of any kind. He also frequently 'kidnapped' visitors, who had expected to leave after a night aboard only to find that the *Lysistrata* was already steaming onward to some far-flung destination. The *Lysistrata*, a horrible great lump of metal, was perhaps the first true super-yacht, and it pointed the way toward the huge deformed pieces of plastic, steel and aluminium that we gawp at in wonder today.

Yes, Bennett had travelled a long and bizarre road since those early days aboard the *Henrietta* with Samuels ruling the roost. A sign of how far Bennett had come from his father's humble working-class roots can be seen in 1890 when, on a brief visit to New York, he observed the new *New York World* headquarters being erected. It was one of the first skyscrapers to puncture the New York skyline and, as Bennett gazed at it with a mixture of horror and disgust, he was heard to mutter: 'Poor parvenu, poor pitiful self deluded parvenu.'

His own contribution to the New York landscape was the somewhat more refined *Herald* building in what is now fittingly known as Herald Square. Completed in 1895 and designed by Stanford White, the structure bore a startling resemblance to the 1476 Venetian Renaissance Palazzo del Consiglio in Verona. It was a gorgeous anomaly, but it did not last long. In 1921, three years after the death of its creator, this great shrine to his own decadence was demolished, replaced by an ugly, drab skyscraper, one of the wonders of its age, no doubt, and described at the time of the *Herald* building's demolition as 'a structure of great income producing capacity'. The only remnant of Bennett is a pair of bronze owls and a sculpture of Minerva that make up a monument in Herald Square. The owls were part of a flock of 22 that adorned his magnificent Herald building. They were one of Bennett's many bizarre ideas, for his original specification was that their eyes must glow green on the hour with the ringing of the clock bell. The building and Bennett are both gone, but the owls still stare down on New York from their lofty perch, their eerie green gaze a fitting epitaph to one of the city's weirdest sons.

As for the *Herald*, that pretty much died with its owner, who remained in exile in France for the rest of his life. He passed away peacefully in 1918 at the age of 77. In latter years, Bennett had lost interest in the paper and, by treating it as his own personal cash cow, left it in a state of penury. He had remained true to his word; the *Herald* genuinely was his own personal plaything. Shortly after his death it amalgamated with the *New York Tribune*, the paper that, years before under the editorship of Horace Greeley, had launched such a savage 'moral war' on Bennett Sr's upstart paper. Both great editors must still be spinning uncontrollably in their graves.

Bennett was far from a perfect human being. Mentally, if not physically, he seems to have been seriously flawed. Yet there was something there to gaze at in wonder. He had flair, if nothing else, and he wasn't ashamed to do things on a grand scale. He also had few illusions about what he was or what his legacy would be. Perhaps it is kindest to head back to New York in 1895 and wander along the wide open pavements of Herald Square. There he is, Bennett himself, standing with his publisher, Blumenfeld, inspecting his own great monument to the gilded age as the crowds swirl by. The media mogul is squinting at the building: 'It looks a little "squattier" than I thought it would. It could have had one more storey,' he comments to Blumenfeld, who responds timidly that perhaps it was unwise to sign only a 30-year-lease on the land where he has built this magnificent structure. 'Never mind, Blumenfeld,' he replies, clapping the man heartily on the back. 'Thirty years from now, the *Herald* will be in Harlem and I shall be in Hell.' And he turned on his heel and walked away.

Let's leave him there, strolling nonchalantly through the streets of a city his father defeated and he himself conquered in his own way. There he goes: one of God's own prototypes. A freak of nature had conspired to create a lethal cocktail of egomania, affluence and improvidence. For all his weirdness, his philandering, his wanton wastefulness, you can never deny that Bennett had a certain style. He and the Jerome brothers were pioneers of a new era of leisure, a wistful age when adventure became a commodity that had to be artificially manufactured for the idle.

Our three heroes, Bennett and the Jerome brothers, were patron saints of profligacy and idle pursuits, but they went about their business with panache. Men like Cornelius Vanderbilt and Jay Gould may have helped to usher in the ceaseless greed and gaping inequality of the gilded age, but it was down to a different calibre of man to make this putrid era actually glitter. Bennett and his cohorts had stepped up to the challenge. It was they who turned being rich into an art form. With the 1866 race they had laid down their first marker in spectacular style.

11
THE FATE OF OUR HEROES

James Gordon Bennett Jr's final years have already been discussed, but there are a few loose ends to tie up. Incredibly, he did eventually marry, though not until he was 73. Maude Potter was the lucky lady. His end was predictably odd. He became obsessed that he would die in his seventy-seventh year. His father had died of a stroke at that age and Bennett was convinced he would go the same way. A bout of pneumonia in 1917 did little to dispel this theory. He headed to a Cote d'Azur holiday home in Beaulieu-sur-Mer to recuperate, but made the error of seeing a clairvoyant who told him that his two Pekingese dogs would die and their deaths would be followed by a member of the Bennett household. The tycoon needed no further convincing. Shortly afterwards, the two dogs obligingly passed on and Bennett sat in his villa patiently awaiting the end. It begun on 10 May 1918. His 77th birthday.

The *New York Times* summed him up nicely in their obituary:

He had his own way through a long life, but he was not an idler. What Editor worked harder? He played hard, he worked hard. He got out of life what he wanted. A vivid figure such as a novelist could not invent, and yet that seems too fanciful for actuality. He was a sort of Fairy Prince to the last.

Samuel Samuels died in 1908 at the grand old age of 85. He was far from discouraged by the chastening defeat of 1871 and in 1887 he was reunited with the *Dauntless* and wheeled out for one more battle with the Atlantic. On this occasion, the old *Dauntless*, now owned by Caldwell Colt, inventor of the Colt revolver, was pitted against the thoroughly modern schooner *Coronet*. The stakes were a more modest $10,000.

Captain Samuels was 64 by this time, but proceeded to drive the *Dauntless* mercilessly, racking up some astonishing day's runs, including a record 328-mile run in 24 hours, a yachting record that stood until 1905. In the meantime, the old vessel, badly strained by decades of racing, leaked mercilessly. Samuels maintained after the race that a small hole had been deliberately bored in her planking below the waterline. Whether this is true or not, *Dauntless* was defeated by her newer, quicker rival and Samuels' racing days finally came to an end.

His death in 1908 was greeted with a genuine outpouring of grief for the passing of one of the most colourful characters of an heroic, swashbuckling era, an era long gone by the time of his death. As the *California Courier* wrote in their eulogy to him: 'He was a man once met not soon to be forgotten. It was his total lack of fear, indefatigable attention to detail and his great executive ability which gave him his success.'

Leonard Jerome never fully recovered the fortune he lost in 1873 and, although his family lived comfortably in Europe until his death in 1891, he was forever trundling to and fro between the new and old worlds trying to rustle up funds. He died in Brighton at the age of 73 in a state of relative penury. His last words to his daughter Jennie were: 'I've given you all I have. Pass it on', and he wasn't talking about money, because all of that was gone. Three years after his death, his magnificent racetrack, Jerome Park, was demolished and replaced by a municipal reservoir.

Larry Jerome passed away in Paris in 1888. Right up to the last, he did his best to keep up with the high jinks of his much younger pal, Bennett, and this may well have contributed to the stroke that eventually did for him.

In Paris, Bennett and Larry had perfected their hedonistic double act and the fun was only curtailed slightly by Jerome's strict wife, Carrie, who had no time for their childish shenanigans. On one occasion, Bennett managed to get around this by sending Larry a telegram late one night stating that he had been involved in a serious coaching accident and was at death's door.

Jerome hurried to the exclusive private hospital where Bennett was being treated and apparently did not have long to live. The grief-struck friend was ushered up to the sick man's quarters, where Bennett lay, wrapped in bandages and apparently in a coma. 'Speak to me, Jimmy boy,' Jerome muttered as he leant down to his stricken friend. 'You're damn right I'll speak to you, you long-faced old bastard,' Bennett yelled, hurling off the sheets and tossing his bandages to one side. 'Bring on the medicine, girls!' Suddenly the hospital room exploded to life, awash with champagne. Jerome realized he was not in a hospital at all; Bennett had coerced him into a high-class brothel. Perhaps it is understandable that Lawrence succumbed early to a stroke.

Henrietta: Bennett's gallant *Henrietta* sailed back home to New York in 1867, but was soon to be replaced in Bennett's affections by the *Dauntless*. She was laid up and sold to the merchant RH Harrington, who placed the fleet little schooner in the fruit trade, where speed was imperative to get your cargo to market before it went off. She was wrecked off the coast of Honduras in 1872.

Fleetwing: Following the 1866 race, the *Fleetwing* was fitted out for leisure and wandered the oceans for 30 years or so, cruising the Mediterranean and the Atlantic. In 1890, she was sold to the American Baptist Home Missionary Society based in New York, who turned the old racer into a 'gospel ship' providing shelter and spiritual guidance to sailors.

A journalist from the *Brooklyn Daily Eagle* penned the following description of her in her final resting place:

> *To-day, lying at the long dock, the old* Fleetwing *extends a cordial welcome to the sailor men who happen to find themselves in the old graveyard as well as to the men who live on the palatial vessels moored in Manning's basin.*
>
> *It is a strange mixture of past and present over in the old 'graveyard'. It is a cemetery without tombstones and with only the bells of those boats still in service to toll the death knell of those that are fast falling into decay.*

Vesta: Pierre Lorillard sold the *Vesta* shortly after the 1866 race to one George W Weld, and he later sold her on to the New England Iron and Metal Co, who worked her as a general trader. She was later sold into the lumber trade and carried deck cargoes of timber between New York and Nova Scotia. She was lost around 1915.

George and Franklin Osgood: This pair of financiers still remain shadowy and uncertain. George went bust in the panic of 1873 after double-crossing his father-in-law, Cornelius Vanderbilt. Never a smart move. Nevertheless, by the time of his death in 1882, he still left his wife a sum of $600,000, so he wasn't quite ruined. Franklin Osgood had the distinction of owning the schooner *Magic*, which was the first successful defender of the America's Cup. I can find no record of his death.

Pierre Lorillard continued to build up the Lorillard tobacco empire that flourishes to this day. Following the 1866 race, he seems to have lost interest in yacht racing to some extent and focused more on the turf. In 1881 his horse Iroquois made history by becoming the first American-bred horse to win the Epsom Derby. He died in 1901 and the aftermath of his death was notable because of the rather messy division of his assets between his wife and mistress, which led to a long drawn-out court case.

George Lorillard was always a keener yachtsman than his brother and he continued to cruise and race avidly. In 1869 he undertook an extended cruise of the Mediterranean aboard his yacht *Meteor*. Catastrophe struck in December when she was wrecked off the coast of Tunisia and, after being rescued, Lorillard was captured and held to ransom by a group of local thugs. Only the payment of $15,000 secured his release. In later years he suffered terribly from rheumatism and he eventually passed away in Nice in 1886.

Jay Gould died comfortably in his bed in 1892. He left a fortune worth somewhere in the region of $600,000,000 and on his death was described by the press as 'a man without a friend'. Not quite true; among his pall bearers were a number of luminaries, including none other than JP Morgan. He has since been voted 'the worst CEO in the history of American business'. Again, this is probably unfair. He was simply the only tycoon who never pretended to be anything other than what he was: a lone wolf, scrupulously dishonest and concerned only with making money – generally out of other people's misfortunes.

After his death his heirs lived a good deal less parsimoniously than old Jay, though his progeny were still marked out as pariahs and they longed to be accepted. Anna Gould, his second daughter and a hard-faced, grasping human being if ever there was one, saw her chance of social acceptance when she met the flamboyant, exotic and splendidly noble Frenchman Boni de Castellane. Boni, the old rascal, saw past Anna's rather plain features to the massive dollar signs behind her eyes. It was a match made in heaven and the Frenchman set about finally putting Jay's ill-gotten gains to good use, managing to run through $10m of his fortune before Anna finally lost patience and divorced him.

William 'Boss' Tweed died in jail in 1878 aged 55. He had been arrested on charges of corruption and embezzlement in 1871 following the *New York Times*'s exposé of the practices of Tammany Hall. Jay Gould posted his $1m bail and he was actually re-elected to the Senate while he awaited his trial. In 1873, he was tried and found guilty on 204 of the 223 counts against him, sentenced to 12 years in jail and fined $12,000. He was released after a year, but New York State then filed a civic suit against him and he was again arrested. A $3m bail was placed on his head. Even Gould wasn't interested this time around. Despite briefly escaping jail and fleeing to Spain by disguising himself as a crew member aboard a freighter, Tweed was recaptured and died in jail.

Prince Albert, 'Bertie', waited patiently for the death of his mother, Queen Victoria, so that he could finally take hold of the reins of power. In the meantime, he seemed to find himself in the soup with almost monotonous regularity. Perhaps the most damning incident came following an alleged affair with the rather promiscuous Harriet Mordaunt in 1868, who was married to Sir Charles Mordaunt MP. Harriet appears to have been bored and in the absence of her husband indulged in a number of affairs. In 1869 she fell pregnant and rashly admitted to her husband that any of three men, including Albert, could be the father. Her family declared she must be insane and at the subsequent divorce hearing, Albert backed up this claim by denying he had ever done anything untoward with Harriet. She spent the rest of her life in an asylum.

In 1901, Queen Victoria finally passed away and Bertie was made king, although he enjoyed only ten years on the throne before he himself passed away. He was noted as an affable and supremely diplomatic monarch, but never got on with his nephew, Kaiser Wilhelm of Germany, and therefore did little to avert the crisis which would overwhelm Europe in 1914.

The Astors: The Astor family has played only a minor role in this tale, but they did set up the stultifying social framework of New York that eventually drove many of our heroes away. Ironically, the family also found itself drawn to England, the very country its own social rules had driven so many 'buccaneers' to in the first place. Waldorf Astor settled at the magnificent stately home of Cliveden in Berkshire. His wife, Nancy Astor, is notable for being the first female MP. She is also often attributed the following exchange with Leonard Jerome's grandson, Winston, in the House of Commons.

Nancy Astor: 'Winston, you are drunk.'

Winston Churchill: 'And you, madam, are ugly. But I shall be sober in the morning.'

Astor got her own back in a later exchange when confronted by Churchill's impolite question about what disguise he should wear so that nobody would recognize him at the Astors' 'stupid' masquerade ball. Nancy responded: 'Why don't you come sober, Prime Minister?'

ENDNOTES

Chapter 1

1 It is a time when one's spirit
   Twain, Mark, *The Gilded Age: a tale of today*, Harper and Brothers, 1915, p317

6 *trip anchors and start*
   New York Herald, 26 September 1866

10 The guns, incidentally
   Josephson, Matthew, *The Robber Barons*, p61

12 a 'carpenter' was paid
   Paine, Albert, *Thomas Nast, His Period and His Pictures*, p144

13 'What do I care
   Josephson, Matthew, *The Robber Barons*, p15

Chapter 2

15 There is no place like it
   Whitman, Walt, *The Brooklyn Eagle*, c1847

16 On that occasion, Bennett
   O'Connor, Richard, *The Scandalous Mr Bennett*, p86

19 On Bennett's death
   Farrell, Mike and Mary Cupito, *Newspapers: A Complete Guide to the Industry*, p29

19 *We do not, as*
   New York Herald, 5 October 1836

20 TO READERS OF THE HERALD
   Ibid., 11 July 1940

21 'New York Society consists
O'Connor, Richard, *The Scandalous Mr Bennett*, p27

21 'You cannot make him a gentleman
Turner, Hy, *When Giants Ruled: The Story of Park Row, New York's Great Newspaper Street*, p234

23 'tall, aristocratic in bearing
Beebe, Lucius, *The Big Spenders*, p127

23 'I eat and drink
Parton, James, *Famous Americans of Recent Times*, p127

25 'tolerably dull place
Hone, Philip, *The Diary of Philip Hone, 1828–51*, p229

27 THE GREAT YACHT RACE
Hudson Daily Star, 28 June 1858

30 *Some distance from Washington*
Carnegie, Andrew, *Gospel of Wealth*, p100

30 'No-one loves their country
Josephson, Matthew, *The Robber Barons*, p57

31 *It is only greenhorns*
Ibid., p50

32 *I found out the hollow*
Hudson, Frederic, *Journalism in the United States*, p431

33 'I begin to believe
Villard, Henry, *Memoirs*, p170

34 *I had seen Bennett*
Ibid., p163

36 *President Lincoln is a joke*
New York Herald, 19 February 1864

37 *As soon as you have*
Kern, Florence, *The United States Revenue Cutters in Civil War*, ch8, p6

39 *squint eyed bibulous youth*
    Ibid., ch8, p7

Chapter 3

43 He turns his head, but
    Binyon, Robert Laurence, 'John Winter', *Modern Poetry*, Dent and Sons,
    1920, p28

43 *I am altogether indifferent*
    Rayner, Dennis and Alan Wykes, *The Great Yacht Race*, p16

45 *Self advertisement is excellent*
    New York World, 17 November 1866

46 *This race we are undertaking*
    Rayner and Wykes, *The Great Yacht Race*, p73

47 'perhaps it is time
    London Daily News, 4 June 1858

48 *In this Atlantic race*
    New York Times, 29 November 1866

49 *By many, yachting is regarded*
    Knight, EF, an essay in *The Badminton Library of Sports and Pastimes*,
    Longmans, Green and Co 1894, p308

50 'Very well, skipper,
    Loomis, Alfred, *Ocean Racing*, p1

50 'It's quite normal
    Barrault, Jean-Michel, *Yachting in the Golden Age*, p113

51 *Lone Yachtsmen looked down*
    McMullen, Richard, *Down Channel*, p61

53 'My step mother and I
    Samuels, Samuel, *From the Forecastle to the Cabin*, p1

54 There is an anecdote
    Lubbock, Basil, *The Western Ocean Packets*, p3

55 'The noble American vessels
Dickens, Charles, *American Notes*, p81

55 'I am disappointed
Dickens, Charles, *The Letters of Charles Dickens: The Pilgrim Edition, Volume 3: 1842–1843*, p156

55 'She possessed the merit
Samuels, Samuel, *From the Forecastle to the Cabin*, p250

56 'taken an oath
Ibid., p268

62 *Nowadays there are no inducements*
Ibid., p2

63 *Some difficulty was experienced*
New York Herald, 12 December 1866

64 'There are classes of men
Melville, Herman, *Redburn, His First Voyage*, p85

66 *They were not intended*
Riis, Jacob, *How The Other Half Lives*, p8

69 'The packet sailors
Samuels, Samuel, *From the Forecastle to the Cabin*, p265

Chapter 4

71 Yes, I can understand that
Balzac, Honoré de, *The Wild Ass' Skin*, Gebbie Publishing co, 1897, p3

72 *I went into his office*
Rayner and Wykes, *The Great Yacht Race*, p86

73 *The instructions of the* Herald
Hudson, Frederic, *Journalism in the United States from 1690 to 1872*, p717

75 A Hearty Adieu
Rochester Daily Union, 12 December 1866

77 *This was not the occasion*
New York Herald, 12 December 1866

79 *I waited in my waxwork semblance*
    Rayner and Wykes, *The Great Yacht Race*, p26

80 *From this time to the start*
    New York Herald, 12 December 1866

80 'looking as if he wished
    Ibid.

81 'The rawest of days,'
    New York Herald, 1 April 1905

85 'Save for the moment
    Rayner and Wykes, *The Great Yacht Race*, p28

85 'They slide up and down
    Fiske, Stephen, for the magazine *The Smart Set*, July 1900

85 'So close you could
    New York Herald, 1 April 1905

86 *We had known before*
    New York Herald, 1 April 1905

89 *At dinner Captain Samuels*
    Fiske, Stephen, *The Smart Set*, July 1900

92 'Talk about racing,'
    New York Herald, 1 April 1905

92 *Captain Samuels jockeyed*
    Fiske, Stephen, *The Smart Set*, July 1900

94 *The crew, certainly*
    Rayner and Wykes, *The Great Yacht Race*, p28

94 *Dayton is not coming up*
    Ibid., p28

Chapter 5

97 There was talk of shortening sail
    Traditional sea shanty, 'The Ballad of John Paul Jones'

98 *I lit my pipe*
Rayner and Wykes, *The Great Yacht Race*, p51

99 *Our party consisted of*
Fiske, Stephen, *The Smart Set*, July 1900

102 'American men are driven
Morris, Lloyd, *Incredible New York: High Life and Low Life from 1850 to 1950*, p50

102 'a jungle where men
Leslie, Anita, *The Remarkable Mr Jerome*, p45

105 'attempting to satisfy
Ibid., p92

105 'One rode better
Ibid., p54

108 'You rob yourself
Twain, Mark, An open letter to Commodore Vanderbilt, *Packard's Monthly Magazine*, 1869

109 *Anyone who has been on board*
Rayner and Wykes, *The Great Yacht Race*, p51

110 *It is some qualification*
London Telegraph, 28 December 1866

112 'I cannot see the first line
Spirit of the Times, 11 June 1875

115 *The weather being warm*
Fiske, Stephen, *The Smart Set*, July 1900

117 *As night closed in*
Ibid.

120 Mystery of the Yacht *Wanderer*
New York Times, 17 December 1858

122 *New York City like*
Vicksburg Daily Whig, 18 January 1860

123 'An aristocracy based
   Josephson, Matthew, *The Robber Barons*, p80

124 *Recommended Captain Dayton*
   Rayner and Wykes, *The Great Yacht Race*, p105

Chapter 6

127 God moves in a mysterious way
   Cowper, William, 'God Moves in a Mysterious Way', *John Newton's Olney Hymns*, William Collins, 1829, p304

128 'Captain, officers and yachtsmen
   Fiske, Stephen, *The Smart Set*, July 1900

128 *For days the yacht*
   Ibid.

130 *Before leaving New York*
   Ibid.

130 *Bennett's devotion to the sea*
   O'Connor, Richard, *The Scandalous Mr Bennett*, p66

133 *With every stitch*
   New York Herald, 1 April 1905

133 'boarded us abreast of
   Rayner and Wykes, *The Great Yacht Race*, p105

134 'That's no loss,'
   Fiske, Stephen, *The Smart Set*, July 1900

134 *Larry Jerome had promised*
   Ibid.

135 *The groaning of timbers*
   Ibid.

135 'One would have thought
   Ibid.

136 *Captain Samuels was solemn*
   Ibid.

140 *I was below at the time*
Rayner and Wykes, *The Great Yacht Race*, p102

142 'nothing but luxury
Ibid., p122

143 'He ain't free no more
Ibid., p122

144 *The ship again started*
Fiske, Stephen, *The Smart Set*, July 1900

144 *No one had the heart*
Rayner and Wykes, *The Great Yacht Race*, p131

Chapter 7

147 He who makes a beast
Hill, George Birkbeck (ed), *Johnsonian Miscellanies*, Vol II, Harper, 1897, p333

148 *As in the middle*
Fiske, Stephen, *The Smart Set*, July 1900

153 *The effect of his potations*
O'Connor, Richard, *The Scandalous Mr Bennett*, p212

154 'Now, Sam,' he observed
Ibid., p213

156 *The summons came at Madrid*
Stanley, Henry, *The Autobiography of Henry Morton Stanley*, p237

158 'I want you fellows
O'Connor, Richard, *The Scandalous Mr Bennett*, P79

160 'My mind has been
Clermont, Camille, *Confessions of Gentle Rebecca*, p63

163 *After dinner he suddenly*
Ibid., p54

166 A STREET ENCOUNTER
New York Times, 3 January 1877

169 BENNETT AND MAY'S DUEL
     New York Sun, 8 January 1877

170 *His great wealth was*
     Clermont, Camille, *Confessions of Gentle Rebecca*, p88

171 *He might have been*
     Ibid., p88

173 *It could not be denied*
     Ibid., p89

174 On one occasion,
     O'Connor, Richard, *The Scandalous Mr Bennett*, p163

174 'Tell Meltzer to cut
     Seitz, Don, *The James Gordon Bennetts, Father and Son, Proprietors of the New York Herald*, p236

176 This ocean race was
     Fiske, Stephen, *Offhand Portraits of Prominent New Yorkers*, p34

Chapter 8

177 We are indeed drifting toward
     Weed, Thurlow, speaking in 1863, *Retrospections of an Active Life*, Vol I, by John Bigelow, 2013, p631

178 *Morning, steady breeze*
     Rayner and Wykes, The Great Yacht Race, p131

179 'Pierre Lorillard's played
     Ibid., p132

179 the glitter of
     Wharton, Edith, *The House of Mirth*, p49

181 'when they [Americans]
     Dickens, Charles, *American Notes*, p266

182 *Union means so many*
     Charles Dickens, writing as editor of the periodical *All the Year Round*, 1862

185 *At the time of which*
Samuels, Samuel, *From the Forecastle to the Cabin*, p258

186 *Bennett's favourite topic*
Clermont, Camille, *Confessions of Gentle Rebecca*, p56

190 *An embodiment in*
New York Independent, 21 October 1860

191 *From Newfoundland to Ireland*
Gordon, John, *A Thread Across the Ocean: The Heroic Story of the Transatlantic Cable*, p38

196 *We are eager to tunnel*
Thoreau, Henry, *Walden*, p35

Chapter 9

199 The first man gets the oyster
Carnegie, Andrew, *The Gospel of Wealth, and Other Timely Essays*, Century Co, 1901, p3

200 *The excitement in regard*
Fiske, Stephen, *The Smart Set*, July 1900

201 *This is the first head*
Rayner and Wykes, *The Great Yacht Race*, p145

202 *The genial Captain nearly*
Fiske, Stephen, *The Smart Set*, July 1900

203 *Some of the officers*
Rayner and Wykes, The Great Yacht Race, p151

206 'Like a well-jockeyed
Fiske, Stephen, *The Smart Set*, July 1900

207 *A Cowes pilot was*
Ibid.

208 *As soon as our colors*
Ibid.

210 *The first question we asked*
New York Herald, 21 March 1887, Extracts from *Vesta's* log

212 *It was Christmas Day*
Fiske, Stephen, *The Smart Set*, July 1900

213 *We would not say*
The Times, 26 December 1866

213 *The Yankees, who can*
The Review, 26 December 1866

217 *It is unfortunate that*
New York Times, 31 December 1866

218 *The sovereigns of Europe*
Stiles, TJ, *The First Tycoon*, p227

219 'The yachts of the English
Ibid., p227

220 *The extraordinary yet very*
The Times, 31 December 1866

221 *I did expect to be*
Ibid.

Chapter 10

223 An aristocracy based on nearly
Johnson, Andrew, speaking in 1866, from *The Reconstruction Years:
The Tragic Aftermath of the War Between the States*, by Walter Coffey,
2014, p31

223 This is an impressive crowd
Bush, George W, speaking at the Alfred Smith Memorial dinner, 2006

229 *Black Friday suddenly illuminated*
Stiles, TJ, *The First Tycoon*, p495

230 *Members of the President's*
Swanberg, WA, *Jim Fisk: The Career of an Improbable Rascal*, p221

233 'clap Bennett in irons'
Ibid.

234 *The speck rapidly approached*
New York Times, 29 July 1870

236 'I am a friend of
Sobel, Robert, *Panic on Wall Street*, p180

238 *Anyone who stood on*
Sobel, Robert, *Panic on Wall Street*, p184

241 'This Mr J seems to be
Sebba, Anne, *Jennie, Winston's American Mother*, p150

241 'I always thought if
Ibid., p150

245 '"Who was Stanley
O'Connor, Richard, *The Scandalous Mr Bennett*, p116

247 The Corsair Raves
New York Herald, 1 March 1888

249 *They* [the newspapers] *cannot help it*
Swanberg, WA, *Pulitzer*, p123

Chapter 11

255 *He had his own way*
New York Times, 15 May 1918

256 'He was a man once met
California Courier, 8 June 1908

256 'I've given you
Leslie, Anita, *The Remarkable Mr Jerome*, p7

257 'Speak to me, Jimmy boy,'
O'Connor, Richard, *The Scandalous Mr Bennett*, p151

258 *To-day, lying at the long*
Brooklyn Daily Eagle, 24 September 1905

BIBLIOGRAPHY

Ashbury, Herbert, *Sucker's Progress: An Informal History of Gambling in America*, Thundermouth Press, 2004

Barrault, Jean-Michel, *Yachting: The Golden Age*, Hachette, 2004

Beebe, Lucius, *The Big Spenders*, Axios Press, 2009

Calonius, Erik, *The Wanderer: The Last American Slave Ship and the Conspiracy That Set Its Sails*, St. Martin's Griffin, 2008

Carnegie, Andrew, *The Gospel of Wealth*, Century, 1901

Clermont, Camille, *Confessions of Gentle Rebecca: A Life Story*, Dranes, 1922

Cookman, Scott, *Atlantic: The Last Great Race of Princes*, Wiley, 2002

Dickens, Charles, *American Notes*, Penguin Classics, 2001

Dickens, Charles, *The Letters of Charles Dickens: The Pilgrim Edition, Volume 3: 1842–1843*, Oxford University Press, 1974

Farrell, Mike and Mary Cupito, *Newspapers: A Complete Guide to the Industry*, Peter Lang Publishing, 2010

Fiske, Stephen, *The Smart Set*, journal, July 1900 (accessed via pdf: http://www.unz.org/Pub/SmartSet-1900Jul)

Fiske, Stephen, *Holiday Stories*, General Books, 2012

Fiske, Stephen, *Offhand Portraits of Prominent New Yorkers*, Cornell University Library, 2010

Gordon, John, *A Thread Across The Ocean: The Heroic Story of the Transatlantic Cable*, Harper Perennial, 2003

Grandison, Henry, *The America Cup: Its Origin and History*, Century, 1914

Greenhalgh Albion, Robert, *Square-Riggers on Schedule; The New York Sailing Packets to England, France, and the Cotton Ports*, Archon Books, 1965

Harper, Robert, *Lincoln and the Press*, McGraw-Hill Book Company, Inc., 1951

Herd, Harold, *Seven Editors*, Allen & Unwin, 1955

Hone, Philip, *The Diary of Philip Hone, 1828–51*, Cornell University Library, 1889

Hudson, Frederic, *Journalism in the United States from 1690 to 1872*, Haskell House Publishers, 1873

Jenkins, Alan, *The Rich Rich: The Story of the Big Spenders*, Putnam, 1978

Josephson, Matthew, *The Robber Barons*, Mariner Books, 1962

Kern, Florence, *The United States Revenue Cutters in Civil War*, USCG publication, 1990

Lawson, Thomas and Winfield Thompson, *History of the America's Cup: A Record of Fifty Years*, Marine & Cannon, 1902

Le Carrer, Olivier, *Yachting: A Visual Celebration of Sailing Past and Present*, Wisden, 2015

Leslie, Anita, *The Remarkable Mr Jerome*, Henry Holt & Co, 1954

Loomis, Alfred, *Ocean Racing*, William Morrow & Company, 1936; Whitley Press, edition, 2011

Lubbock, Basil, *The Western Ocean Packets*, Brown, Son & Ferguson, 1923; Dover Publications edition, 1988

McColl, Gail, *To Marry an English Lord*, Workman Publishing, 2012

McLynn, Frank, *Stanley: Sorcerer's Apprentice*, Oxford University Press, 1992

McMullen, Richard, *Down Channel*, Grafton, 1986

Melville, Herman, *Redburn, His First Voyage*, Modern Library, 2002

Morris, Lloyd, *Incredible New York: High Life and Low Life from 1850 to 1950*, Syracuse University Press, 1996

Myers, Gustavus, *A History of the Great American Fortunes*, Charles H Kerr & Co, 1909

O'Connor, Richard, *The Scandalous Mr Bennett*, Doubleday & Co, 1962

Paine, Albert, *Thomas Nast, His Period and His Pictures*, Princeton: Pyne Press, 1974

Parton, James, *Famous Americans of Recent Times*, Nabu Press, 2012

Rayner, Dennis and Alan Wykes, *The Great Yacht Race*, Peter Davies, 1966

Riis, Jacob, *How the Other Half Lives*, Charles Scribner & Sons, 1890

Rousmaniere, John, *Golden Pastime: A New History of Yachting*, WW Norton & Co, 1987

Rousmaniere, John, *The Low Black Schooner: Yacht America*, WW Norton & Co, 1987

Rousmaniere, John, *The Luxury Yachts*, Time–Life Books, 1981

Sachsman, David (ed), *Words at War – The Civil War and American Journalism*, Transaction Publishers, 2000

Samuels, Samuel, *From the Forecastle to the Cabin*, Seaforth Publishing, 2012

Sebba, Anne, *Jennie Churchill, Winston's American mother*, John Murray, 2008

Seitz, Don, *Dreadful Decade: Detailing Some Phases in the History of the United States From Reconstruction to Resumption, 1869–1879*, Indianapolis Bobbs-Merrill, 1926

Seitz, Don, *The James Gordon Bennetts, Father and Son, Proprietors of the New York Herald*, Indianapolis Bobbs-Merrill, 1928

Sobel, Robert, *Panic on Wall Street: A History of America's Financial Disasters*, Macmillan, 1968

Stanley, Henry, *The Autobiography of Henry Morton Stanley*, Houghton Mifflin, 1909

Stephenson, Ralph (ed), *Small Boats and Big Seas: A Hundred Years of Yachting*, David McKay Co, 1978

Stiles, TJ, *The First Tycoon*, Vintage, 2010

Swanberg, WA, *Jim Fisk: The Career of an Improbable Rascal*, Charles Scribner & Sons, 1959

Swanberg, WA, *Pulitzer*, Charles Scribner & Sons, 1967

Thoreau, Henry David, *Walden, or Life in the Woods*, Dover Editions, 1995

Turner, Hy, *When Giants Ruled: The Story of Park Row, New York's Great Newspaper Street*, Fordham University Press, 1999

Villard, Henry, *Memoirs of Henry Villard – Volume I*, Boston, New York, Houghton, Mifflin and Company, 1904

Whipple, Alfred, *Racing Yachts*, Time-Life Inc, 1981

ACKNOWLEDGEMENTS

I'd like to thank my parents who very kindly devoted many hours to wading through the manuscript and giving it an initial proof. Thanks also to James Cox for his work sourcing images for me. I would also like to thank everyone at Bloomsbury for helping with putting the book together, in particular Clara Jump and Elizabeth Multon who helped massively in different ways. I owe a debt of thanks to Cambridge University Library for their accommodating and inclusive policy to non-alumni, which allowed me extensive access to their enormous archives. Also a thank you to James Gordon Bennett Jr for being so wilfully weird. Sometimes the truth truly is stranger than fiction.

ALSO BY SAM JEFFERSON

Sea Fever: the true adventures that inspired our greatest maritime authors, from Conrad to Masefield, Melville and Hemingway

ISBN: 978-1-4729-0-8841

How did a big-game fishing trip rudely interrupted by sharks inspire one of the key scenes in Hemingway's *The Old Man and the Sea*? How did Robert Louis Stevenson's cruise to the cannibal-infested South Sea islands prove instrumental in his writing of *Treasure Island*? How did Masefield survive Cape Horn and a near-nervous breakdown to write *Sea Fever*?

Behind many a great sea story is a real-life adventure that inspired it, and *Sea Fever* explores the dangerous, exciting and often eccentric escapades of literature's sailing stars, giving us a fascinating insight into how fact fed into fiction.

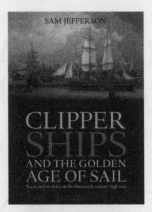

Clipper Ships and the Golden Age of Sail: Races and rivalries on the nineteenth century high seas

ISBN: 978-1-4729-0-0289

In the age of commercial sail, clipper ships were the ultimate expression of speed and grace. Racing out to the gold fields of America and Australia, and breaking speed records carrying tea back from China, the ships combined beauty with breathtaking performance.

This illustrated history recounts some of the most compelling races and rivalries of legendary boats such as *Thermopylae* and *Ariel*, and their wildly talented and often ruthless skippers. Featuring gorgeous paintings and illustrations, and fascinating eyewitness accounts and newspaper reports, this beautiful book celebrates the elegance of these racehorses of the sea, and brings the era vividly to life.